LEGAL CONSTRUCT, SOCIAL CONCEPT

SOCIAL INSTITUTIONS AND SOCIAL CHANGE

An Aldine de Gruyter Series of Texts and Monographs

EDITED BY

Michael Useem • James D. Wright

Larry Barnett, **Legal Construct, Social Concept: A Macrosociological Perspective on Law**

Vern L. Bengtson and W. Andrew Achenbaum, **The Changing Contract Across Generations**

Remi Clignet, **Death, Deeds, and Descendants: Inheritance in Modern America**

Mary Ellen Colten and Susan Gore (eds.), **Adolescent Stress: Causes and Consequences**

Rand D. Conger and Glen H. Elder, Jr., **Families in a Changing Society: Hard Times in Rural America**

G. William Domhoff, **The Power Elite and the State: How Policy is Made in America**

Paula S. England, **Comparable Worth: Theories and Evidence**

Paula S. England, **Theory on Gender/Feminism on Theory**

George Farkas, Robert P. Grobe, and Daniel Sheehan, **Human Capital or Cultural Capital?**

F. G. Gosling (ed.), **Risk and Responsibility**

Richard F. Hamilton and James D. Wright, **The State of the Masses**

Gary Kleck, **Point Blank: Guns and Violence in America**

David Knoke, **Organizing for Collective Action: The Political Economies of Associations**

Dean Knudsen and JoAnn L. Miller (eds.), **Abused and Battered: Social and Legal Responses to Family Violence**

Theodore R. Marmor, **The Politics of Medicare** (*Second Edition*)

Clark McPhail, **The Myth of the Madding Crowd**

Clark McPhail, **Acting Together: The Organization of Crowds**

John Mirowsky and Catherine E. Ross, **Social Causes of Psychological Distress**

Steven L. Nock, **The Costs of Privacy: Survelliance and Reputation in America**

Talcott Parsons on National Socialism (*Edited and with an Introduction by Uta Gerhardt*)

Carolyn C. and Robert Perrucci, Dena B. and Harry R. Targ, **Plant Closings: International Context and Social Costs**

Robert Perrucci and Harry R. Potter (eds.), **Networks of Power: Organizational Actors at the National, Corporate, and Community Levels**

David Popenoe, **Disturbing the Nest: Family Change and Decline in Modern Societies**

James T. Richardson, Joel Best, and David G. Bromley (eds.), **The Satanism Scare**

Alice S. Rossi and Peter H. Rossi, **Of Human Bonding: Parent-Child Relations Across the Life Course**

David G. Smith, **Paying for Medicare: The Politics of Reform**

Martin King Whyte, **Dating, Mating, and Marriage**

James D. Wright, **Address Unknown: The Homeless in America**

James D. Wright and Peter H. Rossi, **Armed and Considered Dangerous: A Survey of Felons and Their Firearms**

James D. Wright, Peter H. Rossi, and Kathleen Daly, **Under the Gun: Weapons, Crime, and Violence in America**

Mary Zey, **Banking on Fraud: Drexel, Junk Bonds, and Buyouts**

LEGAL CONSTRUCT, SOCIAL CONCEPT

A Macrosociological Perspective on Law

LARRY D. BARNETT

ALDINE DE GRUYTER
New York

About the Author

Larry D. Barnett, Professor of Law at Widener University, holds a Ph.D. in demography from Florida State University and a J.D. from the University of Florida. A member of both Phi Beta Kappa and Order of the Coif, he has authored or co-authored three books; has served as a Fulbright Scholar in The Netherlands; and was the founder and first editor of the journal *Population Research and Policy Review.*

ALDINE DE GRUYTER
A division of Walter de Gruyter, Inc.
200 Saw Mill River Road
Hawthorne, New York 10532

This publication is printed on acid-free paper ∞

Library of Congress Cataloging-in-Publication Data

Barnett, Larry D.
Legal construct, social concept : a macrosociological perspective on law / Larry D. Barnett.
p. cm. — (Social institutions and social change)
Includes bibliographical references and index.
ISBN 0-202-30479-5 (cloth : alk. paper)
1. Law—Social aspects—United States. 2. Sociological jurisprudence. 3. Macrosociology. 4. Social change. I. Title. II. Series.
KF380.B36 1993
340'.115—dc20 92-42409
CIP

Manufactured in the United States of America

10 9 8 7 6 5 4 3 2 1

To my parents
Harold and Nancy Barnett
for teaching me to pursue the truth
regardless of where the search might lead

Contents

Preface

It is, I suspect, unusual for the author of a scholarly treatise to advance an argument that is fundamentally at odds with beliefs he held at the start of his project. In the course of preparing the present work, however, I markedly altered my views regarding the role of law in our social system. When I began the treatise, I had no thought of questioning the assumption, dominant in our country and fully accepted by me, that law significantly influences the character and course of society, but within a relatively short time, questions arose that I had not previously considered. As I examined quantitative social science research relevant to these questions—especially research conducted with longitudinal data—I was led to formulate a set of general propositions that could accommodate the findings. Doing so, however, forced me to realize that the results of social science research did not comport with my conception of the societal functions of law. The conflict with my original beliefs was particularly sharp for my conclusion—about which research now leaves little doubt—that the legal institution does not generally alter social behavior and remedy social problems. The process of abandoning the views I held was therefore an uncomfortable one, and the process was not made easier by my awareness that the facts requiring it had only recently become available.

I realize that my thesis is challenging conventional wisdom regarding the role of law in American society and that it will encounter significant resistance among members of both the academic community and the public at large. Given the large investment that has been made in the prevailing conception of law by individuals and organizations, skepticism is unavoidable. However, the empirical evidence supporting the thesis is substantial and cannot be dismissed. I have assembled this evidence in the book, and I hope that it will encourage further work with the thesis and the discipline on which it is based: macrosociology. A macrosociological approach promises to advance significantly our understanding of law and its role in society, and if this book is a step toward fulfilling that promise, it will have achieved its objective.

All scholarship has a unique history, and I would like to acknowledge a small part of the background of the present work. In particular, I want to express my appreciation to Professor Scott Van Alstyne of the University of Florida law school for sparking my interest in the sociology of law in the mid-1980s. Indeed, my collaboration with him on a monograph led directly to the present project. In addition, I want to thank the students at the Widener University law school who added measurably to the book. In the spring semesters of 1988, 1989, 1990, and 1992, I used the evolving manuscript in a seminar and was thus afforded an opportunity to present and defend my argument at length. The students who enrolled were a stimulating audience, and the questions they asked allowed me to refine my ideas. I only hope that they benefited from and enjoyed the seminar as much as I did.

In the preparation of the book, I made extensive use of the resources of the Widener University law school library. The impressive facilities of the library are a credit to the work, ability, and dedication of the library director, Eileen B. Cooper, and her staff. Among the many members of the staff who provided me with assistance, I would particularly like to thank Enza I. Klotzbucher, who was primarily responsible for filling my requests for social science materials that had to be obtained from other libraries. Those materials were essential to the project, and Ms. Klotzbucher processed my requests for them with superb efficiency.

Along more technical lines, Norfleet W. Rives, Jr., provided advice on multiple regression and allowed me to acquire the expertise necessary to conduct the regression analyses reported in chapters 4, 5, and 6. His help was invaluable. It is hardly necessary to say, of course, that any mistakes I made in the regression analyses are wholly my responsibility.

Finally, I must underscore the role of my wife Linda. She not only provided psychological support while the book was being written but on a number of occasions pointed out defects in the manuscript. I believe it was Mark Twain who asserted that marriage is the triumph of hope over experience. Given the divorce rate, I am fully aware of the empirical evidence for Mr. Twain's inimitably expressed rule, but I have had the good fortune to be an exception to it. For that, Linda is solely responsible and I am deeply grateful.

Larry D. Barnett

A Note on Citation Style

References cited in this book follow the Harvard Law Review Association manual *A Uniform System of Citation*, which provides consecutively:

For an article in a journal

last name of author(s), article title, journal volume number, journal title, page on which article begins, page(s) on which a quotation or point appears, and year of publication.

For an article in a book

last name of author(s) of article, article title, the word "in," volume number (if more than one), book title, page on which article begins, page(s) on which a quotation or point appears, names of editor(s), and year of publication.

For a book

volume number (if more than one), name of author(s), book title, page(s) on which a quotation or point appears, edition (if more than one), and year of publication.

For a federal statute, one or both of

Public Law number, the volume of *United States Statutes at Large* (abbreviated Stat.) in which the statute is printed, the abbreviation Stat., the page number on which the statute begins in the designated volume, and the year in which the statute was enacted.

and/or

title number of the *United States Code* (abbreviated U.S.C.) in which the statute is found, the abbreviation U.S.C., section number of the statute in the designated title, and the year in which the Code was published.

For a state statute

citation style varies by jurisdiction.

For a court case

first-named parties to the litigation, volume number, publication, page on which the case begins, page(s) on which a quotation or point appears, court (if not the U.S. Supreme Court), and year in which the decision was announced. The publication is designated by: U.S. for *United States Reports*; S.Ct. for *Supreme Court Reporter*; and F.2d for *Federal Reporter Second Series*.

Citations to an article, book, or court case do not always include a page for a quotation or point. The page that denotes the beginning of an article or court case thus often stands by itself.

The following abbreviations are used in the citations:

Ad.	Administrative
Aff.	Affairs
Am.	American
Ann.	Annotated
App.	Appendix
art.	Article
Ass'n	Association
Bull.	Bulletin
Bus.	Business
C.F.R.	Code of Federal Regulations
cl.	Clause
Comm.	Committee
Cong.	Congress or Congressional
Const.	Constitution
Delinq.	Delinquency
Dep't	Department
Dev.	Development
Econ.	Economic(s)
Educ.	Education
Env't	Environment
Fam.	Family
Hist.	History
H.R.	House of Representatives
Hum.	Human
Indus.	Industrial
J.	Journal
L.	Law
Marr.	Marriage
Mgmt.	Management
Nat'l	National
Persp.	Perspectives
Phil.	Philosophical
Plan.	Planning
Pol.	Political
Pol'y	Policy
Proc.	Proceedings
Pub.	Public
Q.	Quarterly
Rel.	Relations
Rep.	Report(s)
Res.	Research (for journals)
Res.	Resolution (for legislation)
Rev.	Review
S.	Senate
Sci.	Science
sec.	Section
Sess.	Session
So.	Southern
Soc.	Sociological or Sociology
Soc'y	Society
Stat.	Statutes
Stud.	Studies
Supp.	Supplement
Surv.	Survey
Univ.	University
Urb.	Urban
W.	Western

CHAPTER

1

Introduction

This book explores a thesis that has not been adequately elaborated and tested because it requires contributions from two disciplines—sociology and law—that have failed to share extensively their intellectual resources. The limited interaction that has thus far occurred between the two fields is regrettable, for collaboration would benefit both. Particularly valuable to the legal community would be a focus on the structure and values of society, phenomena that are central to the sociological perspective. The structure of a society encompasses the manner in which social life is organized—i.e., the arrangements and patterns characterizing a society—while its values are the ideals and expectations that guide the actions of individuals and groups. The thesis advanced in this book is that societal structure and values are directly related to the nature of the doctrines found in the legal system. The links between societal conditions and law are, I suggest, strong and pervasive.

In the United States, the bulk of legal thought stems from the operation of the judiciary, and I will therefore focus primarily on the doctrines that courts have developed and utilized in resolving the issues they have faced. There are four types of law in our society: constitutions (federal and state), statutes enacted by legislatures (federal and state), regulations that are issued by administrative agencies to explicate statutes, and "common law." The judiciary is the only mechanism in our legal system that deals with all four, and it thus produces the most comprehensive statement of American legal thought. Indeed, common law—the legal principles formulated by courts for issues to which a constitution, statute, or regulation does not apply—stems exclusively from the judiciary. The interpretation of constitutions and statutes is a task of the courts as well; the provisions of constitutions and statutes are necessarily general in nature, inevitably generate disputes regarding their application to concrete situations, and must therefore be construed by courts. In addition, the resolution of challenges to administrative regulations is the responsibility of the judiciary. A regulation may be questioned with regard to whether it is consistent with a constitutional provision and/or authorized by the statute under which it was adopted, and the task of resolving such challenges is imposed on courts.

But while the legal system in the United States may make courts the single most important source of legal doctrine, my concern is not solely with judicial decisions. On the contrary, the thesis I advance encompasses legal thought of all origins, and I will apply it to statutes as well as to court rulings in the chapters that follow. The book thus attempts to specify the manner in which law generally is tied to its social context.[1]

Unfortunately, the ties between society and law have not often been studied. As one observer has concluded, the result is that "[a]t least in the United States, sociology of law has developed to the point where its attitude to and relationship with legal theory urgently require clarification."[2] The problem is an important one. Because legal doctrine involves the assumptions and goals of the legal system, it both specifies the direction in which the system is moving and permits prediction of the way in which the system will behave in particular situations. Doctrine is thus a phenomenon that is central to the legal system and critical to its operation. However, law does not exist in a vacuum, and the social forces that affect it need to be identified. Regrettably, few sociologists and legal scholars have endeavored to do so with quantitative research methods. Sociologists have generally failed to appreciate the social character of legal principles, and "the widespread neglect of this fundamental point among legal sociologists . . . has so far prevented the study of legal thought and legal symbols and concepts from occupying a central place in the sociology of law."[3] Legal scholars, for their part, rarely venture into sociology and have not explored the nature of the ties that exist between legal ideas and society with the data sources and statistical tools available in that discipline.

The present work attempts to help fill this gap. I doubt that many of its arguments are new, but unlike previous writers who have attempted a general analysis of the societal functions of law, I have taken advantage of the enlarged volume and improved quality of quantitative research and data that have appeared in the social sciences since the mid-1970s. The contribution of this book, accordingly, is that it assembles the most credible quantitative evidence that can be brought to bear on the connection between legal thought and society; determines the theoretical propositions regarding the connection that are justified by this material; and illustrates the propositions with several specific topics. In doing so, the book differs sharply from traditional scholarship on the societal role of legal doctrine in the type of proof that it employs. Specifically, while conventional scholarship bases its conclusions on verbal analyses of phenomena—analyses that are unavoidably imprecise—the current book relies on quantitative evidence to investigate the societal environment of legal thought.[4]

At this point it may be helpful to consider a school that has emerged in recent years and that involves some aspects of both traditional jurisprudence scholarship and the approach I am pursuing. I consider the school here, albeit briefly, because some of its positions permit me to delineate more clearly the thrust of my work. The school—Critical Legal Studies—rests on a number of presuppositions.[5] I begin with its contention that legal theories represent social values, not neutral and objective criteria, and that contradictory theories exist because they have incorporated different, and conflicting, values. Although this proposition is not central to my thesis, I do not disagree with it and, indeed, the following chapters will emphasize the relationship of social values and legal thought.

My agreement with Critical Legal Studies can extend no further than this, however, for I believe three important premises of that school are mistaken. First, Critical Legal Studies asserts that social values compete with one another for dominance and that, because the outcome of this competition determines which legal theories prevail, legal thought is not the result of a rational process.

> We should no longer view the project of giving a "rational foundation" for law as a worthwhile endeavor. If morality and law are matters of conviction rather than logic, we have no reason to be ashamed that our deeply felt beliefs have no "basis" that can be demonstrated through a rational decision procedure or that we cannot prove them to be "true" or "right."[6]

I cannot accept this position, because it suggests that a society selects its legal doctrines on the basis of criteria that are either random and/or beyond human understanding. In my view, social values and the legal theories they foster are attributable to societal conditions and needs whose identification is both feasible and important. If this is the case, law can be studied empirically and explained rationally.

A second difference between Critical Legal Studies and my thesis is that Critical Legal Studies has thus far documented its assertions with personal impressions and verbal studies. Quantitative data and statistical techniques, however, offer a more fruitful means to investigate legal thought, for they have a greater ability to produce accurate, precise information and, in turn, conclusions that are correct. It is for this reason I rely on them. Quantitative analyses are not necessarily free of error, but they provide a more rigorous and exacting method of discovery than the approach to evidence utilized to date by Critical Legal Studies.

I come then to the third and final point of disagreement: Critical Legal Studies contends that societal needs and patterns do not exercise a high degree of control over the content of legal doctrine; instead, the school appears to assume that the manner in which legal thought waxes and wanes in one setting is not generalizable to another setting and that the law adopted for a given issue results from a unique configuration of historically specific factors. I reject this position not because it is inconsistent with preconceptions I hold but because it is inconsistent with an impressive body of quantitative evidence. That evidence, which will be considered in the chapters to come, indicates that the links between legal doctrine and the social system are far stronger than advocates of Critical Legal Studies believe.

My approach to legal thought thus derives from the practices and assumptions of the social sciences, particularly sociology, and not from those of Critical Legal Studies. Its closest kin appears to be a body of scholarship known as the "interdisciplinary study of legal evolution"[7] in which social science resources are used to determine how societal change alters law. Unfortunately, scholarship of this genre has been confined largely to economic issues. My concern, however, is with social issues—issues that are substantively different and require their own concepts. In addressing legal thought on social problems with the conceptual framework and quantitative techniques of macrosociology, I will therefore be considering a topic that is infrequently investigated and employing an approach that is infrequently used.

But why undertake an interdisciplinary study of legal change on any issue, social or economic? The answer is that the volume and scope of legal doctrine has expanded during the twentieth century because of alterations in the structure and values of society. Since the increase in legal thought is the product of factors that the social sciences have studied extensively, the increase cannot be understood without these disciplines. The chapters that follow will demonstrate the importance of the social sciences, but at this point I would like to consider the growth of legal doctrine. Table 1.1 presents one measure of that growth—the number of statutes (or, more exactly, public laws) approved by Congress since 1897.

Since legislation rescinds existing measures infrequently, the data in the table indicate the expansion that has taken place in legal doctrine from federal statutes. Excluding bills passed that were negated by a presidential veto, some 27,500 federal statutes became law during the nine decades covered by the table.[8] While the vast majority of these statutes made just minor additions to doctrine, Congress clearly enlarged the number of significant legal principles during the twentieth

Table 1.1. Number of Public Laws Enacted by Congress

Dates of session	*Congresses*	*Number of public laws passed*
1977–1986	95th–99th	2808
1967–1976	90th–94th	3181
1957–1966	85th–89th	4097
1947–1956	80th–84th	4230
1937–1946	75th–79th	3833
1927–1936	70th–74th	3685
1917–1927	65th–69th	2739
1907–1917	60th–64th	2075
1897–1907	55th–59th	2449

Sources: 2 BUREAU OF THE CENSUS, U.S. DEP'T OF COMMERCE, HISTORICAL STATISTICS OF THE UNITED STATES: COLONIAL TIMES TO 1970 1081–82 (1975); BUREAU OF THE CENSUS, U.S. DEP'T OF COMMERCE, STATISTICAL ABSTRACT OF THE UNITED STATES: 1989 250 (109th ed. 1989).

century.[9] I am not aware of data on the number of statutes enacted by state and local governments in the same period, but here too legislative measures have probably become more voluminous.[10] The United States is thus in an era in which legal doctrines are changing in content and growing in number, and the links that exist between social circumstances and those doctrines need to be investigated.

Before examining the thesis that social conditions and legal thought are closely connected, however, two issues should be considered. The first involves the type of evidence necessary to test the thesis and determine its accuracy. The issue is important to chapters 2 through 5, which focus on the elements of the thesis and its ability to generate useful explanations of change in legal thought. The second issue extends the discussion to the problem of prediction, a matter that is central to chapter 6.

DATA TYPES AND CAUSAL INFERENCES

A resource invaluable to social scientists—and increasingly accessible to them—is information from recurring measurements of phenomena over a substantial period of time. For the purpose of identifying causal relationships, such data are superior to a statistical analysis of the characteristics of different individuals, areas, or entities at a single point in time. The latter approach—using what is termed cross-sectional data—compares its subjects on two contemporaneous dimensions. If differences on the dimensions accompany one another and the concomitant variation persists after other factors are statistically held constant, the approach concludes that one of the dimensions is the antecedent of the other. However, causality involves sequences in which phenomena are ordered temporally, and it is more likely to be accurately assessed when the phenomena can be followed over time. Thus, when evaluating the consequences of a particular event, longitudinal data that cover the period both before and after its occurrence are essential, and analyses grounded on cross-sectional data can generate erroneous conclusions.

A pair of studies concerned with the relationship between divorce law and divorce rates illustrates the two types of data and the inconsistent conclusions that can emanate from them. The first study employed cross-sectional data to assess the impact of state statutes governing the dissolution of marriage and found a strong, persistent correlation between the permissiveness of the statutes in 1960 and divorce rates in the same year. The data led the researchers to conclude that "the permissiveness of state divorce laws is a major determinant of state divorce rates. A state that liberalizes its divorce laws . . . may anticipate at least some increase in its divorce rate."[11] However, correlation is not causation, as social scientists are fond of pointing out. A statistical association between phenomena as they exist at the same point in time does not demonstrate that one preceded and produced the other. Indeed, in a later study the same researchers examined marriage termination rates over time in states that had adopted the highly permissive standard of "irretrievable breakdown" as a ground for divorce and, with longitudinal data, arrived at a very different conclusion regarding the impact of statutory liberalization. Specifically, they found that enactment of the new standard was not responsible for subsequent changes in marital dissolution rates. Rates rose following legislation permitting divorce for "irretrievably broken" marriages, but the increases had commenced well before the statutes were revised. In the words of the researchers, "[t]he higher [postreform] rates are part of a trend starting before the reforms and cannot be attributed to a change in the law."[12]

Longitudinal data, then, furnish a more powerful tool for ascertaining whether causal relationships exist—particularly when the time period covered begins substantially in advance of the event being investigated and continues substantially after it. Indeed, definitive conclusions regarding causality would seem to require such data. In this regard, it may be helpful to note that longitudinal data are of two types. The first type—time series data—is based on a group that has a constant physical or social definition but a changing membership. Divorce rates in a state at different dates (e.g., the number of divorces per 1000 population in various years) are an example of time series data; even though the boundaries of the state remain the same, the persons who reside there will change over time as a result of births, deaths, and migration, and the rates that are calculated will involve different people. The second type of longitudinal data—cohort data—is based on a group whose membership is determined by some discrete event (e.g., year of birth or year of graduation from high school). However, unlike the group that generates time series data, a cohort is composed of the same persons, with the result that individuals are observed as they age and their experience (e.g., in terms of marriage, fertility, and divorce) is traced over time.

At the present, it is unclear under what conditions one type of longitudinal data is superior to the other for isolating the societal determinants and consequences of legal doctrine, and future research will need to address this question. Either type, however, is more likely than cross-sectional data to produce accurate conclusions, and longitudinal data will therefore be the principal focus of this book.

SCIENCE AND LEGAL THOUGHT

The thesis I advance is founded upon a tenet of science, viz., that there are relationships between and sequences of events. To the extent the tenet is correct, some phenomena will change before others and the former can be used to predict the latter. If social structure and values are antecedents of legal thought, accordingly, change in societal attributes will predict the emergence of new legal doctrine and the application of existing doctrine to new contexts. Moreover, since societal alterations occur slowly and their effects require a considerable period of time to appear, prediction is in principle feasible years in advance of legal change. The possibility that the evolution and content of law can be anticipated is perhaps the most provocative implication of the thesis to be explored.

As a step toward developing the capacity to predict legal thought from social structure and values, chapter 6 undertakes a sociological examination of euthanasia, an issue with which the American legal system can be expected to grapple over the next two decades, and an hypothesis is advanced regarding the nature of future legal doctrine on the issue. The effort is necessarily exploratory and tentative in nature because of the paucity of sociological research on legal thought. Hopefully, my hypothesis will prove correct, but even if it is found to be mistaken, the reasons for the error can be identified and the experience will be profitable. The effort will also underscore the need for research with multivariate statistical tests to identify the relationships that exist between societal attributes and legal thought. Such research is essential to maximizing the number of accurate predictions.

The value of a sociological approach to law will be determined largely by the extent to which correct predictions concerning the future are generated by the approach, and considerable resources will have to be invested to produce such predictions. In this regard, it may be fruitful to review the outcome of an hypothesis I previously advanced using sociological research.[13] Specifically, I concluded it was "reasonably likely" that, because of urbanization and a lessened commitment to religion, legal restrictions on the marriage of persons of the same gender would be declared unconstitutional, probably on the ground that the restrictions were an unwarranted intrusion into the realm of personal privacy protected by the liberty guarantee of the Constitution. A year following publication of the prediction, however, the U.S. Supreme Court held that government was *not* barred by the right of privacy from criminalizing homosexual activity and penalizing persons who engage in it, even when they do so within their own home.[14] While the issue decided by the Court differed from that of my prediction, the logic of the prediction applies to legal restrictions on private homosexual activity and, if followed, would lead to their invalidation.

The holding of the Supreme Court thus was not anticipated by existing knowledge of the attributes of social structure bearing on the acceptance of homosexual conduct, and it in effect refuted my hypothesis.[15] As to social values, the decision indicates that the factor is only a necessary and not a sufficient condition for the emergence of new constitutional doctrine. Over the eight years preceding the decision, the proportion of Americans favoring the legalization of homosexuality had not changed appreciably. In the three years prior to the decision, there was an increase in persons unfavorable to legalization and a corresponding decline in the number of uncommitted individuals.[16] However, the state of public opinion appears to have been sufficient for judicial invalidation of legal bans on private homosexual activity; when the Supreme Court invalidated restrictions on abortion in 1973, attitudes supporting legalization of the procedure were no more prevalent.[17]

While future research will have to identify the factor(s) not taken into account that caused my prediction to go awry, it is important to recognize that the prediction was not completely inaccurate. The decision of the Court involved a five-to-four split among the justices. Not only was it a vote that was close, but one member of the majority originally believed that a governmental prohibition of homosexuality was unconstitutional and cast his vote accordingly. The justices thus initially favored invalidating the prohibition.[18] Furthermore, after concluding that the governmental policy did not violate the right of privacy and should be upheld on that ground, the same justice broke from the five-member majority and wrote a concurring opinion indicating that he believed imprisonment for private homosexual activity constituted cruel and unusual punishment and consequently violated the Eighth Amendment to the Constitution. "In my view," he wrote, "a prison sentence for such conduct—certainly a sentence of long duration—would create a serious Eighth Amendment issue."[19]

Even though the use of sociological research failed in expecting the complete invalidation of statutes criminalizing homosexuality, the effort at least anticipated judicial turmoil over the issue. The attempt, moreover, can claim success to the extent that constitutional restrictions are imposed under the Eighth Amendment on penalties for homosexual activity between consenting adults in nonpublic areas. The four justices who argued that the right of privacy protects homosexual conduct did not identify the nature of the restraints they believed the Eighth Amendment placed on punishment for such conduct, but given their view that the Constitution is offended when government regulates adult sexual behavior that is voluntary and private, the four would presumably have invalidated its punishment.[20] When their position is juxtaposed with the view advanced by the concurring opinion, it appears that a majority of the Court favored a constitutional principle that permits no more than a modest monetary fine for private, consensual homosexual relationships.

ORGANIZATION OF THE BOOK

The material that follows is organized into six chapters. Chapter 2 describes my thesis and illustrates it with the concept of equal protection, the constitutional guarantee concerned with governmental policies that establish classifications. Chapters 3, 4, and 5 apply the thesis to legal doctrine on three different topics. The topics were selected because they have been of prominent interest to Americans in recent decades and because their social context and impact can be assessed with a substantial body of quantitative data and research. Chapter 3 considers constitutional law on gender, an issue typically treated under equal protection, and examines it with a quantitative measure of sex role egalitarianism, viz., the gender differential in rates of college attendance and graduation during the twentieth century. Chapter 4 deals with a federal statute prohibiting age discrimination in employment-related decisions and relates it to rates of labor force involvement by age. Chapter 5 returns to constitutional law and concentrates on five decisions of the U.S. Supreme Court that invalidated governmental policies regulating contraception and abortion. Birth rates, as well as data on the annual incidence of abortion, are used both to describe the social milieu in which the five decisions developed and to assess the effect of the decisions.

Following chapter 5, the book undergoes a shift in emphasis. Specifically, while the focus of chapters 3, 4, and 5 is the evolution of law in the past, the focus of chapter 6 is the development of law in the future. Chapter 6 thus considers a subject—active forms of euthanasia—on which legal doctrine is likely to change in the next two decades. The chapter identifies the two factors that I believe are creating pressure to alter the present legal status of euthanasia, and it discusses one of them at length—namely, social values. Those values are investigated in depth using data from a series of national sample surveys conducted between 1977 and 1989.

I conclude the book in chapter 7 with a discussion of topics for research and issues for theory. While the thesis of the book constitutes a theoretical framework for the societal functions of law, a full-fledged theory—i.e., a set of propositions that generate a wide range of specific and accurate hypotheses—still does not exist. To aid in the development of such theory, chapter 7 suggests questions that should be addressed and lines of inquiry that should be pursued.

With this overview, we proceed to chapter 2 for a statement and explanation of the thesis.

NOTES

1. In emphasizing the unity of law, my thesis differs from that of G. Rosenberg, The Hollow Hope (1991). Professor Rosenberg focuses on the ability of the judiciary to produce extensive, enduring change in social patterns. His conclusion that courts cannot do so is consistent with mine, but presently available evidence (which I review in the chapters that follow) does not support his argument that such change can result from the legislative and executive branches of government—at least when these branches rely upon regulation. The evidence suggests instead that the ability of the legal system to have an appreciable effect is conditional (1) upon whether social or nonsocial issues are the subject of law that attempts to regulate and (2) upon whether law seeks to achieve its aims by regulation or by the distribution of resources that allow individuals to pursue their goals. A discussion of the two distinctions appears in chapter 7.

2. Cotterrell, *Jurisprudence and Sociology of Law, in* The Sociology of Law 21, 22 (W. Evan ed., 1980).

3. *Id.* at 25.

4. In his recent book (*supra* note 1), Professor Rosenberg utilizes quantitative data to assess the ability of courts to initiate social change. While his work is a welcome addition to the literature on the societal functions of law, it fails to mention a number of previously published quantitative studies that are directly

relevant and of considerable importance. In addition, the data on which Professor Rosenberg appears to rely most heavily are not subjected to any multivariate statistical test. As a result, his evidence is unnecessarily weak and his argument is more easily dismissed. In terms of the impact of law on the frequency with which women terminate unwanted pregnancies, conclusions of greater credibility can be drawn from my study of birth rates (reported in chapter 5) than from the analysis undertaken by Professor Rosenberg.

5. My discussion of Critical Legal Studies draws upon the following articles: Singer, *The Player and the Cards: Nihilism and Legal Theory*, 94 YALE L.J. 1 (1984); Gordon, *Critical Legal Histories*, 36 STANFORD L. REV. 57 (1984).

6. Singer, *supra* note 5, at 57.

7. Clark, *The Interdisciplinary Study of Legal Evolution*, 90 YALE L.J. 1238 (1981).

8. Congress enacted 29,097 statutes during the period covered by the table. Of these, approximately 1558 were the subject of a presidential veto that was sustained. Calculated from the sources shown for table 1.1.

9. Using simple random sampling, I selected fifty public laws (from *United States Statutes at Large*) that were enacted by the eightieth through the ninety-ninth Congresses. Five-digit numbers were used to choose the Congress and the law jointly; acts dealing solely with foreign affairs were excluded from the analysis. Of the fifty statutes examined, I found that none rescinded existing legislation and that four constituted (in my subjective judgment) major legislation. If I accurately distinguished major from minor legislation, just a small fraction of all enacted bills added substantially to legal doctrine. However, major legislation augmented doctrine not only by increasing the number of statutes. It also was explicated in judicial decisions and agency regulations; indeed, major legislation was undoubtedly the subject of more extensive interpretation by courts and administrative agencies than was minor legislation.

10. Growth in the number of state and local government employees who were engaged in functions other than education may indicate an increase in the volume of law at these levels. Such employees were 1.6% of all persons 15 years of age and older in 1929 and 3.5% in 1986. Calculated from 2 BUREAU OF THE CENSUS, U.S. DEP'T OF COMMERCE, HISTORICAL STATISTICS OF THE UNITED STATES: COLONIAL TIMES TO 1970 1104 (1975); BUREAU OF THE CENSUS, U.S. DEP'T OF COMMERCE, STATISTICAL ABSTRACT OF THE UNITED STATES: 1989 294 (109th ed. 1989); Bureau of the Census, U.S. Dep't of Commerce, *Estimates of the Population of the United States, by Single Years of Age, Color, and Sex: 1900 to 1959*, CURRENT POPULATION REP. Series P-25, No. 311, at 64–65 (1965); Bureau of the Census, U.S. Dep't of Commerce, *United States Population Estimates, by Age, Sex, and Race: 1980 to 1987*, CURRENT POPULATION REP. Series P-25, No. 1022, at 12–13 (1988).

11. Stetson & Wright, *The Effects of Laws on Divorce in American States*, 37 J. MARR. & FAM. 537, 546 (1975).

12. Wright & Stetson, *The Impact of No-Fault Divorce Law Reform on Divorce in American States*, 40 J. MARR. & FAM. 575, 577 (1978). Marital dissolution rates in states adopting "irretrievable breakdown" as a basis for divorce were first adjusted to eliminate change that presumably would have occurred if the grounds for divorce had remained unaltered. The adjustment involved subtracting from

the marital dissolution rates of these jurisdictions the mean change in the rate of states that did not accept the criterion of "irretrievable breakdown."

13. Barnett & Reed, Law, Society, and Population: Issues in a New Field 172–76 (1985).

14. Bowers v. Hardwick, 478 U.S. 186 (1986).

15. Unfortunately, in hypothesizing that bans on same-sex marriages would be ruled unconstitutional, I limited myself to one source of change in legal doctrine. I failed to consider the possibility that state and/or municipal governments would respond to social conditions within their jurisdiction and would enact legislation approving same-sex relationships. Such a response by local governments may now be occurring. Wilson, *Same-Sex Marriage: A Review*, 17 Wm. Mitchell L. Rev. 539 (1991). Illustrative of legislation at the municipal level is an ordinance adopted in 1989 by the Board of Supervisors for the City and County of San Francisco. The ordinance allows unmarried couples of the same sex, as well as unmarried couples of the opposite sex, to confer a legal status on their relationships by executing a Declaration of Domestic Partnership. A Declaration is effective under the ordinance when the original is filed with the municipal government or, in the case of a Declaration whose execution was witnessed, a notarized copy is provided to the witness. San Francisco, Cal., Ordinance 176–89 (May 22, 1989). See also Bishop, *San Francisco Grants Recognition to Partnerships of Single People*, New York Times, May 31, 1989, at A17.

16. *Majority Say Opinion of Gays Unchanged by AIDS Epidemic*, Gallup Rep. Nos. 244–45, at 2, 3 (Jan.–Feb. 1986); Barnett & Reed, *supra* note 13, at 174–75.

17. Barnett & Reed, *supra* note 13, at 33–35.

18. Kamen, *Powell Changed Vote in Sodomy Case*, Washington Post, July 13, 1986, at A1; Greenhouse, *When Second Thoughts in Case Come Too Late*, New York Times, Nov. 5, 1990, at A14.

19. Bowers v. Hardwick, 478 U.S. 186, 197 (1986) (Powell, J., concurring).

20. *Id.* at 202–3 n.2 (Blackmun, Brennan, Marshall, and Stevens, JJ., dissenting).

CHAPTER

2

The Thesis

Intellectual disciplines normally change incrementally rather than dramatically, but there are grounds for believing that legal scholarship and education are entering a period in which an appreciable change of orientation will occur. With such a change, the manner of conceptualizing and resolving issues will be substantially altered. Shifts in paradigms have taken place in the past in law[1] as well as in the sciences,[2] and they can be expected to occur again. The prospect of such a change in law is suggested by the presence of a daylong workshop at the 1987 meeting of the Association of American Law Schools (AALS) on five "emerging traditions in legal education and legal scholarship."

The paradigm shift that seems to be looming in law will, I believe, stem from the social sciences. Indeed, four of the five approaches considered by the 1987 AALS workshop significantly implicated these disciplines.[3] The social sciences have made major advances in recent years, and their increased power will lead the legal community to utilize their research techniques and data for a wide range of issues. As that occurs, the legal profession will adopt fresh approaches to questions, both new and old, and will answer those questions with a degree of rigor not previously attainable.

One question that can be usefully investigated with the resources now available in the social sciences is the societal foundations of the legal system—and especially of the doctrines that govern the system. The essence of law is rules that have been formulated through political and judicial processes, and the rules that emanate from these processes reflect the dominant needs and ideology of the public.[4] It could not be otherwise if a democratic form of governance is to persist. To the extent that the rules of a legal system create friction, the rules will be revised or eliminated. Though it is hardly a novel observation,[5] the links between the attributes of society and its law are necessarily close.

Unfortunately, the ties that exist between society and law have yet to be studied with the full range of sampling, measurement, and statistical procedures that have emerged in the social sciences.[6] There appear to be at least three reasons for this. First, the emphasis on the individual that permeates our culture[7] has directed attention away from the societal causes of phenomena. Individualism is not conducive to a focus on group-level properties, and the aspects of the social system that mold law have thus rarely been investigated. Second, the legal profession and its law schools are primarily concerned with resolving the problems of particular clients. A concern with specific parties, however, inhibits interest in the large-scale forces that determine the nature of law. Finally, and perhaps most importantly, the social sciences have developed rapidly in recent years, and their resources have yet to be fully appreciated and exploited. In the last two decades, social scientists have been increasingly able to obtain data (especially longitudinal data) that are based on well-measured variables and on samples that are drawn from the population as a whole or important segments of it. Simultaneously, statistical techniques for the analysis of data have become more powerful. As a consequence, social scientists and legal scholars now have the opportunity to explore systematically the relationships that exist between society and law—an opportunity they need to pursue.

The failure to employ fully the resources currently available to study the social context of law has negative consequences both for the legal system and for society: The effectiveness of the former is not maximized and the operation of the latter is to that extent impaired. These consequences are especially important with regard to the doctrines that govern law. The legal profession is often concerned with predicting whether a particular practice violates a statute, and at times it must consider whether a statute (or regulation) is acceptable under a constitutional provision. It must also deal occasionally with a case that may lead to a major change in the common law. Such situations involve legal principles, and when dealing with them, the accuracy of the predictions that lawyers must make for their clients—and the social utility of the decisions that judges must render—will be enhanced by knowledge of the societal attributes that determine the content of legal doctrine.

A MACROSOCIOLOGICAL APPROACH

The thesis that I am advancing emanates from macrosociology, the social science discipline that focuses on the nature, causes, and consequences of social organization and change. Rather than investigating processes and experiences that occur in small groups and organizations—the focus of microsociology—macrosociology emphasizes the broad patterns that characterize social systems. For example, while microsociology studies particular organizations concerned with sex discrimination, macrosociology examines the manner in which gender is involved in the structure of occupations, industries, and family life.

The perspective being utilized here can be understood more fully by noting the differences that exist between it and the Critical Legal Studies school. Although macrosociology and Critical Legal Studies both assert that law is a product of society and must be understood in terms of its social context, the approaches differ in at least two important respects.[8] First, Critical Legal Studies argues that law results from the contest of competing socioeconomic groups and functions to legitimize the societal organization and philosophy (or worldview) that emerges from this contest. Critical Legal Studies thus regards law as a political mechanism that justifies the dominant social order. A macrosociological perspective, on the other hand, contends that law operates to maintain the stability of the social system. In the latter view, law serves society by helping it to respond to forces such as technological and demographic change that threaten to damage its equilibrium. Macrosociology is, accordingly, a form of systems theory rather than of political theory. Second, Critical Legal Studies is concerned with altering society and its legal system. A macrosociological perspective, on the other hand, focuses on explaining the nature and predicting the future course of law. Its orientation is strictly that of science, and it has no political agenda.

Macrosociology thus differs significantly from Critical Legal Studies. Yet while it falls within the tradition of Legal Realism, it also deviates from that school in at least one key assumption.[9] Macrosociology, unlike Legal Realism, assumes that a society responds effectively to social forces even though its participants are not aware of all of the reasons for their actions. In a macrosociological framework, a social system has a life of its own that is independent of the individuals in it at a particular time; the system adapts to imperatives in its environment; and individuals need not be fully cognizant of the factors responsible for change. The conscious use of law to manipulate the system—i.e., social engineering—may improve the adaptation if the manipulation is based on accurate and complete information, but the improvement will be one of degree since the system on its own will normally satisfy societal needs reasonably well within a relatively short period of time.

Given this background, let me state the principal propositions of my thesis—the propositions that I believe describe the nature and behavior of legal doctrine in the social system of the United States. The evidence for these propositions will also be presented; since the propositions are interrelated and interdependent, evidence for any one supports the entire set. The propositions are outlined in the current chapter; the evidence on which they are based appears in this and the next three chapters.

I. The doctrines that govern issues in the legal system are determined by the characteristics of society.

It is essential to keep in mind that the subject of this book is the conditions responsible for the nature of legal thought—the factors that cause the legal system to specify certain types of conduct as acceptable and other types as unacceptable. The book is not concerned with activities that occur within existing legal doctrine. Thus, to the extent they involve the processes by which established principles of law are implemented, the resolution and prevention of disputes are not relevant to the discussion—even though these functions seem to be primarily responsible for the central importance of law in an urbanized, technologically complex society. Similarly, factual questions such as whether the tort of fraud or the crime of robbery was committed by a particular person are not pertinent, for these questions presuppose the existence of certain legal doctrines. The focus, rather, is on the determinants of those doctrines—the conditions under which law defines fraud as a tort and robbery as a crime. The factors that determine legal thought, it is argued, lie outside the legal system and are found in the attributes of the society in which the system is immersed. From this perspective, then, the debate is irrelevant as to whether the Constitution should be interpreted in accord with the intent of the persons who wrote and ratified it.[10] Individual rights and government powers are not granted by the Constitution (or by statutes) but determined by the needs and values of society.

Let me illustrate the first proposition with a 1979 decision of the U.S. Supreme Court.[11] The case arose from a program operated by a private employer to provide on-the-job training for craft positions. With the consent of the union, half of the openings were reserved for Blacks until the labor force of the employer and that of the surrounding community were similar in racial composition. The use of a racial quota for selecting persons for the program was challenged under a provision of Title VII of the federal Civil Rights Act of 1964 that explicitly prohibits employers and unions from discriminating on the basis of race in admitting individuals to job training programs. The Supreme Court, however, concluded that no violation of Title VII had occurred even though the use of race in the selection process was prohibited by the terms of the statute. In the view of the Court, the wording of the legislation did not determine its interpretation; rather, the statute had to be construed in a manner that was consistent with the social conditions leading to its enactment. In the case at hand, Title VII was believed to be aimed at eliminating the disproportionately high rate of unemployment and low-paying jobs that existed among Blacks while preserving maximum latitude of action for employers. Given this, the Court concluded it was unreasonable to believe that Congress intended the statutory ban on discrimination in apprenticeship programs to apply to employers that voluntarily adopted racial quotas in programs of relatively limited duration. Notably, the Court did not mention that during the 1970s the labor force participation rate of men, while falling among both Blacks and Whites, declined substantially faster among Blacks. Even though the racial gap diminished in terms of the earnings of employed men, it increased in terms of access to the job market.[12] The societal need for affirmative action programs in employment was thus mounting along with pressure for their approval.

II. Legal doctrines, being functional for the social system rather than disruptive of it, change as the needs and values of society evolve.

In the thesis being developed here, the ideas that dominate law are considered to be a product of social circumstances and a means of promoting social cohesion. Legal thought, I argue, responds to the needs and values of society rather than molds them, and new legal doctrines emerge with change in the social order. Three justices of the U.S. Supreme Court recently alluded to this principle in the context of constitutional law:

> Courts . . . do not sit or act in a social vacuum. Moral philosophers may debate whether certain inequalities are absolute wrongs, but history makes clear that constitutional principles of equality, like constitutional principles of liberty, property, and due process, evolve over time; what once was a "natural" and "self-evident" ordering later comes to be seen as an artificial and invidious constraint on human potential and freedom. Shifting cultural, political, and social patterns at times come to make past practices appear inconsistent with fundamental principles upon which American society rests, an inconsistency legally cognizable under the Equal Protection Clause.[13]

The contention that legal doctrine reflects the nature of the social system, and does not initiate substantial change in that system, receives support from a growing body of empirical evidence on the inability of law to contribute significantly to the solution of social problems. Simply stated, the evidence (which I consider at length in the chapter appendix) indicates that the overall course of social issues is modified just marginally by regulatory measures. Economic problems may respond to law, but social problems generally do not.[14] Legal thought thus appears to operate as a mirror of the social order rather than as an important influence on it.[15]

III. Legal doctrines do not necessarily react immediately to change in society, but they conform to its needs and values within a reasonably short period of time.

At least in a society having a democratic form of government, problems must come into existence and develop to the point where they attract public attention before the legal system will attempt to devise solutions for them. Law is thus a reaction to societal circumstances and concerns.

The fact that legal thought may appear to respond slowly to its social context should not, however, cause one to forget that it does respond. My thesis has been criticized for failing to recognize that, in spite of the severe economic difficulties facing the United States during the 1930s, New Deal legislation was judicially invalidated on constitutional grounds.[16] But rather than providing evidence contrary to the thesis, this historical episode supports the thesis, for only a half-decade after New Deal programs commenced, the U.S. Supreme Court began to bestow constitutional approval on them.[17] The legal system may act independently of social problems and trends, but it does not and cannot do so for very long.

IV. Individuals, regardless of their prominence or position, do not determine the nature of legal thought.

An issue inherent in my thesis is the role of the individual in society. In particular, the thesis raises the question whether individuals are able to affect the progress and outcome of events. Because the question implicates the strongly held American belief in personal autonomy and limitless achievement, it will generate unnecessary controversy unless two types of situations are distinguished, viz., those in which social needs and values do not change and those in which they do. The contention here is that individuals and their special interest groups have an influence only in situations of the former type: Persons can mold events within established societal patterns but they cannot alter the patterns themselves. In a situation in which established social patterns continue, furthermore, the impact of individuals and groups is dependent on the personal talents and resources of the participants; for example, the effectiveness of an attorney within prevailing legal rules is determined to a large extent by his/her competence and the financial means of his/her client.

It is important to keep in mind, however, that the present book is concerned with settings in which patterns of social behavior change and not with settings in which they endure. Specifically, the book focuses on the adoption of novel concepts and the extension of existing concepts to entirely new issues—a process of cultural evolution—and argues that large-scale social forces, not individuals, control the process.[18] In this regard, it is significant that political protest seeking new types of public policy appears to be initiated after—not before—there has been widespread change in social values[19] and in social structure.[20] This suggests that innovation in legal doctrine is a response to an altered social milieu and that the persons who participate in such innovation—whether through legislative or judicial processes—exert no appreciable independent influence on the content of the doctrine.

EQUAL PROTECTION: AN ILLUSTRATION

The explanatory power of the four propositions outlined above will be illustrated in the pages to follow. In the remainder of the present chapter, I will show that the use of a particular principle of constitutional law (namely, equal protection) increased dramatically in a short span of time in the United States. Because it is improbable that the change can be explained satisfactorily by simultaneous decisions on the part of a large number of individuals acting without environmental stimuli (proposition IV), sociological research will be employed to identify two societal attributes that apparently contributed to the change (proposition I). This will take us to chapter 3, where one issue cognizant under equal protection will be examined, namely, gender distinctions in public policy. I will review the case law on the issue that has arisen in the twentieth century, relate it to quantitative measures of sex role ideology and behavior in the United States, and show that the change found in legal thought was congruent with change that occurred in sex roles (propositions II and III). The second and third propositions will be supported further by data demonstrating that a constitutional prohibition on sex discrimination did not emerge until differences in gender roles had declined for an appreciable period of time and were being rapidly eliminated.

The discussion of sex discrimination in chapter 3 will be followed by a treatment of age discrimination in chapter 4. While age discrimination may present an equal protection issue, chapter 4 will focus on the substantive provisions, not the constitutionality, of a statute prohibiting age discrimination in employment and will underscore the applicability of my thesis to legislation and its legal doctrines. Chapter 5 will extend the analysis to sexuality and the control of procreation. The chapter will examine U.S. Supreme Court cases declaring that constitutionally assured rights to liberty and equal protection do not permit government severely to curtail access to contraception and abortion. The context and impact of the decisions will be studied with data on birth rates and abortion.

As many readers are aware, the American judicial system in the 1970s decided a number of cases under the equal protection guarantee of the U.S. Constitution with regard to governmental policies that distinguished between males and females. However, the factors causing the frequency of constitutional challenges to gender-based classifications to increase at this point in time are not my focus here. Rather, I want to consider the fact that equal protection was the basis for court decisions on a wide variety of questions that arose in the same historical period—a fact that seems not to be widely recognized. Distinctions in public policy that were grounded on gender were challenged as part of a much broader attack on classifications made by government. The data in table 2.1, which are drawn from the *Decennial Digest*, indicate the relative magnitude and rapidity of the change that enveloped federal and state courts.

The table suggests that, starting in the latter part of the 1960s, Americans became significantly more sensitive to classifications in governmental policies than they had been previously.[21] Equal protection questions in federal and state courts increased by a factor of more than three-and-a-half in the 1966–1976 period. However, another measure—in which each decade is subdivided into five-year periods—indicates that the precipitous growth in public sensitivity to governmental classifications

Table 2.1. Equal Protection Case Law in the *Decennial Digest*

Period	*Number of headings and subheadings with cases involving equal protection*	*Number of pages with cases involving equal protection*[a] *Total*	*Mean per year*
1897–1906	48		
1907–1916	48		
1916–1926	48		
1926–1936	48		
1936–1946	48		
1946–1956	48	87	8.7
1956–1966	48	113	11.3
1966–1976	173	441	44.1
1976–1981	173	335	67.0
1981–1986	173	317	63.4

[a] The page format and type style of the *Decennial Digest* differed markedly between volumes published in 1897–1946 and those published in 1946–1986; among the volumes of the earlier period, there are differences as well. Accordingly, a page count was made only for 1946–1986. Within this period, the data shown are comparable and indicate the relative increase in equal protection decisions.

Table 2.2. Number of Decisions That Were Rendered by Federal Courts Using the Term *Equal Protection*[a]

Period	*Number of decisions*	*Increase from preceding period (%)*
1945–1949	235	—
1950–1954	252	7
1955–1959	343	36
1960–1964	717	109
1965–1969	1567	119
1970–1974	3750	139
1975–1979	3851	3
1980–1984	4394	14
1985–1989	5687	29

[a] The number of decisions shown was obtained from Westlaw (using the ALLFEDS database). Only federal court decisions were examined, because Westlaw did not cover all states until the mid-1960s and a count of state court decisions before this time would have been affected by changes in the inclusiveness of the data source. However, for decisions in the federal courts, a comparison of different time periods was possible, permitting change over time to be assessed.

commenced in the early 1960s.[22] Table 2.2 presents the number of federal court opinions since World War II that utilized the term *equal protection*. The equal protection guarantee was not necessarily the basis for the holding in each case, but the concept was explicitly used in the opinion. The table shows that the number of decisions more than doubled in each of the three five-year periods starting in 1960, that the rapid increases in 1960–1974 occurred with little forewarning, and that they ended even more abruptly.

It is difficult to attribute the greatly increased reliance on the concept of equal protection that emerged in the 1960s to coincidence. The argument that, without external motivation, individuals suddenly began to attack governmental classifications is simply not plausible. A more credible hypothesis is that there were forces broadly affecting society that caused the incidence of equal protection questions to rise rapidly. The focus of constitutional law was altered, then, not because individuals acting on their own became dissatisfied with and sought to reform the existing legal order but, rather, because fundamental changes were occurring in the nature of society.

What were the forces that were responsible for redirecting constitutional law? While their identification unavoidably involves considerable speculation, two factors were probably instrumental: an expanding body of knowledge and increasing population density. Other influences were undoubtedly present, but growth in knowledge and in population concentration appear to have contributed significantly to the increasing sensitivity to governmental classifications. Indeed, these two factors may be relevant to numerous aspects of the legal system; elsewhere I have outlined the manner in which the factors seem to mold the need for lawyers and the prestige of the legal profession.[23] I would like to discuss here the ways in which each apparently contributed to the increase in equal protection challenges, relying on sociological research to suggest the principal means by which the factors operated.

KNOWLEDGE AND POPULATION SIZE AS SOCIETAL ATTRIBUTES

Knowledge, and its physical manifestation in technology, must be distinguished from education. Knowledge is an attribute of society; education, the product of the transmission of knowledge, is a characteristic of the individual. Under some conditions, average educational achievement may be used as an indicator of the volume of knowledge possessed by a society, but it is knowledge that is critical. Not only is the quantity of knowledge a determinant of the extent to which individuals pursue education,[24] but it appears to have important ramifications for the ideas that develop and dominate a society.[25]

There seems to be no argument with the proposition that knowledge has increased significantly in the past century.[26] The proposition that growth in knowledge is in large measure responsible for the rise in equal protection challenges requires justification, however. By what means did the former produce the latter? The answer appears to be threefold. First, the expansion of knowledge promotes a focus on the individual and the economic functions he or she performs, thereby diminishing the salience in human relationships of demographic characteristics such as gender and race. With the growth of knowledge, then, the importance of the individual is magnified and the acceptability of social divisions is reduced.[27] Second, additions to knowledge increase both the capacity of a society to exercise control over events and the level of its affluence—changes that provide greater opportunities for individual freedom.[28] Third, the augmentation of knowledge generally increases the complexity of tasks performed in the occupational system. In turn, advances in the substantive complexity of work enhance the intellectual flexibility of employed persons, their willingness to adopt new concepts, and their inclination to question authority.[29] However, all three effects of knowledge growth—a strengthened concept of the individual, an enlarged perimeter for personal autonomy, and a heightened analytical capacity and progressive orientation for labor force participants—are impeded by or adverse to classifications, and challenges to classifications thus become more frequent as knowledge grows.

The second factor that appears to have promoted sensitivity to classifications in governmental policies was increased population concentration. As population density rises, the values and customs of a society become more heterogeneous.[30] By enlarging the number of subgroups that exist, population growth appears to foster variety in subcultural patterns within a society, and as a result, it increases the frequency with which behavior occurs that is unconventional by the standards of the dominant culture.[31] Three mechanisms are believed to be involved:

> First, large population size increases the likelihood that any individual, no matter how unusual his or her characteristics, will be able to find others to whom he or she is similar. Second, large population size increases the likelihood that any such group of similar persons will be large enough to attain "critical mass" and so be able to support distinctive subcultural institutions. Finally, to the extent that subcultural institutions emerge and are maintained, the characteristics on which the subculture was based in the first instance are intensified. Thus, heterogeneity and unconventionality are maintained.[32]

A society with a growing population is characterized not only by an expanded number of diverse subcultures but also—as a consequence of that diversity—by a greater rate of interaction between the members of different subcultures. As subcultures become more numerous, all else being equal, the probability rises that there will be interaction between groups that possess different values and customs. This interaction will be accompanied by a higher rate of intermarriage between subculture members and, in turn, by a melding of the subcultures.[33] As a result, greater population density causes social divisions to become more fluid as well as more common, and both the utility and durability of classifications are reduced. It should not be surprising, then, that the frequency with which governmental classifications are challenged rises with the concentration of people.

Having outlined the reasons that knowledge and population density affect the frequency of equal protection challenges, the question remains as to why there was a dramatic upsurge in such challenges commencing in the 1960s. Unfortunately, a definitive answer is not possible at this time, but the question is important because it deals with the nature of the relationships that exist between increasing population and knowledge, on the one hand, and the incidence of equal protection concerns, on the other. Identification of these relationships is critical if practicing lawyers, judges, and scholars are to anticipate the content and timing of the legal doctrines that are likely to emerge in the future.

There is evidence that knowledge grew at a sustained rate following World War II.[34] The impact of increasing knowledge apparently took place (1) through a time lag, which was necessary before the social system could respond, and/or (2) through a threshold, which was approached gradually but was finally surpassed in the 1960s. If a time lag was involved, the effect of the quantity of knowledge on the number of equal protection challenges was constant but delayed. If a threshold was involved, the volume of knowledge had an effect that varied in magnitude, and there was little or no impact on the frequency of equal protection issues until knowledge volume attained a certain level.

Human numbers and density seem to have affected sensitivity to governmental classifications through elevated rather than constant rates of growth. The number of Americans who were at least 18 years of age rose at an increasing rate between the 1950s (10.6%), the 1960s (16.5%), and the 1970s (21.2%). It may be particularly important that, as part of this demographic change, the number of young adults 18–24 years of age expanded rapidly in the 1960s and 1970s as the result of the post–World War II baby boom. After declining slightly during the first half of the 1950s and returning to its initial level during the last half, the number of 18- to 24-year-olds went from 16.1 million in 1960 to 24.7 million in 1970 and to 30.3 million in 1980.[35] The necessity of incorporating the enlarged cohorts of young adults into the social system may have intensified pressure on all sources of structural rigidity, including dysfunctional classifications in government policy.[36] Existing practices of a society, that is, may constrain its adaptability, and the lines of demarcation drawn by the American social system and its law may have come under greater scrutiny in the process of absorbing the large and growing number of young adults. This proposition is made more plausible by the fact that persons 18–24 years of age contract marriages at a high rate; the mean age at first marriage among Americans who were born between 1943 and 1950—and who were 18–24 years old during the 1960s and 1970s—fluctuated between 23.3 and 23.7 for males and between 21.4 and 21.8 for females.[37] To the extent its members crossed subcultural lines in selecting their marriage partners, the group was an important catalyst for assimilation and a source of pressure on classifications in public policy.

CONCLUSION

In this chapter, I have outlined a macrosociological approach to legal thought. Specifically, I have argued that legal doctrine reflects social needs and values rather than affects them and that changes in doctrine are the work of forces broadly influencing the social system rather than of individuals. The argument, which has its intellectual roots in the structuralist/functionalist conception of law,[38] receives considerable support from existing quantitative research and will be bolstered by evidence presented in the next three chapters. However, additional research is required, especially research applying multivariate statistical procedures to longitudinal data, and in the last chapter I will suggest topics that should be investigated. I fully expect that future research will identify conditions under which the thesis does not operate; e.g., further investigation may conclude that, while law does not appreciably influence social patterns through penalties, it may modify social patterns in certain circumstances through financial subsidies and incentives.[39] Nonetheless, situations in which the thesis does not apply are likely to be small in number and relatively minor limitations on it.

For legal education and scholarship, there are two important and related ramifications of the thesis. One is the need to identify the social forces that determine legal thought. In the preceding pages, I have considered the constitutional principle of equal protection, shown that the period from 1960 to the mid-1970s was characterized by rapid growth in its use, and suggested that an expanding body of knowledge and an increasing concentration of population were critical forces in that growth. Additional aspects of the social system undoubtedly contributed to the change, and empirical research is needed to identify them. For instance, in the area of sex roles—the subject of the next chapter—the ratio of males to females in the population may influence legal doctrine.[40] However, increasing knowledge and population concentration are factors on which research seems likely to prove particularly fruitful. The factors apparently promote the importance of law to society and the demand for legal training.[41] They thus appear to be critical for many aspects of the legal system in an industrialized nation.[42]

In addition to promoting a focus on the forces that govern legal thought, the thesis of this book directs attention to the role of law in American society. Specifically, the legal community must come to understand that law is valuable to society primarily because it is a mechanism to avoid and resolve disputes between particular parties, not because it alters social patterns and solves social problems. As a result of the American penchant for rapid and simple solutions to problems, law is often assigned the task of curing social ills, a task for which it is not suited. The result is a substantial waste of resources on legislation and litigation to correct maladjustments in the social system. That waste can only reduce the efficiency of society and ultimately damage the prestige of the legal profession.

Let me end with an additional point. While a macrosociological approach to law can be expected to make a significant contribution to understanding the nature and operation of the legal system, that understanding will not occur unless there is extensive collaboration between legal scholars and quantitatively oriented social scientists. Unfortunately, law schools have generally resisted such collaboration,[43] a resistance that recently led a prominent academician to warn legal educators that "we ignore the social sciences at our peril, for their techniques grow steadily more refined."[44] The reluctance of law school faculties to address legal issues with the measurement, sampling, and statistical procedures available in the social sciences is regrettable. Quantitative research will promote the utility and increase the benefits of the legal system, and the time has come for its value to be recognized.

With this statement and explication of my framework, I turn to two demographic characteristics that are central to the organization of American society, namely, gender (which I consider in chapter 3) and age (which I consider in chapter 4). The key roles that gender and age play in ordering the social system have necessarily made them subjects of law, and the forces that have altered their social definitions have brought change in their treatment by the legal system. As a result, gender and age are critical topics in the sociology of legal thought, and the next two chapters are devoted to them.

APPENDIX

The contention that regulation by the legal system normally does not alter social patterns to a meaningful extent is supported by a large body of social science research, particularly research using longitudinal data. The research is reviewed here at length because it is important to my thesis (see proposition II). Studies whose findings seem to be inconsistent with it are also examined.

I

While discrimination in employment has attracted considerable public attention, a federal statute prohibiting such discrimination on the basis of gender and race appears not to have generally reduced work- and occupation-related differences between males and females and between Blacks and Whites.[45] Some investigators, however, have reached a different conclusion, and I therefore discuss their research in some detail.

One study of males reported that the federal statute (the Civil Rights Act of 1964) and ensuing federal measures had some effect during the period from 1965 to 1975 in diminishing the economic gap that existed between nonwhites and Whites. At the same time, however, the investigators found that, while governmental policy lessened the disparity between White median income and nonwhite median income, the impact was confined to the South, was small in magnitude (only two percentage points per year), and was readily suppressed by deleterious economic change such as a rise in the unemployment rate.[46] A substantially smaller impact—also occurring only in the South—was found for black females.[47] Other research indicates that the benefit of the Act to nonwhite men and women varies in amount with the manner in which the benefit is measured. Unfortunately, the size of the benefit reported by this research for each measure is likely to obscure important regional differences; even though the effects of the Act seem to be restricted to the South, the research estimated benefits just for the nation as a whole and not for each region separately. The results of the research are also potentially inaccurate because extensive interpolation and extrapolation were required to obtain the data used in the regression analysis for one of the three control variables (viz., attitudes).[48]

A further aspect of the Civil Rights Act should not be overlooked. While the Act may have provided a nontrivial benefit to nonwhite women, much of that benefit may have come at the expense of White women, for whom the statute may have damaged employment opportunities.[49] Negative side effects must be included in assessments of the net impact and social desirability of a policy, but they are rarely investigated. One examination of the Act considered some of these effects in terms of gender.[50] In comparing men and women, however, the examination suffered from two deficiencies: It failed to distinguish racial groups—i.e., it compared men of all races to women of all races—and it had an insufficient number of observations for the statistical technique it used.[51] As a result, the findings of the examination are of limited utility and questionable accuracy.

A number of studies have concluded that enforcement of the federal statute reduced gender and racial differences in income and occupation.[52] However, unlike the research cited above, the studies failed to examine trends in these differences over a substantial period of time prior to the Act. As emphasized in chapter 1, consideration of such trends is essential for determining whether change that occurs after adoption of a policy is likely to have materialized without the policy.

A study of unemployment rates reported that, from 1965 to 1976, the Civil Rights Act of 1964 appreciably narrowed the difference in joblessness that existed between Blacks and Whites.[53] Unfortunately, the study did not control for the influence of several potentially important factors (e.g., region, gender, education, and occupation), and its conclusion regarding the impact of the Act is therefore open to question. Indeed, a subsequent investigation, using data for 1968 to 1988, indicates that from the late 1960s onward the Act did not materially reduce the gap in unemployment between Blacks and Whites.[54] However, if the initial study is correct in concluding that the Civil Rights Act was of major assistance to Blacks during 1965–1976, another of its findings becomes relevant—namely, that rates of joblessness among Blacks diverged from rates of joblessness among Whites between 1977 and 1983 and that the magnitude of this divergence each year was six times larger than the yearly convergence between 1965 and 1976.[55] Just two years of the 1977–1983 period were thus needed to eliminate the gains that had accrued to Blacks in the preceding twelve years. While the role of the Civil Rights Act in the later period is not known, the Act, in reducing the racial difference in joblessness, may have contributed to the subsequent widening of that difference. In particular, if the law forced change on societal patterns between 1965 and 1976, it could have engendered stress in the social system, and a reaction to that stress may have occurred that increased the Black-White gap in unemployment.

A study of the textile industry has reported that the Civil Rights Act produced significant employment gains for Black men and women in at least one southern state.[56] If correct, the conclusion is an exception to the contention that law usually has little effect on social patterns, but it does not disprove the contention because there will be occasional situations deviating from any generalization (see chapter 7). Moreover, the conclusion may well be incorrect even though it is based on data for a relatively long period before the statute was in force. The study itself recognizes that a labor shortage existed at the time the law was implemented (1965); that the growth of Black employment that followed may have stemmed from the shortage; and that the statute may have acted only to provide employers with the social excuse they needed to hire Blacks. "What cannot be dismissed and indeed seems quite plausible is that in 1965 entrepreneurs seized on the new federal legislation and decrees to do what they wanted to do anyway."[57] If this was the case, it is likely that, had the statute not been enacted, the textile industry would have found other means to enlarge its minority work force and alleviate its labor shortage, and the gains made by Blacks would have materialized without the law (though perhaps at a somewhat slower pace).[58]

II

Like employment discrimination, abortion has been a politically salient issue, and law designed to restrict it has not had a major impact on its frequency—at least among adult women.[59] Adults account for the vast majority, and a rising proportion, of all pregnancy terminations in the United States—87% in 1976 and 90% in 1988[60]—and they therefore must be the primary focus in assessing the effect of law on abortion.

Regrettably, the impact of law on pregnancy termination among minors has been the subject of little research. Two studies suggest that legislation may exercise a considerable influence on the frequency with which minors abort pregnancies, but they are far from definitive. One of the studies found that the abortion rate among females 15–17 years old was reduced in a state that adopted a statute requiring minors either to (1) advise their parents at least forty-eight hours in advance of having an abortion or (2) obtain the approval of a court for the abortion. The statute, however, seems not to have prevented minor females from obtaining abortions but, rather, led them to avoid pregnancies through contraception.[61] Moreover, the statute of another state that required minors to secure the approval of their parents or of a court prior to terminating a pregnancy did not have a clear effect on the incidence of abortion among minors.[62]

The second study suggesting that law may be a major determinant of the number of pregnancies aborted by minors examined births to New York City residents who were less than 20 years old. The study reported that legislation easing the legal requirements for abortion had a substantial, sustained impact on the fertility of Blacks but that, for Whites, the impact of the legislation was limited to approximately one year.[63] Unfortunately, mothers who were under age 18 at the time of delivery were not distinguished from mothers who had reached age 18, but the findings are consistent with the hypothesis that law markedly affects the likelihood a minor will undergo an abortion.

III

A popular assumption in the United States is that government policies and agencies have a major influence on the crime rate. Research, however, does not support the assumption. Thus, statutes that define certain conduct as criminal and authorize punishment for it appear not to deter the conduct to an appreciable extent.[64] Legal requirements (e.g., permits) for the acquisition and possession of guns do not have an impact on the rate at which gun-related crimes occur,[65] and a mandatory minimum prison sentence for possession of a gun during the commission of a felony seems not to affect the frequency of assaults, homicides, and robberies.[66] A state statute that imposed a mandatory minimum prison sentence for unlicensed possession of a firearm, however, was reported by one study to have produced a net decline in armed robberies and homicides.[67] Unfortunately, the study could not determine whether the statute had a lasting impact because its data covered only a brief period after the law took effect. More importantly, the conclusion of the study regarding robbery and homicide was reached by comparing a city in the state that adopted the law with cities located in states where comparable legislation did not exist. Such a procedure is inherently risky. The city that was subject to the statute undoubtedly differed in many ways from the cities with which it was compared, and the course of armed robbery and homicide in the former thus cannot be attributed with any confidence to the legislation. The study also examined armed assault, however, and its conclusions regarding the impact of the law are more certain with regard to this offense than with regard to robbery and homicide because rates of armed assault prior to the statute were available for a longer period. The data indicated that the legislation curtailed the use of guns in armed assaults but did not affect the total number of armed assaults—i.e., the law caused a decrease in assaults with a gun but an offsetting increase in assaults with other types of weapons. Another investigation of the statute with longitudinal data was inconclusive because of a defective statistical analysis.[68]

Arrest for criminal conduct has been found to reduce the frequency with which persons who are arrested commit criminal acts in the future.[69] The finding suggests that, even if punishment is not a deterrent to criminal conduct, the state may control crime through arrests. However, while arrest may affect the individuals directly involved, it does not necessarily influence the rate at which criminal acts occur in a social system. Indeed, the proportion of crimes for which an arrest is made seems to have at most a small effect on the crime rate.[70]

Even if the state is able to prevent crime to a meaningful degree, however, an examination of its role requires consideration of the alternative to government involvement in crime control. A principal concern of my thesis is the contribution that law makes to society, and an understanding of that contribution with respect to crime necessitates an estimate of the extent to which behavior of a criminal nature would occur if private persons and groups rather than the state were responsible for dealing with that behavior. If government were to eliminate its criminal law, police, and criminal justice system, individuals and groups not affiliated with the state (e.g., victims, their friends, and/or their relatives) would respond to acts presently defined as criminal. The issue, therefore, is whether the state or private parties would be more effective in minimizing the frequency of acts of a criminal character. Unfortunately, direct quantitative evidence on the issue is lacking, but I find no compelling reason to believe that the state is markedly more effective than private parties would be in curtailing conduct of the type the state defines as criminal. Indeed, the size of a municipal police force does not appreciably influence either the ratio of arrests to crimes or the rate of crime.[71] If state involvement does not improve deterrence, a social system does not need—and presumably does not employ—criminal law, police, and a criminal justice system to minimize socially dangerous behavior. Rather, other objectives are advanced by the state. In condemning certain forms of conduct through its criminal law, the state endorses prevailing social ideals and strengthens the commitment to society of individuals who hold those ideals. Criminal law in this regard performs a symbolic function. In addition, through its criminal justice system, the state both centralizes and monopolizes the administration of punishment. The result is a reduced incidence of two types of situations that impair the operation of society. First, inequality in penalties for the same type of offense is diminished, and as a consequence, perceptions of social injustice are decreased.[72] Second, punishment is less likely to be administered by private parties to persons who have injured them, and retaliation and internecine conflict are accordingly curtailed.[73]

IV

Numerous attempts have been made by government during the last half of the twentieth century to lessen, if not eliminate, racial separation in the United States, and these attempts have largely focused on education. The programs undertaken, however, seem not to have met with much success. In particular, judicially mandated school desegregation has evidently not been able to promote racial integration substantially in either school systems or associated housing patterns.[74] A study of 122 major desegregation efforts in public school districts from 1967 to 1985 concluded that the efforts increased racial integration in the schools,[75] but their net effect was nonetheless limited. During implementation of the desegregation programs, the decline in segregation (as measured by the dissimilarity index) exceeded the decline experienced in the year prior to implementation, but the integration that occurred would evidently have materialized in a relatively short time without the programs. Specifically, the reduction in segregation levels that was found during program implementation would have been achieved in approximately nine and one-half years in the absence of the programs if integration continued to advance at the pace observed in the year before implementation.[76] However, since the programs lasted a mean of 1.65 years,[77] the net gain was less than eight years. Moreover, the programs were responsible for the withdrawal of White students from the public school systems involved: "[D]esegregation efforts lower the index of racial dissimilarity, and they also reduce enrollments of White students."[78] Although the study found that the exposure of minority to nonminority students within the public schools improved as a result of desegregation,[79] evaluation of desegregation programs must include the White students who changed schools. The latter presumably were less likely to be exposed to minority classmates in their new schools than they would have been in the schools from which they withdrew. If so, the enrollment loss caused by desegregation programs is contrary to the purpose of the programs and offsets their benefit to at least some degree.

Apart from the net effect of court orders on the racial composition of schools, integration may not promote interracial contact in the classroom or academic achievement by minority students.[80]

V

Legislation to improve the safety of motor vehicle operation has been a concomitant of the growing density of automobiles in the United States and has been the subject of a number of studies. The research indicates that statutes requiring the use of seat belts in motor vehicles have not substantially decreased accident fatalities among vehicle occupants. A study of nine states that had relatively high rates of motor vehicle deaths and/or that had mandatory seat belt use statutes in operation for a relatively long time found that, after they had been in force for three months, the statutes in seven of the states had no impact on fatalities among front-seat occupants of passenger vehicles involved in accidents. In one of the two remaining states, the compulsory seat belt use law produced a statistically significant decline in front-seat fatalities that lasted more than three months, but in the other state, fatalities exhibited a statistically significant rise after the law had been in effect for three months. Notably, the rise in the latter state was roughly equal in magnitude to the decline in the former state.[81]

A statute that requires seat belts to be used and that makes their use more common may increase deaths by providing motor vehicle operators with a sense of greater safety that leads them to take more frequent and/or more serious risks while driving. The extent of such a reaction is uncertain, however.[82]

A reduction in front-seat fatalities of approximately 6% has been found in all jurisdictions with mandatory seat belt use legislation that has been in force for more than three months.[83] However, the estimate is influenced by states having relatively brief experience with seat belt use statutes and/or relatively few motor vehicle fatalities. The effect of statutes requiring seat belt use in such states cannot be estimated as reliably as the effect of the statutes in states having comparatively long experience with the statutes and/or comparatively large numbers of accident fatalities.

Mandating the use of seat belts has not been the only means that legislators have adopted to minimize injuries and deaths from motor vehicle operation. In addition, statutes establishing the minimum age for the purchase of alcoholic beverages have been revised. Research, however, indicates that such statutes have little or no impact on the incidence of alcohol-related fatalities from traffic accidents.[84] One study that suggests the statutes can have a beneficial effect found higher levels of alcohol-related, nonfatal motor vehicle accidents among 18- to 20-year-old drivers in a state following a reduction in the minimum age for buying alcoholic beverages, but of the two measures employed by the study of alcohol involvement in accidents, one was conceded to be unreliable while the other was indirect and produced results which for the most part were not statistically significant.[85] Indirect measures of (proxies for) alcohol involvement have frequently been used in research, but they seriously compromise the credibility of the conclusions reached.[86]

A study that relied on a direct measure—police judgments regarding alcohol use by drivers involved in accidents in the state of Michigan—concluded that an increase in the minimum age from 18 to 21 reduced injury-producing accidents stemming from the consumption of alcohol among drivers less than 21 years of age. The study examined the ratio between (1) drivers in a given age range who were involved in injury-producing accidents while under the influence of alcohol and (2) all drivers in the same age range who were involved in injury-producing accidents. Thus, among drivers who had been in injury-causing motor vehicle mishaps, the proportion who had consumed alcohol was calculated. Over a five-year period, the statutory change in the minimum age was estimated to have produced a 9% decline in the proportion among 18- to 20-year-old drivers, while at the same time a 7% rise occurred among drivers who were 21 years of age and older.[87] The investigator argues that the 7% rise in alcohol-related, injury-producing accidents among drivers 21 years of age and older would have occurred among 18- to 20-year-old drivers had the statutory minimum age not been increased, and he therefore adds that percentage to the 9% decline experienced by 18- to 20-year-old drivers. By doing so, he concludes that the statutory change was responsible for a 16% reduction in the proportion of injury-causing accidents involving drivers 18–20 years old who were under the influence of alcohol. However, it is mere assumption that, if the minimum age had not been altered, the increment in the accident rate experienced by older drivers would have occurred among those who were 18–20 years old. To estimate the impact of the statutory change at more than 9% is therefore unwarranted. Moreover, insofar as it delayed access to alcoholic beverages, the increase in the minimum age may have augmented the use of such beverages once that age was attained. If this is the case, some of the rise in the rate of injury-producing, alcohol-related accidents among drivers 21 years of age and older offsets, and should be subtracted from, the decline among drivers 18–20 years old. But even without an offset, there was little effect from raising the minimum legal age to purchase alcoholic beverages. Two points are important in this regard. First, visual inspection of the time series plot reveals that, within a year after the new minimum age was implemented, the proportion of 18- to 20-year-olds who were involved in alcohol-related, injury-producing accidents was as high as it had been prior to the change in the law.[88] The benefit of the new minimum age was therefore short-lived. Second, the impact of the change in the minimum age was measured in percentages, not percentage points; among 18- to 20-year-old drivers involved in injury-producing accidents, the proportion who were under the influence of alcohol was curtailed by 9%, not 9 percentage points. However, impact is preferably assessed in terms of percentage points, since percentages must be considered in relation to the initial level of the phenomenon under investigation; a 9% decline is far more impressive if the initial level is high than if it is low. When examined in terms of percentage points, the new minimum age appears to have had only a small effect, for it eliminated substantially less than two percentage points from the rate of alcohol-related, injury-producing accidents among drivers 18–20 years old.[89]

Statutes fixing a minimum age for the purchase of alcoholic beverages have been found to influence the consumption only of beer.[90] However, the conclusion regarding beer consumption is based on cross-sectional, not longitudinal, data. When beer consumption is studied with time series data for several years after the minimum age is altered and when no contemporaneous events have occurred that can influence consumption, little if any long-term impact on beer use is observed.[91] In one state (New Hampshire), a statistically significant increase in total sales of package beer followed a reduction in the minimum age from 21 to 18. However, visual inspection of the moving average in the time series plot discloses that the increase lasted only about one year, after which sales volume remained constant for almost three years.[92] The failure of aggregate sales to continue expanding beyond one year cannot be attributed to a lack of population growth; the number of persons 18 years of age and older who resided in the state rose throughout the period.[93] By lowering the minimum age, the state may only have concentrated into a single year the increase in package beer sales that would have been spread over several years without a change in the law. The time series plot shows a rise in total sales before the minimum age was altered, and the rise should have continued throughout the period under study since population was growing. It thus seems at least plausible that the lower minimum age compressed the expansion of demand that would have materialized over a relatively long period into a short one.

VI

Research has been conducted on an array of other issues and has found that law is generally ineffective in changing social patterns. The research can be summarized succinctly as follows:[94]

- Legislation designed to influence the size and composition of community populations has not on the whole accomplished its objectives.[95]
- The enrollment of Blacks and Hispanics in law schools and medical schools was minimally affected by a decision of the U.S. Supreme Court that invalidated quotas designed to increase the number of minority students in institutions of higher education.[96] Similarly, neither a 1972 federal statute that prohibited sex discrimination in graduate and professional programs of institutions of higher education while those programs receive financial assistance from the federal government, nor litigation commenced against all medical schools in the United States, had a material impact on the number of women admitted to medical schools.[97]
- Statutes requiring that minors attend school have had little or no influence on rates of enrollment in primary and secondary schools.[98]
- Legislation to enforce child support awards has had no more than a small effect on the probability that noncustodial fathers will provide judicially ordered financial assistance to their children.[99] Moreover, the type of child custody ordered by courts (custody by both parents jointly versus custody by the mother only) has just a limited influence on the amount paid by fathers for the support of their children.[100]
- Changes in the statutory grounds for divorce have generally had no more than a minimal impact on the incidence of divorce.[101]
- Neither federal legislation nor policing of the border has appreciably curbed illegal immigration into the United States from Mexico.[102]
- Legislation to improve the safety of work sites and products on the market has not materially reduced injury and death rates among

employees and consumers.[103] At the same time, regulation by the federal government to protect the safety of work sites appears to have diminished economic productivity.[104]

- Legislation that requires a protective helmet to be worn while operating a motorcycle has been of negligible benefit in averting fatalities among cyclists involved in accidents.[105]

NOTES

1. Grey, *Langdell's Orthodoxy*, 45 UNIV. OF PITTSBURGH L. REV. 1 (1983).

2. T. KUHN, THE STRUCTURE OF SCIENTIFIC REVOLUTIONS (2nd ed. 1970).

3. Ass'n of Am. Law Schools, 1987 Annual Meeting Program (1987). The four were Law and Society, Feminist Jurisprudence, Critical Legal Studies, and Law and Economics. The fifth approach considered in the workshop was Clinical Education.

4. Page & Shapiro, *Effects of Public Opinion on Policy*, 77 AM. POL. SCI. REV. 175 (1983); Wright, Erikson, & McIver, *Public Opinion and Policy Liberalism in the American States*, 31 AM. J. POL. SCI. 980 (1987); T. MARSHALL, PUBLIC OPINION AND THE SUPREME COURT (1989).

Research finds that law follows public opinion on most issues but not all. A majority of the instances in which law and opinion seem to diverge are probably the result of two factors. One is measurement error: The items used in surveys to assess attitudes are worded succinctly and at times fail to convey the complexity of the issues confronting courts and legislatures. Items that do not portray the critical features of an issue may result in data that suggest legal doctrine deviates from public opinion when in fact it does not.

A second factor probably responsible for instances of divergence between law and public opinion is that certain components of society will often determine legal thought when attitudes toward the issues involved differ markedly, in content and/or intensity, across the social system. In these circumstances, law will not be formulated by a process of compromise on the part of the populace as a whole but will manifest the ideology of particular social subsystems, e.g., certain occupational or age groups. Regrettably, research to date has not investigated how legal doctrine responds when attitudes differ from one segment of society to another. Where large differences exist, however, erroneous conclusions regarding the link between public opinion and legal thought can be reached if legal doctrine is compared to the attitudes of the population in general rather than to the attitudes of the most influential societal components.

5. L. FRIEDMAN, THE LEGAL SYSTEM 139–43 (1975).

6. *See* Galliher, *The Study of the Social Origins of Criminal Law*, in 3 RESEARCH IN LAW AND SOCIOLOGY 301 (S. Spitzer ed., 1980).

7. Inkeles, *American Perceptions*, 9 CHANGE 25, 27 (Aug. 1977).

8. For this discussion of Critical Legal Studies, I have relied on Russell, *The Critical Legal Studies Challenge to Contemporary Mainstream Legal Philosophy*, 18 OTTAWA L. REV. 1 (1986).

9. *See* Gordon, *Critical Legal Histories*, 36 STANFORD L. REV. 57, 59–67 (1984).

10. *E.g.*, Meese, *The Supreme Court of the United States: Bulwark of a Limited Constitution*, 27 SOUTH TEXAS L. J. 455 (1986); M. PERRY, THE CONSTITUTION, THE COURTS, AND HUMAN RIGHTS (1982).

11. United Steelworkers of America v. Weber, 443 U.S. 193 (1979).

12. J. SMITH & F. WELCH, CLOSING THE GAP: FORTY YEARS OF ECONOMIC PROGRESS FOR BLACKS 6, 81 (1986); J. Robinson, A Cohort Analysis of Trends in the Labor Force Participation of Men and Women in the United States: 1890 to 1985 (1988) at 214 (unpublished Ph.D. dissertation, University of Pennsylvania).

13. City of Cleburne v. Cleburne Living Center, 473 U.S. 432, 466 (1985) (Marshall, Brennan, and Blackmun, JJ., concurring in part and dissenting in part) (citations omitted).

14. The distinction between social and economic issues is discussed further in chapter 7.

15. This conclusion receives additional support from the finding that decisions of the U.S. Supreme Court normally are consistent with American public opinion and do not markedly influence that opinion. MARSHALL, *supra* note 4, at 78–79, 146.

16. Schoeman, *Book Review: Larry D. Barnett and Emily F. Reed, Law, Society, and Population*, 11 POPULATION & DEV. REV. 776 (1985).

17. *E.g.*, Steward Machine Co. v. Davis, 301 U.S. 548 (1937).

18. *See* Brunk & Minehart, *How Important Is Elite Turnover to Policy Change?*, 28 AM. J. POL. SCI. 559 (1984).

19. Orcutt & Bayer, *Student Protest and Sex-Role Attitude Change, 1967–1971: A Log-Linear Analysis of Longitudinal Data*, 4 SEX ROLES 267 (1978); Burstein, *Public Opinion, Demonstrations, and the Passage of Antidiscrimination Legislation*, 43 PUB. OPINION Q. 157 (1979).

20. Evidence bearing on the changes that have occurred in sex roles—the subject of the study by Orcutt and Bayer cited *supra* note 19—can be found in: BUREAU OF THE CENSUS, U.S. DEP'T OF COMMERCE, 1 HISTORICAL STATISTICS OF THE UNITED STATES: COLONIAL TIMES TO 1970, at 132 (1975); BUREAU OF THE CENSUS, U.S. DEP'T OF COMMERCE, STATISTICAL ABSTRACT OF THE UNITED STATES: 1986, at 392 (106th ed. 1985); Sorensen & McLanahan, *Married Women's Economic Dependency, 1940–1980*, 93 AM. J. SOC. 659 (1987).

Data on changes between Blacks and Whites—the focus of the study by Burstein *supra* note 19—appear in Smith & Welch, *supra* note 12, and in Bureau of the Census, U.S. Dep't of Commerce, *The Social and Economic Status of the Black Population in the United States: An Historical View, 1790–1978*, CURRENT POPULATION REP. Series P-23, No. 80 (no date), at 74, 93.

21. Of the pages in the *Decennial Digest* devoted to equal protection, the proportions concerned with race and sex discrimination were, respectively, only 7.9 and 3.7% in 1966–1976 and 5.8 and 6.6% in 1976–1981. Given their small share of the total, race and sex discrimination cases cannot account for the increase in equal protection decisions. Moreover, while the space needed for sex discrimination cases rose from roughly 0.3% of the pages occupied by equal

protection decisions in 1956–1966 to 3.7% in 1966–1976, the space required for race discrimination cases fell from 17.4 to 7.9%.

22. Further evidence that the change began in the early 1960s can be found in the enactment by Congress of the Civil Rights Act of 1964. The statute banned discrimination on the basis of several demographic characteristics (e.g., race, religion, and gender) in employment and other settings. Pub. L. No. 88–352, 78 Stat. 241. Adoption of the statute was preceded by a marked rise in civil rights demonstrations commencing about 1960. Burstein, *supra* note 19, at 169.

The section of the statute dealing with employment (Title VII) did not apply to state and local governments until 1972. Pub. L. No. 92–261, 86 Stat. 103. While this may suggest that the public was intolerant of classifications only in the private sector when the statute was enacted in the 1960s, the extension of the law to state and local governments in 1972 was explicitly considered by Congress not to involve establishment of a new policy but, rather, to be a means of enforcing an existing policy. H.R. REP. No. 238, 92d Cong., 2d Sess., *reprinted in* 1972 U.S. CODE CONG. & AD. NEWS 2137, 2152–2154.

23. S. VAN ALSTYNE, J. JULIN, & L. BARNETT, THE GOALS AND MISSIONS OF LAW SCHOOLS 48–61 (1990).

24. Rubinson & Ralph, *Technical Change and the Expansion of Schooling in the United States, 1890–1970*, 57 SOC. OF EDUC. 134 (1984); Inkeles & Sirowy, *Convergent and Divergent Trends in National Educational Systems*, 62 SOCIAL FORCES 303 (1983).

25. Leavitt, *Ideology and the Materialist Model of General Evolution: A Cross-Cultural Test of Subsystem Relationships*, 65 SOCIAL FORCES 525 (1986).

26. *E.g.*, Bohme & Stehr, *The Growing Impact of Scientific Knowledge on Social Relations*, *in* THE KNOWLEDGE SOCIETY 7 (G. Bohme & N. Stehr eds., 1986). Empirical evidence on the increase is found in: Price, *Ups and Downs in the Pulse of Science and Technology*, 48 SOC. INQUIRY 162 (1978); F. MACHLUP, THE PRODUCTION AND DISTRIBUTION OF KNOWLEDGE IN THE UNITED STATES 382–88 (1962); *cf.* D. Grusky, American Social Mobility in the 19th and 20th Centuries 52–55, 98–100 (1986) (unpublished Ph.D. dissertation, University of Wisconsin-Madison). While there is widespread agreement that the quantity of knowledge has expanded, questions exist about particular procedures used to measure the change. Gilbert, *Measuring the Growth of Science*, 1 SCIENTOMETRICS 9 (1978).

27. *See* Jackman & Muha, *Education and Intergroup Attitudes: Moral Enlightenment, Superficial Democratic Commitment, or Ideological Refinement?*, 49 AM. SOC. REV. 751 (1984); Semyonov, *The Social Context of Women's Labor Force Participation: A Comparative Analysis*, 86 AM. J. SOC. 534 (1980).

28. Lesthaeghe, *A Century of Demographic and Cultural Change in Western Europe: An Exploration of Underlying Dimensions*, 9 POPULATION & DEV. REV. 411 (1983); Booth, Johnson, White, & Edwards, *Women, Outside Employment, and Marital Instability*, 90 AM. J. SOC. 567 (1984).

29. C. Nass, Society as Computer: The Structure and Skill of Information Work in the United States, 1900–1980 123 (1986) (unpublished Ph.D. dissertation, Princeton University); Kohn & Schooler, *Job Conditions and Personality: A Longitudinal Assessment of Their Reciprocal Effects*, 87 AM. J. SOC. 1257 (1982);

Miller, Slomczynski, & Kohn, *Continuity of Learning-Generalization: The Effect of Job on Men's Intellective Process in the United States and Poland*, 91 AM. J. SOC. 593 (1985).

30. Carneiro, *On the Relationship Between Size of Population and Complexity of Social Organization*, 42 J. ANTHROPOLOGICAL RES. 355 (1986).

31. Fischer, *Toward a Subcultural Theory of Urbanism*, 80 AM. J. SOC. 1319 (1975).

32. Wilson, *Community Population Size and Social Heterogeneity: An Empirical Test*, 91 AM. J. SOC. 1154–1155 (1986). Copyright 1986 by The University of Chicago. All rights reserved. *Accord*, Wilson, *Urbanism and Tolerance: A Test of Some Hypotheses Drawn from Wirth and Stouffer*, 50 AM. SOC. REV. 117 (1985); Fischer, *Urban-to-Rural Diffusion of Opinions in Contemporary America*, 84 AM. J. SOC. 151 (1978); Wilson, *Urbanism, Migration, and Tolerance: A Reassessment*, 56 AM. SOC. REV. 117 (1991). *See* Stephan & McMullin, *Tolerance of Sexual Nonconformity: City Size as a Situational and Early Learning Determinant*, 47 AM. SOC. REV. 411 (1982).

33. Blau, Beeker, & Fitzpatrick, *Intersecting Social Affiliations and Intermarriage*, 62 SOCIAL FORCES 585 (1984); Blau, Blum, & Schwartz, *Heterogeneity and Intermarriage*, 47 AM. SOC. REV. 45 (1982); Rytina, Blau, Blum, & Schwartz, *Inequality and Intermarriage: A Paradox of Motive and Constraint*, 66 SOCIAL FORCES 645 (1988).

34. Price, *supra* note 26, at 169.

35. Calculated from Bureau of the Census, U.S. Dep't. of Commerce, *Projections of the Population of the United States, By Age, Sex, and Race: 1983 to 2080*, CURRENT POPULATION REP. Series P-25, No. 952 (1984), at table E.

36. Research has found that, with growth in the size of young adult cohorts, some forms of political alienation become more prevalent in the population as a whole. Kahn & Mason, *Political Alienation, Cohort Size, and the Easterlin Hypothesis*, 52 AM. SOC. REV. 155 (1987). The finding is consistent with the argument here. Political alienation presumably stems in part from government classifications that frustrate the ability of individuals to achieve their goals, and as the level of alienation rises, an increase logically occurs in the number of constitutional challenges to such classifications. *Cf.* Orcutt & Bayer, *supra* note 19, and Burstein, *supra* note 19. From this perspective, political alienation is a mechanism (or, in sociological terminology, intervening variable) through which the relative size of young adult cohorts influences the frequency of equal protection challenges: Enlargement of these cohorts magnifies problems from dysfunctional government classifications and promotes alienation, which in turn fosters litigation contesting the constitutionality of the classifications.

37. Schoen, Urton, Woodrow, & Baj, *Marriage and Divorce in Twentieth Century American Cohorts*, 22 DEMOGRAPHY 101, 103, 105 (1985).

38. R. KIDDER, CONNECTING LAW AND SOCIETY 58–82 (1983).

39. Burkhauser & Quinn, *Is Mandatory Retirement Overrated? Evidence from the 1970s*, 18 J. HUM. RESOURCES 337 (1983); Copeland & Meier, *Gaining Ground: The Impact of Medicaid and WIC on Infant Mortality*, 15 AM. POLITICS Q. 254 (1987); Gratton, *The Labor Force Participation of Older Men: 1890–1950*, 20 J. SOC. HIST. 689

(1987); Hendershott & Smith, *Transfer Programs and Aggregate Household Formations*, 8 POPULATION RES. & POL'Y REV. 227 (1989); Klerman & Leibowitz, *Child Care and Women's Return to Work After Childbirth*, 80 AM. ECON. REV. 284 (May 1990); Whittington, *Taxes and the Family: The Impact of the Tax Exemption for Dependents on Marital Fertility*, 29 DEMOGRAPHY 215 (1992); Whittington, Alm, & Peters, *Fertility and the Personal Exemption: Implicit Pronatalist Policy in the United States*, 80 AM. ECON. REV. 545 (1990). *See also* Buttner & Lutz, *Estimating Fertility Responses to Policy Measures in the German Democratic Republic*, 16 POPULATION & DEV. REV. 539 (1990).

40. *See* South & Trent, *Sex Ratios and Women's Roles: A Cross-National Analysis*, 93 AM. J. SOC. 1096 (1988).

41. I have developed the reasons and evidence for this in VAN ALSTYNE, JULIN, & BARNETT, *supra* note 23.

42. *See* C. Colella & W. McIntosh, The Social Foundations of Litigation (paper presented at the 1988 meeting of the Law and Society Association); Kasarda & Friedrichs, *Comparative Demographic-Employment Mismatches in U.S. and West German Cities*, 3 RESEARCH IN THE SOCIOLOGY OF WORK 1 (I. Simpson & R. Simpson eds., 1985); Roncek, *Dangerous Places: Crime and Residential Environment*, 60 SOCIAL FORCES 74 (1981); S. Kim, Dimensions of Social Integration: Solidarity and Deviance in American Cities 112–121 (1986) (unpublished Ph.D. dissertation, University of Virginia).

43. Zimring, *Where Do the New Scholars Learn New Scholarship?*, 33 J. LEGAL EDUC. 453 (1983).

44. Bok, *A Flawed System of Law Practice and Training*, 33 J. LEGAL EDUC. 570, 582 (1983).

45. Smith & Welch, *Black Economic Progress After Myrdal*, 27 J. ECON. LITERATURE 519 (1989); J. SMITH & M. WARD, WOMEN'S WAGES AND WORK IN THE TWENTIETH CENTURY (1984); Butler & Heckman, *The Government's Impact on the Labor Market Status of Black Americans: A Critical Review*, *in* EQUAL RIGHTS AND INDUSTRIAL RELATIONS 235 (L. Hausman, O. Ashenfelter, B. Rustin, R. Schubert, & D. Slaiman eds., 1977). *See also* Shapiro & Stelcner, *The Persistence of the Male-Female Earnings Gap in Canada, 1970–1980: The Impact of Equal Pay Laws and Language Policies*, 13 CANADIAN PUB. POL'Y 462 (1987); *see generally* Gunderson, *Discrimination, Equal Pay, and Equal Opportunities in the Labour Market*, *in* WORK AND PAY: THE CANADIAN LABOUR MARKET 219 (W. Riddell ed., 1985). *See* Lichter, *Racial Differences in Underemployment in American Cities*, 93 AM. J. SOC. 771 (1988).

46. McCrone & Hardy, *Civil Rights Policies and the Achievement of Racial Economic Equality, 1948–1975*, 22 AM. J. POL. SCI. 1 (1978).

47. Hardy & McCrone, *The Impact of the Civil Rights Act of 1964 on Women*, 7 POL'Y STUD. J. 240 (1978).

48. P. BURSTEIN, DISCRIMINATION, JOBS, AND POLITICS 46–47, 141, 149 (1985).

49. Smith & Welch, *Affirmative Action and Labor Markets*, 2 J. LABOR ECON. 269, 288 (1984).

50. Uri & Mixon, *Effects of U.S. Affirmative Action Programs on Women's Employment*, 13 J. POL'Y MODELING 367 (1991).

51. *See* R. McCleary & R. Hay, Jr., Applied Time Series Analysis for the Social Sciences 20 (1980).

52. *E.g.*, Leonard, *The Impact of Affirmative Action on Employment*, 2 J. Labor Econ. 439 (1984); Beller, *The Impact of Equal Opportunity Policy on Sex Differentials in Earnings and Occupations*, 72 Am. Econ. Rev. 171 (May 1982).

53. Rice & Whitby, *Racial Inequality in Unemployment: The Effectiveness of the Civil Rights Act of 1964*, *in* Affirmative Action 61 (M. Combs & J. Gruhl eds., 1986).

54. F. Wilson, M. Tienda, & L. Wu, Racial Equality in the Labor Market: Still An Elusive Goal? (Center for Demography & Ecology, University of Wisconsin, Madison, Wisconsin, Working Paper No. 91–33, 1992).

55. Rice & Whitby, *supra* note 53, at 66.

56. Heckman & Payner, *Determining the Impact of Federal Antidiscrimination Policy on the Economic Status of Blacks: A Study of South Carolina*, 79 Am. Econ. Rev. 138 (1989).

57. *Id*. at 174.

58. *Id*. at 144.

59. Hogan, *An Intervention Analysis of the Effects of Legalized Abortion Upon U.S. Fertility*, 3 Population Res. & Pol'y Rev. 201 (1984); Johnson & Bond, *Coercive and Noncoercive Abortion Deterrence Policies*, 2 Law & Pol'y Q. 106 (1980). See also *infra* chapter 5.

60. S. Henshaw & J. Van Vort, Abortion Services in the United States, Each State & Metropolitan Area, 1984–1985, at table 1 (1988); Henshaw, *Abortion Trends in 1987 and 1988: Age and Race*, 24 Fam. Plan. Persp. 85, 86 (1992).

61. Rogers, Boruch, Stoms, & DeMoya, *Impact of the Minnesota Parental Notification Law on Abortion and Birth*, 81 Am. J. Pub. Health 294 (1991).

62. Cartoof & Klerman, *Parental Consent for Abortion: Impact of the Massachusetts Law*, 76 Am. J. Pub. Health 397 (1986).

63. T. Joyce & N. Mocan, The Impact of a Ban on Legalized Abortion on Adolescent Childbearing in New York City 18 (National Bureau of Economic Research Working Paper No. 3002, 1989).

64. Paternoster, Saltzman, Waldo, & Chiricos, *Perceived Risk and Social Control: Do Sanctions Really Deter?*, 17 Law & Soc'y Rev. 457 (1983); Saltzman, Paternoster, Waldo, & Chiricos, *Deterrent and Experiential Effects: The Problem of Causal Order in Perceptual Deterrence Research*, 19 J. Res. Crime & Delinq. 172 (1982); Piliavin, Gartner, Thornton, & Matsueda, *Crime, Deterrence, and Rational Choice*, 51 Am. Soc. Rev. 101 (1986); Meier & Johnson, *Deterrence as Social Control: The Legal and Extralegal Production of Conformity*, 42 Am. Soc. Rev. 292 (1977); Bailey & Peterson, *Murder and Capital Punishment: A Monthly Time-Series Analysis of Execution Publicity*, 54 Am. Soc. Rev. 722 (1989); Peterson & Bailey, *Murder and Capital Punishment in the Evolving Context of the Post-Furman Era*, 66 Social Forces 774 (1988); Singer & McDowall, *Criminalizing Delinquency: The Deterrent Effects of the New York Juvenile Offender Law*, 22 Law & Soc'y Rev. 521 (1988); Wilkinson, *Reducing Drunken Driving: Which Policies Are Most Effective?*, 54 So. Econ. J. 322 (1987); L. Shannon, A More Precise Evaluation of the Effects of Sanctions (Executive Report, Aug. 1986) (Report to the Nat'l Institute of Justice, U.S. Dep't of

Justice). *See* J. Marsh, A. Geist, & N. Caplan, Rape and the Limits of Law Reform 26–28 (1982). *See also* Ross, *Social Control Through Deterrence: Drinking-and-Driving Laws, in* 10 Annual Review of Sociology 21 (R. Turner & J. Short eds., 1984) (even when law lowers the frequency with which motor vehicles are driven by persons who have consumed an excessive amount of alcohol, the effect is transient and limited to no more than a few years).

65. DeZee, *Gun Control Legislation*, 5 Law & Pol'y Q. 367 (1983); Murray, *Handguns, Gun Control Laws and Firearm Violence*, 23 Social Probs. 81 (1975); Magaddino & Medoff, *An Empirical Analysis of Federal and State Firearm Control Laws, in* Firearms and Violence: Issues of Public Policy 225 (D. Kates ed., 1984).

66. Loftin & McDowall, *The Deterrent Effects of the Florida Felony Firearm Law*, 75 J. Crim. L. & Criminology 250 (1984); Loftin, Heumann, & McDowall, *Mandatory Sentencing and Firearms Violence: Evaluating an Alternative to Gun Control*, 17 Law & Soc'y Rev. 287 (1983).

67. Pierce & Bowers, *The Bartley-Fox Gun Law's Short-Term Impact on Crime in Boston*, Annals Am. Academy Pol. & Social Sci. 120 (May 1981).

68. *See* Hay & McCleary, *Box-Tiao Time Series Models for Impact Assessment: A Comment on the Recent Work of Deutsch and Alt*, 3 Evaluation Q. 277 (1979).

69. Smith & Gartin, *Specifying Specific Deterrence: The Influence of Arrest on Future Criminal Activity*, 54 Am. Soc. Rev. 94 (1989).

70. Greenberg & Kessler, *The Effect of Arrests on Crime: A Multivariate Panel Analysis*, 60 Social Forces 771 (1982); Greenberg, Kessler, & Logan, *A Panel Model of Crime Rates and Arrest Rates*, 44 Am. Soc. Rev. 843 (1979); Pogue, *Offender Expectations and Identification of Crime Supply Functions*, 10 Evaluation Rev. 455 (1986). *Contra*, Corman, Joyce, & Lovitch, *Crime, Deterrence and the Business Cycle in New York City: A VAR Approach*, 69 Rev. Econ. & Statistics 695 (1987).

71. Liska, Chamlin, & Reed, *Testing the Economic Production and Conflict Models of Crime Control*, 64 Social Forces 119 (1985); Loftin & McDowall, *The Police, Crime, and Economic Theory: An Assessment*, 47 Am. Soc. Rev. 393 (1982); Greenberg, Kessler, & Loftin, *The Effect of Police Employment on Crime*, 21 Criminology 375 (1983).

72. *Cf.* Tittle & Curran, *Contingencies for Dispositional Disparities in Juvenile Justice*, 67 Social Forces 23 (1988).

73. *See* McDowall & Loftin, *Collective Security and the Demand for Legal Handguns*, 88 Am. J. Soc. 1146 (1983).

74. Clark, *Judicial Intervention as Policy: Impacts on Population Distribution and Redistribution in Urban Areas in the United States*, 1 Population Res. & Pol'y Rev. 79 (1982); Klaff, *Metropolitan School Desegregation: Impact on Racial Integration of Neighborhoods in the United States*, 1 Population Res. & Pol'y Rev. 259 (1982); Clark, *School Integration Impacts on Residential Change: Evaluation and Tests*, 6 Env't & Plan. C 475 (1988); Scott, *Desegregatory Effects in Charlotte-Mecklenburg County Schools: Longitudinal Demographics on Black Achievement and Middle Class Flight*, 25 Mankind Q. 47 (1984); Clark, *Demographic Change, Attendance Area Adjustment and School System Impacts*, 6 Population Res. & Pol'y Rev. 199 (1987). *See also* Massey & Denton, *Trends in the Residential Segregation of Blacks, Hispanics, and*

Asians: 1970–1980, 52 AM. SOC. REV. 802 (1987); Welch, *A Reconsideration of the Impact of School Desegregation Programs on Public School Enrollment of White Students, 1968–76,* 60 SOC. OF EDUC. 215 (1987).

75. F. WELCH & A. LIGHT, NEW EVIDENCE ON SCHOOL DESEGREGATION (1987).

76. This estimate, which assumes that the integration occurring in the year prior to implementation was not affected by the prospect of court desegregation orders, was calculated by dividing the mean decline in the dissimilarity index during program implementation by the change in the year before implementation (.217/.023 = 9.4 years). *See id.* at 55.

77. Calculated from *id.* at table A-4.

78. *Id.* at 56; *see generally* Rossell, *Is It the Busing or the Blacks?,* 24 URB. AFF. Q. 138 (1988).

79. *Id.* at 67.

80. Singer, Gerard, & Redfearn, *Achievement, in* SCHOOL DESEGREGATION 69 (H. Gerard & N. Miller eds., 1975); Gerard, Jackson, & Conolley, *Social Contact in the Desegregated Classroom, in id.* at 211.

81. D. SKINNER & P. HOXI, EFFECTS OF SEATBELT LAWS ON HIGHWAY FATALITIES: UPDATE—APRIL 1988 (Project DOT-TSC-HS870-PM-88–5) (1988) (preliminary report; available from the Operator/Performance and Safety Analysis Division, Transportation Systems Center, Research and Special Programs Administration, U.S. Dep't of Transportation, Cambridge, MA). *But see* A. Wagenaar, R. Maybee, & K. Sullivan, Effects of Mandatory Seat Belt Laws on Traffic Fatalities in the First Eight States Enacting Seat Belt Laws (May 1987) (available from Transportation Research Institute, University of Michigan, Ann Arbor, MI) (Mortality among front-seat occupants declined in three states after implementation of a seat belt law; the study, however, failed to separate short-term effects from long-term effects, and its figures [A.1, A.3, and A.5] reveal a trend toward declining mortality in two of the states before their laws were adopted, suggesting that the mortality change that followed the laws in these states would have occurred without any legislation, albeit more slowly.)

82. *Compare* Asch, Levy, Shea & Bodenhorn, *Risk Compensation and the Effectiveness of Safety Belt Use Laws: A Case Study of New Jersey,* 24 POL'Y SCI. 181 (1991), Garbacz, *More Evidence on the Effectiveness of Seat Belt Laws,* 24 APPLIED ECON. 313 (1992), *and* Garbacz, *Do Front-Seat Belt Laws Put Rear-Seat Passengers At Risk?,* 11 POPULATION RES. & POL'Y REV. 157 (1992) *with* Wagenaar, Maybee, & Sullivan, *supra* note 81, at 19.

83. SKINNER & HOXIE, *supra* note 81, at 4.

84. Males, *The Minimum Purchase Age for Alcohol and Young-Driver Fatal Crashes: A Long-Term View,* 15 J. LEGAL STUD. 181 (1986); Asch & Levy, *Does the Minimum Drinking Age Affect Traffic Fatalities?,* 6 J. POL'Y ANALYSIS & MGMT. 180 (1987); Cook & Tauchen, *The Effect of Minimum Drinking Age Legislation on Youthful Auto Fatalities, 1970–1977,* 13 J. LEGAL STUD. 169, 187 (1984). *Contra* Saffer & Grossman, *Drinking Age Laws and Highway Mortality Rates: Cause and Effect,* 25 ECON. INQUIRY 403 (1987).

85. R. Douglass & J. Freedman, Alcohol-Related Casualties and Alcohol

Beverage Market Response to Beverage Alcohol Availability Policies in Michigan: Final Report. Vol. I, at 23–32 (Aug. 1977) (available from the Highway Safety Research Institute, University of Michigan, Ann Arbor, MI).

86. *E.g.*, T. Klein, The Effect of Raising the Minimum Legal Drinking Age on Traffic Accidents in the State of Maine (1981) (available from the National Technical Information Service).

87. Wagenaar, *Effects of Minimum Drinking Age on Alcohol-Related Traffic Crashes, in* 1 ADVANCES IN SUBSTANCE ABUSE: BEHAVIORAL AND BIOLOGICAL RESEARCH 119 (H. Holder ed., 1987).

88. *Id.* at 124 (figure 3).

89. Calculated from *id.* at 124 (figure 3).

90. Coate & Grossman, *Effects of Alcoholic Beverage Prices and Legal Drinking Ages on Youth Alcohol Use*, 31 J. LAW & ECON. 145 (1988); Ornstein & Hanssens, *Alcohol Control Laws and the Consumption of Distilled Spirits and Beer*, J. CONSUMER RES. 200 (1985).

91. A. WAGENAAR, ALCOHOL, YOUNG DRIVERS, AND TRAFFIC ACCIDENTS 80–92 (1983).

92. *Id.* at 90, 91.

93. Bureau of the Census, U.S. Dep't of Commerce, *Estimates of the Population of States, by Age: July 1, 1971 to 1979*, CURRENT POPULATION REP. Series P-25, No. 875 (1980).

94. In addition, see Hardy & Newcomer, *The Impact of Reapportionment on Policy Expenditures*, 3 LAW & POL'Y Q. 464 (1981); Karnig & Sigelman, *State Legislative Reform and Public Policy: Another Look*, 28 Western Pol. Q. 548 (1975); Mansfield, *The R&D Tax Credit and Other Technology Policy Issues*, 76 AM. ECON. REV. 190 (May 1986); McNiel & Yu, *Blue Laws: Impact on Regional Retail Activity*, 8 POPULATION RES. & POL'Y REV. 267 (1989); Witwer, *Wisconsin's Grandparent Liability Law Saved Very Little State Money and Averted Few Teenage Births*, 21 FAM. PLAN. PERSP. 230 (1989).

95. D. VARADY, NEIGHBORHOOD UPGRADING (1986); Logan & Zhou, *Do Suburban Growth Controls Control Growth?*, 54 AM. SOC. REV. 461 (1989).

96. Gruhl & Welch, *The Impact of the Bakke Decision on Black and Hispanic Enrollment in Medical and Law Schools*, 71 SOCIAL SCI. Q. 458 (1990).

97. *See* Cole, *Sex Discrimination and Admission to Medical School, 1929–1984*, 92 AM. J. SOC. 549 (1986).

98. J. FOLGER & C. NAM, EDUCATION OF THE AMERICAN POPULATION 24–27 (1976); Landes & Solmon, *Compulsory Schooling Legislation: An Economic Analysis of Law and Social Change in the Nineteenth Century*, 32 J. ECON. HIST. 54 (1972).

99. Beller & Graham, *The Effect of Child Support Enforcement on Child Support Payments*, 10 POPULATION RES. & POL'Y REV. 91 (1991).

100. Seltzer, *Legal Custody Arrangements and Children's Economic Welfare*, 96 AM. J. SOC. 895 (1991).

101. Peters, *Marriage and Divorce: Reply*, 82 AM. ECON. REV. 686 (1992); Marvell, *Divorce Rates and the Fault Requirement*, 23 LAW & SOC'Y REV. 543 (1989); Frank, Berman, & Mazur-Hart, *No-Fault Divorce and the Divorce Rate: The Nebraska Experience—An Interrupted Time Series Analysis and Commentary*, 58 NEBRASKA L.

REV. 1 (1978); Wright & Stetson, *The Impact of No-Fault Divorce Law Reform on Divorce in American States*, 40 J. MARR. & FAM. 575 (1978); Schoen, Greenblatt, & Mielke, *California's Experience With Non-Adversary Divorce*, 12 DEMOGRAPHY 223 (1975). *Cf.* Jacob, *Another Look at No-Fault Divorce and the Post-Divorce Finances of Women*, 23 LAW & SOC'Y REV. 95 (1989).

102. Donato, Durand, & Massey, *Stemming the Tide? Assessing the Deterrent Effects of the Immigration Reform and Control Act*, 29 DEMOGRAPHY 139 (1992); Kossoudji, *Playing Cat and Mouse at the U.S.-Mexican Border*, 29 DEMOGRAPHY 159 (1992). *See also* Espenshade, *Policy Influences on Undocumented Migration to the United States*, 136 PROC. AM. PHIL. SOC'Y 188 (1992).

103. Bartel & Thomas, *Direct and Indirect Effects of Regulation: A New Look at OSHA's Impact*, 28 J. LAW & ECON. 1 (1985); Viscusi, *Consumer Behavior and the Safety Effects of Product Safety Regulation*, 28 J. LAW & ECON. 527 (1985); Viscusi, *The Impact of Occupational Safety and Health Regulation, 1973–1983*, 17 RAND J. ECON. 567 (1986); Wallace, *Dying for Coal: The Struggle for Health and Safety Conditions in American Coal Mining, 1930–82*, 66 SOCIAL FORCES 336 (1987); Peltzman, *The Health Effects of Mandatory Prescriptions*, 30 J. LAW & ECON. 207 (1987).

104. Gray, *The Cost of Regulation: OSHA, EPA and the Productivity Slowdown*, 77 AM. ECON. REV. 998 (1987).

105. Sass & Leigh, *The Market for Safety Regulation and the Effect of Regulation on Fatalities: The Case of Motorcycle Helmet Laws*, 73 REV. ECON. & STATISTICS 167 (1991).

CHAPTER

3

Gender

I would like now to undertake a test of the thesis developed in chapter 2 using constitutional doctrine on the issue of gender. The issue is particularly suitable. Not only has it been the subject of constitutional adjudication by the U.S. Supreme Court over an extended period of time, but a substantial body of empirical sociological research has accumulated that can help to identify the social context of the legal thought found in the opinions of the Court.

I begin with a synopsis of the case law. The provision of the Constitution involved in these cases was not necessarily equal protection, but that is immaterial since, with regard to gender, the provision in question seems largely irrelevant to the expression of the legal doctrine required by the structure and values of society.[1] The first case arose at the start of the twentieth century and involved a state statute limiting the number of hours that women (but not men) could work in certain types of employment. Writing in 1908, the U.S. Supreme Court in *Muller v. Oregon* upheld the statute even though three years earlier it had invalidated similar legislation for men. Its opinion emphasized the role that the state would be permitted to play in protecting the health of women and their ability to bear children:

> Even though all restrictions on political, personal, and contractual rights were taken away, and [a woman] stood, so far as statutes are concerned, upon an absolutely equal plane with [a man], it would still be true that she is so constituted that she will rest upon and look to him for protection; that her physical structure and a proper discharge of her maternal functions—having in view not merely her own health, but the well-being of the race—justify legislation to protect her from the greed as well as the passion of man. The limitations which this statute places upon her contractual powers, upon her right to agree with her employer as to the time she shall labor, are not imposed solely for her benefit, but also largely for the benefit of all.[2]

With this as a baseline, we proceed to the 1920s and 1930s, where we encounter a pair of cases involving statutes that established a minimum wage for women but not for men. In the first, decided in 1923, the Court invalidated the statute because change in the status of women was seen as having been marked over the preceding fifteen years and as having largely erased political and legal differences based on gender.[3] Because of social change, the Constitution could not tolerate special protections for women and a result different than in *Muller* was reached. However, in 1937 the Court faced the same issue and reversed itself. The principles advanced in *Muller* were reaffirmed, and a statute setting a minimum rate of pay for women but not men was upheld. "What," asked the Court, "can be closer to the public interest than the health of women and their protection from unscrupulous and overreaching employers?"[4] Significantly, both the 1923 and 1937 decisions are consistent with trends in the earnings gap between men and women. In the three decades preceding the first decision, the earnings disparity between working men and women was appreciably reduced, but starting in the 1920s it began to widen, a divergence that was continuing at the time of the second decision.[5]

We next go to 1948 and a decision of the Supreme Court on a state statute that, in regulating the sale of liquor, required bartenders to be licensed. The statute, however, precluded a female from receiving a license unless the owner of the establishment was a male and the female was the wife or daughter of the owner. In upholding the statute in *Goesaert v. Cleary*,[6] the Court acknowledged that changes had occurred in sex roles but concluded that the state may act to protect the morals of women. The Court noted that "[t]he Constitution does not require legislatures to reflect sociological insight, or shifting social standards, any more than it requires them to keep abreast of the latest scientific standards."[7] However, the question is *not* whether a judicially imposed requirement exists that constitutional doctrine and legislation conform to the nature of society. The question, rather, is whether they in fact do so. The evidence suggests that the holding in *Goesaert* and the statute at issue accurately reflected social structure and values in the late 1940s: At least two out of three white married women at this time made no contribution to family income and thus were completely dependent economically on their husbands;[8] and the egalitarian ideology for sex roles that was manifested in later years was only getting under way.[9]

A similar decision occurred thirteen years later in *Hoyt v. Florida*, a case involving an unsuccessful challenge to a statute that exempted women from jury service unless they volunteered for such service. Under the statute, only men were required to serve on juries, but the Supreme Court held in 1961 that there was no constitutional violation since the state could take into account that, in American society, the "woman is still regarded as the center of home and family life."[10] In basing its decision on this observation, the Court kept legal thought in line with social conditions. Egalitarianism was increasing, but for 55% of white married women in 1960, family income still derived solely from the earnings of their husbands;[11] even among college seniors in 1964, three out of four men and women endorsed the view that a wife should give priority to the career of her husband rather than to a career for herself.[12]

It was not until the early 1970s that the Supreme Court exhibited a sustained willingness to evaluate critically and invalidate public policies that made distinctions on the basis of gender, but it would be erroneous to conclude that constitutional doctrine in the preceding decades was designed to block change in sex roles. For instance, a year and a half before its decision in *Hoyt*, the same justices who decided that case found no fault in an indictment charging a wife with conspiracy to commit a crime with her husband. The argument that a wife was an appendage and under the control of her husband—and was therefore legally incapable of conspiring with him—was rejected on the ground that it "implies a view of American womanhood offensive to the ethos of our society."[13] Rather than hostility to women, constitutional doctrine prior to the 1970s can best be viewed as reflecting a deference to the actions of the legislative and executive branches of government in the area of gender roles.

The reticence of the Supreme Court to intrude into the domains of other branches of government was abandoned in 1971 when it held in *Reed v. Reed*[14] that a statute was unconstitutional in requiring a preference for males over females in appointments to administer the estates of persons who died intestate. *Reed* was the first in a series of cases involving gender distinctions which the Court accepted for review and in which it demonstrated a willingness to invalidate public policies seen as having an invidious discriminatory purpose. Indeed, in 1975 an exemption of women from jury service—upheld in *Hoyt* fourteen years earlier—was found to be unconstitutional.[15]

Change that had occurred in sex roles was explicitly acknowledged in the constitutional doctrine that developed in the 1970s. As will be seen, however, this doctrine did not emerge at an early stage of the change. Rather, traditional conceptions of sex roles became impermissible under the Constitution only after social structure and values had clearly experienced a substantial transformation. For instance, in responding to a challenge to a statute that established a lower age of majority for females than for males—with the result that daughters lost child support payments from a noncustodial parent at a younger age than did sons—the State contended that the age differential was necessitated by the obligation imposed by society on males to support a wife and children financially. Because of that obligation, the State argued, males required a longer period of education—and hence economic assistance from parents—than females. In finding the argument insufficient to justify the statute, the Court in 1975 recognized the major shift in gender roles that had taken place and concluded that the change undermined the acceptability of the argument under the Constitution:

> No longer is the female destined solely for the home and the rearing of the family, and only the male for the marketplace and the world of ideas. . . . Women's activities and responsibilities are increasing and expanding. Coeducation is a fact, not a rarity. The presence of women in business, in the professions, in government and, indeed, in all walks of life where education is a desirable, if not always a necessary, antecedent is apparent and a proper subject of judicial notice. If a specified age of minority is required for the boy in order to assure him parental support while he attains his education and training, so, too, is it for the girl.[16]

I would like now to relate the foregoing review of constitutional doctrine on sex roles to a measure of long-term change in those roles in order to test the premise that shifts in legal thought are a response to alterations in society rather than a spontaneous product of the legal system. The measure—which I treat as an indicator (not a cause) of role dissimilarity—is male-female differences in rates of college enrollment and graduation, and I believe it provides credible evidence for the premise that change in social conditions precedes change in legal thought.[17] Educational attainment is preferable to earned income for measuring gender disparities over time, because earnings are the result of complex components—e.g., years of employment, number of hours of employment annually, and skill levels—that are not necessarily moving in the same direction.[18] As an indicator of social differences between men and women, educational achievement seems to possess fewer dimensions and to be less susceptible to difficulties in interpretation.[19]

Table 3.1 shows the proportion of male and female high school graduates who went on to and completed college. It is arranged by birth cohort—i.e., by year of birth—and thus permits a comparison over time. The pursuit of higher education appears to be an accurate indicator of the degree to which nontraditional sex roles prevail,[20] at least in part because college attendance is associated with financial success—especially for those who graduate—and therefore with personal independence.[21] For women, then, access to higher education signifies egalitarian values and the opportunity for equality.[22]

The table discloses that the proportion of female high school graduates who continued to higher education and the proportion who completed it increased from the cohort of 1866–1870 to the cohort of 1896–1900. Among men in these cohorts who graduated from high school, however, the proportion attending college remained roughly constant and the proportion completing college declined. The result was, as the fourth and seventh columns show, a steady erosion of the greater probability that a male would enroll in and graduate from college. Women born in 1896–1900 or earlier were of college age during the decades prior to the 1923 decision of the Supreme Court that held unconstitutional a statute establishing a minimum wage for women but not for men, and their growing equality of access to higher education was reflected in the decision. The Court itself noted that, in terms of political status and legal rights, gender "differences have now come almost, if not quite, to the vanishing point."[23] When measures of educational attainment in addition to those in table 3.1 are considered, it is clear that considerable egalitarianism had been attained between men and women; in the 1886–1890 cohort, for instance, the proportion of females who completed twelve years of schooling was substantially lower than the proportion of males who did so, but the proportion of females who completed more than twelve years was somewhat higher.[24]

In 1937, the Supreme Court overruled its 1923 decision and concluded that there was no constitutional violation when a state created a minimum rate of pay for women only. Table 3.1 shows that, compared to their predecessors in the 1906–1910 cohort, high school graduates in the 1916–1920 cohort—i.e., those who reached age 18 in the middle and later part of the 1930s—experienced declines in rates of college attendance and completion. However, the declines were substantially larger among females than among males, and the result was the widening disparity between the sexes that is seen in the fourth and seventh columns of the table.[25] The depression of the 1930s apparently intensified traditional conceptions of sex roles, and the decision of the Court reflected the change.

In 1948, the Supreme Court rendered its decision in *Goesaert v. Cleary*, validating a statute that made a woman ineligible for a bartending license unless a man owned the establishment where she was employed and the male owner was her husband or father. The decision was consistent with trends in sex roles. As table 3.1 shows, the increase in the male advantage that occurred between the 1906–1910 and 1916–1920 cohorts continued with the 1926–1930 cohort. The result was a substantial widening of the gender disparity in higher education from the cohort that reached age 18 in the 1920s to the cohort that reached age 18 in the 1940s. *Goesaert* was thus decided after two decades of increasing conventionalism in sex roles.

The expansion of the male advantage in higher education ceased with the 1926–1930 cohort, and a decline began with the 1936–1940 cohort, which reached age 18 in the middle to late 1950s. However, in spite of the inception of a trend toward gender equality, a comparison of the

Table 3.1. College Attendance and Graduation Rates Among High School Graduates

Birth cohort	Proportion (%) attending college[a]		Male advantage: probability (%) that a male was more likely than a female to attend college[b]	Proportion (%) completing college[a]		Male advantage: probability (%) that a male was more likely than a female to complete college[b]
	Male	*Female*		*Male*	*Female*	
1866–1870	51.9	36.8	41	27.8	13.5	106
1876–1880	50.2	38.9	29	27.0	14.9	81
1886–1890	51.3	42.3	21	26.3	15.7	68
1896–1900	50.0	42.8	17	25.2	16.5	53
1906–1910	45.6	40.1	14	23.6	16.6	42
1916–1920	39.8	30.5	30	19.3	12.2	58
1926–1930	44.8	31.1	44	25.1	12.6	99
1936–1940	44.3	33.6	32	23.4	14.4	63
1946–1950	53.4	43.7	22	25.4	19.7	29

[a] *Source:* J. Smith & M. Ward, Women's Wages and Work in the Twentieth Century 39 (1984).
[b] Probability = (proportion of males minus proportion of females) divided by proportion of females and multiplied by 100.

1936–1940 cohort with its predecessors discloses that the cohort was still markedly traditional. It therefore should not be surprising that the Supreme Court upheld an exemption of women from jury service in 1961. The present-day movement toward egalitarianism had commenced, but the differences in sex roles that existed at the time of the Court decision were large by historical standards.

Table 3.1 thus suggests that change in and the nature of sex roles foreshadow the state of gender-relevant constitutional doctrine. Legal thought, that is, appears to be a direct reflection of social structure and values. The reflection is also seen in the current era of constitutional law on gender distinctions that began in 1971 with the decision of the Supreme Court in *Reed v. Reed*. Let me now turn to that era.

Table 3.1 shows that, from the 1926–1930 cohort to the 1936–1940 cohort, rates of college attendance and graduation increased among women but not men. The increase among women continued with the 1946–1950 cohort. In that group—i.e., among women who finished high school in the middle to late 1960s—rates of college attendance and graduation were approximately one-third higher than they had been in the cohort born ten years earlier. While men in the 1946–1950 cohort also experienced increases in these rates, their increases were substantially smaller than those experienced by women.[26] The result was that, from the cohort completing high school in the middle to late 1940s to the cohort completing high school in the middle to late 1960s, there was a significant narrowing of the gender disparity in higher education. Indeed, the male advantage during this twenty-year period fell by one-half in the case of college attendance and by more than two-thirds in the case of college graduation.

Table 3.1 does not include persons who finished high school in the 1970s, but the male advantage in higher education apparently continued to fall during the decade. At 25–29 years of age, the male advantage among persons who were born between 1952 and 1956—and who would have completed high school in the first part of the 1970s—was approximately one-half the level existing among persons who were born five years earlier (i.e, between 1947 and 1951) and who would have graduated from high school in the last part of the 1960s.[27] While these data are not comparable to those in table 3.1,[28] they are consistent with the conclusion that the 1970s witnessed an extension of the trend toward less sex role traditionalism. Other considerations suggest the same conclusion. The most important is that social values favoring egalitarianism in gender roles became more prevalent between the early and middle years of the decade; the decline occurring in the male advantage prior to the onset of the 1970s was thus followed by a further advance in egalitarian values after the decade began.[29] In addition, it is relevant that constitutional jurisprudence disapproving sex role stereotypes was articulated by the Supreme Court as the high school graduates of the early 1970s were entering and attending college. Since the gender disparity in enrollment rates was already narrowing, that jurisprudence is unlikely to be a significant cause of reduced traditionalism in the cohort; rather, it is an indicator of the level of sex role egalitarianism that existed and of the direction in which change was occurring.

Cohort data thus show that a substantial convergence in sex roles commenced well before the 1970s when the Court undertook its critical assessment of gender-based public policies, and movement toward egalitarianism evidently continued during the 1970s. The convergence can also be seen in the period data appearing in table 3.2, which presents the college enrollment rates of men and women who were 20–24 years of age in 1950, 1960, 1970, and 1980 (second and third columns),[30] the relative advantage possessed by males in the acquisition of higher education (fourth column), and the amount and rate of change in that advantage over ten-year intervals (fifth and sixth columns).

The last three columns of the table are the most revealing. The third-to-last column presents the relative advantage of men over women in their likelihood at age 20–24 of being in college, i.e., the probability that a male was more likely than a female to be enrolled. That advantage was clearly shrinking between 1950 and 1980; indeed, by 1980, the probability of college enrollment was only 11% greater for a man than for a

Table 3.2. College Enrollment Rates Among Persons 20–24 Years Old: United States

	Proportion (%) enrolled in college		*Male advantage: probability (%) that a male was more likely than a female to be enrolled*[a]	*10-year change in the male advantage: amount and rate of change*	
Year	*Men*	*Women*		*Amount: percentage point change*[b]	*Rate: percentage change*[c]
1950	13.6	5.2	162		
1960	15.7	7.4	112	−50	−31
1970	25.3	15.6	62	−50	−45
1980	23.7	21.4	11	−51	−82

[a] Probability = (proportion of men enrolled minus proportion of women enrolled) divided by the proportion of women enrolled and multiplied by 100.
[b] Percentage point change = probability at time 1 minus probability at time 2.
[c] Percentage change = (probability at time 1 minus probability at time 2) divided by probability at time 1 and multiplied by 100.

woman. Equally important, the gap between men and women was being closed by an amount that remained steady from decade to decade and by a rate that accelerated over time. With regard to amount of change, the next-to-last column shows that the probability a man was more likely than a woman to be enrolled fell by approximately 50 percentage points each decade. Given the shrinking size of the male advantage, the continued fixed amount of the decline involved an increasing rate of change. Looking at the last column, we see that the male advantage diminished at a rate of 31% between 1950 and 1960, 45% between 1960 and 1970, and 82% between 1970 and 1980.

The willingness of the Supreme Court in the 1970s to utilize the Constitution to invalidate statutes and regulations that distinguished on the basis of gender thus occurred after sex role differences had diminished substantially in magnitude and after the rate of increase in egalitarian values had started to escalate.[31] As in earlier years, change in legal thought was preceded by alteration in social patterns, suggesting that legal doctrine reflects the society in which it is found. If legal thought is a response to social structure and values, however, the key to explaining the development of law in the past and predicting its course in the future does not lie with the particular personalities who are involved in the legal system (e.g., as judges, legislators, and leaders of pressure groups). Rather, it lies with the forces that slowly but pervasively transform society.

EQUAL RIGHTS AMENDMENT

Given the apparent primacy of social forces in determining legal thought, the manifestations of such thought—e.g., constitutional provisions, statutes, and court opinions—should be approached with less emphasis than at present on their internal logic and with increased attention to their societal context. Failure to understand that context has had unfortunate consequences by creating unrealizable expectations for the legal system. The effort invested in the unsuccessful attempt to place an Equal Rights Amendment (ERA)[32] in the federal Constitution—an attempt that may well be repeated[33]—is illustrative. The political, economic, and psychological resources that were expended on the ERA could have been invested more fruitfully in identifying the options created by the social forces that affect gender roles and pursuing the most attractive among them.[34] This could have been done, of course, only with a well-developed and empirically grounded macrosociological framework for legal doctrine—a situation requiring a substantial body of research that has yet to be conducted—but the framework would have allowed us to recognize that the proposed ERA was no more than a barometer of the social system and that its ratification would not have appreciably influenced the nature of sex roles.

The contention that the ERA would not have had a marked impact on social life requires justification, for it is important to my thesis as well as controversial. Definitive proof is of course not possible that an unratified constitutional amendment would have had little or no effect, but the data in table 3.2 suggest such a conclusion. When the ERA emerged from Congress in 1972, social differences between males and females had been waning for at least two decades and the advance of egalitarianism was proceeding at a substantial and increasing pace. Moreover, since the ERA never became part of the Constitution, the Amendment could not have contributed to the acceleration of gender equality during the 1970s or to the virtual disappearance by 1980 of the male-female difference in college enrollment rates.

Another indication the ERA would have been an ineffective agent for social change may be obtained from the experience of states that adopted comparable provisions for their own constitutions and that did so during the 1970s when ratification of the ERA would have placed the Amendment into the federal Constitution.[35] While statutory bans on sex discrimination existed in many states, constitutional provisions presumably carry more weight since they are part of the basic document of government. Indeed, the ERA was proposed by Congress several years after federal legislation was enacted to forbid sex discrimination in employment,[36] and the movement for ratification of the Amendment continued even though Congress was concurrently adopting additional legislative prohibitions on sex discrimination.[37] The effort made to ratify the Amendment in spite of the existence of such statutory enactments is evidence that a constitution is viewed by the public generally as a more productive source of law than a statute.

Since 1970, fourteen states have adopted a constitutional measure similar to the broad prohibition on sex discrimination found in the ERA.[38] Only two, however, will be considered here: Illinois and Pennsylvania. Unlike the provisions in a number of states, those in Illinois and Pennsylvania deal exclusively with gender and do not encompass other demographic characteristics.[39] If a constitutional provision in fact promotes egalitarianism in sex roles, one that focuses only on gender would seem the most likely to show an effect since it presumably provides sex discrimination with a high level of salience in the legal system.

In addition to their sole concern with gender, the equal rights provisions of the Illinois and Pennsylvania constitutions have an important advantage for studying the impact of constitutional doctrine: Each became effective at roughly the same time that the 1970 census was taken.[40] As a result, data from that census can be used to gauge the status of sex roles at the point when the provisions were adopted and can be compared to other censuses to show change over ten-year periods. Comparisons that are based on at least one full decade prior to and following an event make possible conclusions of some credibility.

The measure of change that will be used here is enrollment rates in institutions of higher education. The measure is superior to years of school completed or receipt of a degree, because a resident of a state may have moved there after finishing his/her education elsewhere and the state where education is acquired cannot be determined from the census. Students currently enrolled in college, however, are enumerated in the state in which they reside.[41] For eight out of ten students, this is the state in which their college is located,[42] but even for those who commute to a college in another state, the environment where they reside presumably contributes significantly to their motivation to pursue higher education.

Table 3.3 presents the proportion of men and women 20–24 years of age in Illinois and Pennsylvania who were enrolled in college.[43] For comparison, the enrollment rates are shown (from table 3.2) for the United States as a whole.

Table 3.3 discloses no clear evidence that the status of women improved as the result of the equal rights provisions in the two states. In Illinois, the proportion of women 20–24 years of age who were in college was essentially the same as the proportion in the United States for each of the years shown. If the state constitutional provision was benefiting women, however, the Illinois rate should have moved from equality with the national rate in 1970 to a level noticeably exceeding the national rate in 1980. In Pennsylvania, the enrollment rate for women was consistently lower than in the United States, but the disparity narrowed somewhat on a proportional basis (though not in absolute terms) between 1970 and 1980.[44] The narrowing may stem from other factors, but at least on the surface it supports the hypothesis that the equal rights provision had an effect. Unfortunately for the proponents of such provisions, the experience in Pennsylvania suggests that the effect was small and the experience in Illinois suggests that an effect was not general.

Further analysis of college enrollment rates fails to reveal convincing evidence that change in gender roles is the result of legal doctrine. Table 3.4 extends the data in table 3.3 by presenting (in the top panel) the probability that a male 20–24 years old was more likely than a female of the same age to be enrolled in college. The middle and bottom panels of the table respectively show the amount by which and the rate at which this probability changed from 1950 to 1960, from 1960 to 1970, and from 1970 to 1980.

Table 3.3. College Enrollment Rates Among Persons 20–24 Years Old: Illinois, Pennsylvania, and the United States

	Proportion enrolled (%)					
	United States		*Illinois*		*Pennsylvania*	
Year	*Men*	*Women*	*Men*	*Women*	*Men*	*Women*
1950	13.6	5.2	14.4	5.8	12.6	4.4
1960	15.7	7.4	16.0	7.2	15.7	6.9
1970	25.3	15.6	27.4	15.9	25.7	14.4
1980	23.7	21.4	23.5	21.1	22.8	20.2

The top panel of table 3.4 shows that the relative advantage in college attendance enjoyed by males declined steadily and appreciably from 1950 to 1980 in the United States as a whole and in the two states. However, in both 1960 and 1970, the male advantage found in each of the states exceeded that in the nation, and there was no diminution in the magnitude of the disparity during the period. By 1980, on the other hand, the state-national difference had disappeared in Illinois and was minimal in Pennsylvania. Thus, in the two states, egalitarianism during the ten years prior to the constitutional provision was less than in the United States and the size of the disparity did not change, but subsequently the difference was either eliminated or reduced.

Before the increasing similarity of the two states with the country as a whole is taken as evidence for the effectiveness of the state constitutional provisions, it is critical to note (in the bottom panel of table 3.4) the rapid abatement that occurred during the 1970s in the probability that a male was more likely than a female to be enrolled in college at age 20–24. The rate of the reduction from 1970 to 1980 in the United States and in each state was such as virtually to eliminate the male advantage, and it made increased similarity between the nation and the states a mathematical inevitability. Illinois and Pennsylvania converged on the national average, that is, not because of the constitutional provisions in the two states but because of the dramatic rate of decrease in the male advantage that brought the advantage close to the vanishing point.

Two additional points emerge from table 3.4 and are worthy of mention. First, the rate of the reduction in the male advantage between 1970 and 1980 was essentially identical for the United States, which had not adopted a constitutional prohibition against sex discrimination, as it was for Illinois and Pennsylvania, which had. (The rates, shown in the bottom panel, were 82, 85, and 83%, respectively.) This suggests that the constitutional provisions did not affect gender roles.

Table 3.4. Male–Female Differences in College Enrollment Rates Among Persons 20–24 Years Old

Year(s)	*United States*	*Illinois*	*Pennsylvania*
Probability (%) that a male was more likely than a female to be enrolled in college			
1950	162	148	186
1960	112	122	128
1970	62	72	78
1980	11	11	13
Amount of change (percentage point change) in the probabilities in the top panel			
1950–1960	−50	−26	−58
1960–1970	−50	−50	−50
1970–1980	−51	−61	−65
Rate of change (%) in the probabilities in the top panel			
1950–1960	−31	−18	−31
1960–1970	−45	−41	−39
1970–1980	−82	−85	−83

Source: Tables 3.2 and 3.3. For the manner in which the data in each panel were calculated, see Table 3.2.

Second, the amount of the decline in the male advantage (presented in the middle panel)—which remained constant from one decade to the next for the United States as a whole—was noticeably greater in both states between 1970 and 1980 than between 1960 and 1970, and the magnitude of the decline in the states substantially exceeded that in the country generally during the 1970s. In addition, the rate at which gender role differences were waning (shown in the bottom panel) accelerated from the 1960s to the 1970s more in Illinois and Pennsylvania than in the nation. The rate of decline was 44 percentage points faster in the two states between 1970 and 1980 than between 1960 and 1970 (e.g., in Illinois, 85−41 = 44), while in the nation it was only 37 percentage points faster (82−45 = 37). Viewed in another way, the rate of decline in the male advantage more than doubled from the 1960s to the 1970s in the two states but increased by a smaller ratio in the United States as a whole. These findings suggest that the state constitutional provisions were effective in reducing gender differences.

However, the experience of Illinois prior to adoption of its provision undermines any assertion that the constitutional bans on discrimination were responsible for the greater movement toward equality in the two states than in the nation during the 1970s. Three aspects of the middle and bottom panels of table 3.4 are important in this regard.

First, the amount of change in Illinois (middle panel) virtually doubled between 1950–1960 and 1960–1970 (from 26 to 50 percentage points), but the increment between 1960–1970 and 1970–1980 was much smaller in both relative and absolute terms. The amount of change in Illinois continued to expand after adoption of the constitutional provision, that is, but the decade-to-decade increase was appreciably less than before adoption. Second, while the rate of change in Illinois (bottom panel) more than doubled between 1960–1970 and 1970–1980, it more than doubled between 1950–1960 and 1960–1970. The trend in the rate of change in the state was thus uninterrupted in spite of the appearance of the constitutional ban on sex discrimination. Third, rates of change (bottom panel) accelerated between 1950–1960 and 1960–1970 substantially more in Illinois than in the United States as a whole (23 versus 14 percentage points). The increase in rates was thus greater in Illinois than in the United States even before the state constitutionally prohibited sex discrimination. The finding negates the importance of a greater rise in rates of change in Illinois than in the United States after the ban. While these patterns are not found in Pennsylvania, the experience of Illinois in the 1950s and 1960s makes it doubtful that state constitutional provisions generally affected the progress of egalitarianism during the 1970s.

A final issue remains, however. The course of college enrollment rates among men and women in Illinois is evidence only for the proposition that an equal rights measure in a state constitution does not influence gender roles in all circumstances. The behavior of enrollment rates in Pennsylvania, on the other hand, may indicate that such a measure can have an impact under certain limited conditions. In this regard, Pennsylvania may be compared to the adjacent state of New Jersey, the constitution of which does not ban sex discrimination. A comparison of just two states is hazardous because substantial differences may exist between them on factors relevant to the phenomenon being assessed. For example, population density and personal affluence were greater in New Jersey than in Pennsylvania throughout the 1950–1980 period,[45] and these differences may obscure an effect of the equal rights mandate in Pennsylvania. Nonetheless, the experience of New Jersey provides an opportunity to assess at least tentatively the impact of the Pennsylvania constitutional provision on gender equality.

In New Jersey, the probability that a male 20–24 years old was more likely than a female of the same age to be enrolled in college was 236% in 1950, 138% in 1960, 81% in 1970, and 11% in 1980.[46] A comparison of New Jersey and Pennsylvania with regard to the amount and rate of change in these probabilities permits an evaluation of the effect of the constitutional ban on sex discrimination in the latter state. Three points emerge from such an analysis and support the conclusion that gender roles are not altered by a constitutional requirement of equal rights. First, even though the New Jersey constitution did not contain an equal rights measure and the Pennsylvania constitution did, the male advantage declined between 1970 and 1980 at least as much in New Jersey as in Pennsylvania both in terms of amount (70 versus 65 percentage points) and in terms of rate (86 versus 83%). Second, the amount of change in New Jersey fell from 1950–1960 to 1960–1970 (from 98 to 57 percentage points) and then rose (to 70 percentage points in 1970–1980). The increase that appeared in Pennsylvania after the state approved a constitutional ban on sex discrimination was thus paralleled by New Jersey and was not unique to Pennsylvania; indeed, the increment between 1960–1970 and 1970–1980 was virtually identical in New Jersey and Pennsylvania (13 and 15 percentage points, respectively). Third, the rate of change roughly doubled between 1960–1970 and 1970–1980 in New Jersey (from 41 to 86%) as well as in Pennsylvania (from 39 to 83%). The rate of change accordingly accelerated as much in a state that adopted an equal rights mandate as in one that did not.

A comparison of Pennsylvania and New Jersey, in short, provides no evidence for the contention that a state constitutional measure banning sex discrimination has a significant impact on gender roles. Support for the argument would require that, in magnitude and rate, movement toward social equality between men and women be more substantial in a state having such a measure than in a state not having one. This, however, was not found. Instead, the gender differential in college enrollment rates behaved uniformly in the two states, suggesting that a constitution expresses societal ideals rather than advances them.

CONCLUSION

The macrosociological aspects of legal thought may be understood more fully by returning to the constitutional doctrine on gender that has been articulated by the U.S. Supreme Court since the early 1970s. That doctrine possesses two features: It is hostile to government policies that have incorporated traditional sex role stereotypes, and it is favorable to policies designed to assist women. For example, even though retirement benefits under the federal Social Security Act were calculated by a procedure that was more advantageous to eligible women than to men, the Court in 1977 found no constitutional violation because the statutory purpose was considered to be that of compensating women for their generally lower earnings in the labor market:

> The more favorable treatment of the female wage earner enacted here was not a result of "archaic and overbroad generalizations" about women or of "the role-

typing society has long imposed" upon women such as casual assumptions that women are "the weaker sex" or are more likely to be child-rearers or dependents. Rather, "the only discernible purpose of [the provision is] the permissible one of redressing our society's longstanding disparate treatment of women."[47]

A social system is most likely to experience minimal disruption in moving from a structure characterized by gender stratification to a structure characterized by gender equality if its legal doctrines disapprove manifestations of traditional sex roles and approve assistance to those who have experienced social and economic disadvantages because of gender. The constitutional doctrine on gender that emerged in the 1970s was thus congruent with and supportive of the transformation under way in social structure and values. A philosophy was eliminated that was believed to be an obstacle to the social change that was occurring, and help was endorsed to those who were burdened by the societal form being discarded.

Change in legal doctrine illustrates the macrosociological principle that a social system generally fulfills its needs and protects its interests, is viewed by its members as equitable,[48] and acts to minimize disequilibrium from change in its structure. Sex roles, which have been at the heart of American society, are evidence of this principle. The viability of a social system is dependent upon the rearing of children, a task that has traditionally been performed by their mothers within stable marital relationships.[49] The commitment of the wife-mother to child rearing has in turn been a significant factor in the weaker labor force attachment of women than of men[50] and in the lower earnings of women who are employed.[51] At the present time, the gender disparity in compensation from employment is a political and legal issue, but the disparity is defined as invidious discrimination only because of the societal context in which it is found.[52] A condition is socially deemed a problem, that is, as a result of its historical setting.[53] More specifically, the earnings differential between employed men and women is currently viewed as a problem because a transition is occurring from one type of societal organization to another, a transition requiring change in the manner in which women are afforded economic justice. However, one must not forget that, in protecting its means for rearing children, the social structure that is now being abandoned generally provided women with economic equity relative to men: In terms of family (rather than personal) income, the economic return obtained from each year of education has been substantially greater for married women than for married men.[54]

The marital relationship has thus historically been the mechanism by which society, guarding its arrangement for rearing children, has treated women fairly,[55] and the mechanism was effective until recent decades because virtually all women married and relatively few divorced.[56] However, in the last half of the twentieth century the instability of marital relationships has limited the ability of marriage to provide women with economic justice and has encouraged women to enter the labor force.[57] As a consequence, the need for gender equality in employment emerged as a societal imperative and legal problem.

A social system, in sum, possesses components that facilitate its operation and that change when necessary to maintain it. As one of those components, legal doctrine appears to have at least two functions. First, legal doctrine is the means by which the ideals of society are officially stated and the problems of society are formally acknowledged. Even though law does not in general contribute significantly to the alteration of social ideals or the solution of social problems, it provides recognition to prevailing social values and perceived problems, and in so doing it helps to bond individuals to their society. Legal ideas perform a symbolic function in this regard, creating for the members of society an identification with and a commitment to their social system. Second, legal doctrine provides judicial bodies with justification for the manner in which disputes are settled. Given the widespread endorsement of the doctrinal principles employed in the resolution of disputes, persons and groups are likely to abide by adjudicative decisions with which they disagree, thereby minimizing social disharmony.

Legal thought in case law and statutory law, accordingly, appears to reinforce the existing social system by acting as a mirror of societal ideals and needs. As such, it functions in a manner that is more limited than most Americans believe and many desire. The United States is currently in an era of rapid social change, and the temptation has been frequent to utilize the legal system to cure the problems accompanying that change. Law, however, appears not to be an effective means for treating social problems, and the inevitable result has been disappointment and frustration. Nevertheless, law is an essential as well as enduring aspect of our social system, and it should be appreciated for what it does rather than criticized for what it cannot do.

NOTES

1. Under some conditions the use of one constitutional provision rather than another may affect the doctrine that emerges. When different provisions implicate different social values, the outcome of litigation will depend on both the issue and the provision jointly. In statistical terminology, an interaction effect can exist. I do not believe, however, that such an effect has occurred in the context of gender distinctions.

2. Muller v. Oregon, 208 U.S. 412, 422 (1908). *Accord*, Miller v. Wilson, 236 U.S. 373 (1915).

3. Adkins v. Children's Hospital, 261 U.S. 525 (1923).

One year later, however, the Court upheld a state statute that, with certain exceptions, prohibited the employment of women by restaurants in large cities after a specified time at night. Radice v. New York, 264 U.S. 292 (1924). Restrictions of this nature were viewed as involving physical health and biological differences between men and women, and the social values they implicated differed from the values affected by the regulation of economic matters such as compensation. Although today the statutes in *Muller v. Oregon* and *Radice v. New York* would be viewed differently and would be unconstitutional, gender-based biological differences and their health ramifications continue to be an important basis for justifying the dissimilar treatment of men and women. Michael M. v. Superior Court, 450 U.S. 464 (1981).

4. West Coast Hotel Co. v. Parrish, 300 U.S. 379, 398 (1937).

5. J. Smith & M. Ward, Women's Wages and Work in the Twentieth Century 16–20 (1984). The gap between the earnings of men and women increased until 1960 and then apparently narrowed somewhat. *Id.* It is significant that deterioration in the relative position of women came to a halt, and some improvement in their position possibly commenced, *before* constitutional doctrine changed and the Supreme Court exhibited a willingness to invalidate gender-based public policies. See the text accompanying notes 14–16 *infra*.

6. 335 U.S. 464 (1948).

7. *Id.* at 466.

8. Sorensen & McLanahan, *Married Women's Economic Dependency, 1940–1980*, 93 Am. J. Soc. 659, 669 (1987).

9. B. Duncan, O. Duncan, & J. McRae, Sex Typing and Social Roles 3 (1978).

10. 368 U.S. 57, 62 (1961).

11. Sorensen & McLanahan, *supra* note 8, at 669.

12. Mason, *Studying Change in Sex-Role Definitions Via Attitude Data*, Proc. Am. Statistical Ass'n. (Social Statistics Section) 138 (1973).

13. United States v. Dege, 364 U.S. 51, 53 (1960).

14. 404 U.S. 71 (1971).

15. Taylor v. Louisiana, 419 U.S. 522 (1975).

16. Stanton v. Stanton, 421 U.S. 7, 14–15 (1975).

17. The rate of school attendance and completion in a population may be employed as a measure of the volume of knowledge possessed by a society, but subgroup rates do not appear to be suitable for this purpose. The discussion accompanying the tables in the remainder of the chapter is thus concerned with an indicator of social change rather than a cause.

18. Smith & Ward, *supra* note 5, at 49–67, 85.

19. The complexity of earned income may help to explain the disagreement that exists among social scientists over whether gender differences in earnings result from discrimination. *E.g.*, Kamalich & Polachek, *Discrimination: Fact or Fiction? An Examination Using an Alternative Approach*, 49 So. Econ. J. 450 (1982);

Goldberger, *Reverse Regression and Salary Discrimination*, 19 J. HUM. RESOURCES 293 (1984).

Occupation too is a problematic indicator of the course of sex roles over time because of the substantial changes that have occurred in job titles. *See* England, *Assessing Trends in Occupational Sex Segregation, 1900–1976 in* SOCIOLOGICAL PERSPECTIVES ON LABOR MARKETS 273 (I. Berg ed., 1981).

20. Mason, Czajka, & Arber, *Change in U.S. Women's Sex-Role Attitudes, 1964–1974*, 41 AM. SOC. REV. 573 (1976).

21. Goodman, *The Economic Returns of Education: An Assessment of Alternative Models*, 60 SOCIAL SCI. Q. 269 (1979).

22. Substantial differences exist between men and women in their fields of specialization in college, and the differences are responsible for much of the gender disparity that is found in earnings from employment after graduation. Daymont & Andrisani, *Job Preferences, College Major, and the Gender Gap in Earnings*, 19 J. HUM. RESOURCES 408 (1984). Selection of a field of study, however, appears to be a matter of preference rather than of coercion. *See* Fiorentine & Cole, *Why Fewer Women Become Physicians: Explaining the Premed Persistence Gap*, 7 SOC. FORUM 469 (1992). As a result, the opportunity for equality between men and women is measured more accurately by the gender differential in college attendance and completion than by the gender differential in fields of study.

23. Adkins v. Children's Hospital, 261 U.S. 525, 553 (1923).

24. SMITH & WARD, *supra* note 5, at 36.

25. The drop in the proportion attending college between the 1906–1910 and 1916–1920 cohorts was 12.7% for men and 23.9% for women, while the drop in the proportion completing college was 18.2% for men and 26.5% for women. (The decline is calculated in terms of the percentage by which the proportions changed between the cohorts of 1906–1910 and 1916–1920. The decline is *not* measured by the number of percentage points by which the rates changed. For instance, among male high school graduates who went on to college, the decline between the two cohorts was 5.8 percentage points but 12.7%. The latter figure was calculated as follows: $[(45.6 - 39.8)/45.6] \times 100 = 12.7$.)

26. Between the 1936–1940 and 1946–1950 cohorts, rates of college attendance among high school graduates increased 20.5% for men and 30.1% for women; rates of college graduation rose by 8.5% for men and 36.8% for women. These figures represent the proportional increments in rates of attendance and graduation, not the number of percentage points by which rates increased between the two cohorts.

27. The male advantage at age 25–29 for completion of one or more years of college was 30% in the 1947–1951 birth cohort and 12% in the 1952–1956 cohort. For completion of four or more years of college, the male advantage at age 25–29 was 37% in the 1947–1951 cohort and 18% in the 1952–1956 cohort. Calculated from Bureau of the Census, U.S. Dep't of Commerce, *Educational Attainment in the United States: March 1981 and 1980*, CURRENT POPULATION REP. Series P-20, No. 390, at table A (1984).

28. The male advantages considered here and in table 3.1 differ with respect to both the persons covered and their age at the time educational attainment was

measured. The male advantage being discussed at this point encompasses all persons in their respective cohorts, with their educational attainment assessed at age 25–29. The data in table 3.1, on the other hand, apply only to high school graduates and do not have an age limitation.

29. Cherlin & Walters, *Trends in United States Men's and Women's Sex-Role Attitudes: 1972–1978*, 46 Am. Soc. Rev. 453 (1981).

30. The proportions enrolled in college (second and third columns of table 3.2) were calculated from:

Bureau of the Census, U.S. Dep't of Commerce, Census of Population: 1950. Vol. II: Characteristics of the Population. Part 1: United States Summary tables 94, 112 (1953).

Bureau of the Census, U.S. Dep't of Commerce, Census of Population: 1960. Vol. I: Characteristics of the Population. Part I: United States Summary table 167 (1964).

Bureau of the Census, U.S. Dep't of Commerce, 1970 Census of Population. Vol. I: Characteristics of the Population. Part 1: United States Summary—Section 2 tables 196, 197 (1973).

Bureau of the Census, U.S. Dep't of Commerce, 1980 Census of Population. Vol. 1: Characteristics of the Population. Chapter D: Detailed Population Characteristics. Part 1: United States Summary. Section A: United States table 260 (1984).

Bureau of the Census, U.S. Dep't of Commerce, 1980 Census of Population. Vol. 1: Characteristics of the Population. Chapter B: General Population Characteristics. Part 1: United States Summary table 43 (1983).

31. *Accord*, Duncan, *Indicators of Sex Typing: Traditional and Egalitarian, Situational and Ideological Responses*, 85 Am. J. Soc. 251, 257 (1979).

The principle that the alteration of legal doctrine is an effect of social change rather than a cause also explains the low frequency with which individuals file formal complaints alleging statutory violations. A study of union members found that less than 4% had filed a charge of sex discrimination. Hoyman & Stallworth, *Suit Filing by Women: An Empirical Analysis*, 62 Notre Dame L. Rev. 61, 79 (1986). The infrequent use of the legal system suggests that change in social structure and values carries individuals along with it and is not appreciably promoted by pressure exerted through the system.

32. The proposed Amendment read as follows:

> Section 1. Equality of rights under the law shall not be denied or abridged by the United States or by any State on account of sex.
>
> Section 2. The Congress shall have the power to enforce, by appropriate legislation, the provisions of this article.
>
> Section 3. The amendment shall take effect two years after the date of ratification.

Congress submitted the Amendment to the states in March 1972 and allowed seven years for its ratification. H.R.J. Res. 208, 92d Cong., 2nd Sess., 86 Stat. 1523 (1972). For an amendment to be incorporated into the Constitution, ratification is required by three-fourths of the states. U.S. Const. art. V.

33. Johnson, *New ERA Push: Some Ready, Some Say the Time's Not Right*, *Sunday News J.* (Wilmington, DE), Jan. 18, 1987, at A8. Associated Press report.

34. That the ERA was not, and was unlikely to be, ratified is not surprising in light of the findings of a study of political involvement in the United States. K. BECKWITH, AMERICAN WOMEN AND POLITICAL PARTICIPATION (1986). The study, which included the period for ratifying the ERA, found that political participation did not differ markedly between women and men and that participation was not closely and consistently related to endorsement of a feminist philosophy. *See also* Fleming, *Women Against Men? Gender as a Base of Support for Change in Women's Rights and Roles,* 2 RESEARCH IN POLITICS AND SOCIETY 105 (G. Moore & G. Spitze eds., 1986). Without a distinctive commitment to political action on the part of the two groups with a special interest in the status of women in our society—viz., women and feminists—a necessary condition for acceptance of the ERA would seem to be absent.

Whether women endorse the ERA, moreover, is evidently a function in large part of social-demographic attributes (age, educational attainment, race, religious affiliation, and region of residence) whose configuration in a society changes slowly; endorsement seems no more than minimally dependent on situational factors (viz., employment and family life) that can alter rapidly. Plutzer, *Work Life, Family Life, and Women's Support of Feminism,* 53 AM. SOC. REV. 640 (1988). Adoption of the ERA would thus appear to require a gradual but significant shift in the composition of the population and the nature of the social system.

35. At least in the short run, a state constitutional provision that forbids sex discrimination may widen the disparity in earnings that exists between men and women. Medoff, *The Effect of the Equal Rights Amendment on the Economic Status of Women,* 13 ATLANTIC ECON. J. 60 (1985).

36. The Equal Pay Act was approved by Congress in June 1963. Pub. L. No. 88–38, 77 Stat. 56 (codified at 29 U.S.C. § 206(d) (1982)). Title VII of the Civil Rights Act of 1964 was adopted in July 1964. Pub. L. No. 88–352, 78 Stat. 253 (codified at 42 U.S.C. § 2000e et seq. (1982)).

37. *E.g.,* Pub. L. No. 93–87, § 301(f), 87 Stat. 250, 295 (1973); Pub. L. No. 93–203, §§ 208(f), 603, 612(a), 87 Stat. 839, 856, 878, 882 (1973); Pub. L. No. 93–383, §§ 109(a), 808(a), 808(b), 88 Stat. 633, 649, 728, 729 (1974); Pub. L. No. 93–495, § 503, 88 Stat. 1500, 1521 (1974).

A few months after submitting the ERA to the states, Congress approved a statute to ban sex discrimination by institutions of higher education in programs receiving financial assistance from the federal government. The statute was Title IX of the Education Amendments of 1972 and was enacted in June 1972. Pub. L. No. 92–318, 86 Stat. 373 (codified at 20 U.S.C. § 1681 (1988)).

Since the present chapter employs gender roles to illustrate my thesis that law results from but does not cause appreciable social change, Title IX merits comment. Gender roles have been measured here by the college enrollment rates of men and women, but if the statute substantially diminished the male-female difference in college attendance during the 1970s, my thesis is erroneous. As table 3.2 shows, the gender difference abated between 1970 and 1980, suggesting that the legislation had an effect. However, Title IX clearly did not initiate the change, because college enrollment rates among men and women began to converge long before the statute was enacted. Nor did Title IX increase the magnitude of the change, since the number of percentage points by which the male advantage diminished between 1970 and 1980 was the same as in earlier ten-year periods. The issue is thus only whether Title IX contributed to the acceleration in the rate of the convergence that occurred during the 1970s. (The reasoning applicable to Title IX is also relevant to the constitutional doctrine that developed in the 1970s with regard to sex roles; if the statute did not diminish the gender disparity in higher education, it is likely that the Constitution did not either. *See* NOTE, *Grove City College v. Bell: Restricting the Remedial Reach of Title IX*, 16 LOYOLA CHICAGO L.J. 319 (1985).)

While the evidence is less than ideal, it appears that the acceleration was not the result of Title IX but of other factors. Discussion of the factors responsible for the acceleration requires a focus on males and females separately, because their college attendance rates between 1970 and 1980 changed in opposite directions. As table 3.2 discloses, a small decrease occurred among men, while a substantial rise took place among women. *See generally* Alexander, Pallas, & Holupka, *Consistency and Change in Educational Stratification: Recent Trends Regarding Social Background and College Access, in* 6 RESEARCH IN SOCIAL STRATIFICATION AND MOBILITY 161 (R. Robinson ed., 1987).

The factor that appears to have been decisive with regard to males was the termination of military conscription in 1973. 50 U.S.C. APP. § 467(c) (1982). Only men had been subject to conscription, 50 U.S.C. APP. § 453 (1982), and a deferral had been provided to those who were under 24 years of age and who were full-time undergraduates in institutions of higher education. Pub. L. No. 90–40, 81 Stat. 100 (1967). The threat of conscription thus motivated young men to attend college in 1970 but not in 1980, and elimination of the threat was probably central to lowering their enrollment rate in the latter year.

The change in the enrollment rate of women during the 1970s appears to possess a number of roots. Title IX was intended to protect females from discrimination in the educational system, H.R. REP. No. 554, 92d Cong., 2d Sess., *reprinted in* [1972] U.S. CODE CONG. & AD. NEWS 2462, 2511–12, but it is doubtful that the legislation was a significant factor encouraging them to pursue higher education. Indeed, the college enrollment rate of females 20–24 years old rose faster in the 1960s—the decade before Title IX was enacted—than in the 1970s. (As calculated from the third column of table 3.2, the rise between 1960 and 1970 was 8.2 percentage points or 111%, but the rise between 1970 and 1980 was only 5.8 percentage points or 37%.) The increase in the enrollment rate of women between 1970 and 1980 may be attributed to the forces that operated in earlier decades and to an important event that occurred shortly after Title IX was adopted—a major surge in the price of energy and the cost of living. That surge forced a substantial number of wives into the job market. Sternlieb & Hughes, *Running Faster to Stay in Place*, 4 AM. DEMOGRAPHICS 16 (June 1982); *cf.* Shapiro & Shaw, *Growth in the Labor Force Attachment of Married Women: Accounting for Changes in the 1970s*, 50 SO. ECON. J. 461, 468 (1983) (enlargement of the labor force participation rate of white married women during the 1970s was retarded to the extent there was a rise in the purchasing power of their husbands' income). It is likely that the same economic pressures also increased the number of women who pursued higher education, since a college degree provides a considerable financial reward to individuals who are employed. Goodman, *supra* note 21; Nord, *Schooling and Changes in the Inequality in Male and Female Earnings in the United States over the 1970s*, 19 APPLIED ECON. 1083 (1987). The economic benefit of college training can be expected to attract women who plan only to supplement the income of their husbands as well as women who desire to be financially independent. *See* Sorensen & McLanahan, *supra* note 8, at 675.

In sum, the accelerated pace of egalitarianism in higher education during the 1970s involved a decline in the college enrollment rate of men and an increase in that of women. It is probable that the decline among men resulted largely from the elimination of military conscription and that the increase among women can be explained by preexisting forces and newly manifested pressures on the standard of living. The accelerated rate of convergence in college participation that occurred between 1970 and 1980 thus appears not to have been caused by Title IX. This conclusion is buttressed by the evidence (cited in the appendix to chapter 2) that regulation by the legal system generally does not induce substantial social change and especially by the finding that Title IX did not play a significant role in the growing representation of women among medical school students during the 1970s. Cole, *Sex Discrimination and Admission to Medical School*, 1929–1984, 92 AM. J. SOC. 549 (1986).

Data from the 1980s provide additional support for the argument that Title IX did not foster college attendance among women. The probability of completing college within four years after high school was greater among women than men in the classes that graduated from high school in 1972 and in 1980, but the female advantage declined from 12% in the 1972 class to 8% in the 1980 class. The decline between the two classes occurred because the probability of college graduation in the four years following high school increased at a more rapid rate among men than women (59 versus 53%). Calculated from T. Baker, Gender Differences in the Expectation and Attainment of Higher Education: A Comparative Cohort Analysis of American High School Seniors Since 1960 (paper presented at the 1988 meeting of the Midwest Sociological Society), table 2. Title IX, it should be noted, became effective in July 1972. Pub. L. No. 92–318, 86 Stat. 236. Since both classes were covered by the statute, the larger gain in college completion among men than women between the two classes suggests that, at least during the four years after high school, Title IX did not benefit women in their pursuit of a college degree.

38. Avner, *Some Observations on State Equal Rights Amendments*, 3 YALE L. & POL'Y REV. 144 (1984).

Sixteen states, according to Avner, have added an equal rights measure to their constitutions since 1970. *Id.* at 144 note 1. However, two states on her list did so earlier: Wyoming in 1890 and Utah in 1896. Fourteen states have thus acted since 1970.

In the discussion that follows in the text, 2 of the 14 states (viz., Illinois and Pennsylvania) are compared with the United States as a whole in order to assess the impact of a constitutional provision that broadly requires equal rights for males and females. The comparison is possible because only 3 out of 10 Americans reside in states with constitutions banning gender discrimination, and even if the residents of these states had a uniform response to an equal rights mandate, the weight of their numerical representation in the population would not automatically make their experience that of the country generally. Residents of the 14 jurisdictions approving a broad constitutional ban on sex discrimination since 1970 comprised 29.8% of the U.S. population in 1970 and 29.7% in 1980. Residents of the 16 jurisdictions having such a ban constituted 30.5% of the population in 1970 and 30.6% in 1980. Calculated from BUREAU OF THE CENSUS, U.S. DEP'T OF COMMERCE, STATISTICAL ABSTRACT OF THE UNITED STATES: 1987 20 (107th ed. 1986).

39. In Illinois, the provision states: "The equal protection of the laws shall not be denied or abridged on account of sex by the State or its units of local government and school districts." ILL. CONST. art. I, § 18.

In Pennsylvania, the provision is worded as follows: "Equality of rights under the law shall not be denied or abridged in the Commonwealth of Pennsylvania because of the sex of the individual." PA. CONST. art. 1, § 28.

The provisions in Alaska, Connecticut, Hawaii, Massachusetts, Montana, New Hampshire, Texas, and Virginia include demographic criteria in addition to gender. ALASKA CONST. art. I, § 3; CONN. CONST. art. I, § 20; HAWAII CONST. art. I, § 3; MASS. CONST. part 1, art. I; MONT. CONST. art. II, § 4; N.H. CONST. part 1, art. II; TEX. CONST. art. I, § 3a; VA. CONST. art. I, § 11.

40. The 1970 census was conducted during a period surrounding April 1, 1970. BUREAU OF THE CENSUS, U.S. DEP'T. OF COMMERCE. 1970 CENSUS OF POPULATION. Vol. I: CHARACTERISTICS OF THE POPULATION. Part 1: UNITED STATES SUMMARY V (1973). The equal rights provisions were incorporated into the two state constitutions within 15 months of the census. In Illinois, the provision was ratified by the electorate on December 15, 1970, and became effective on July 1, 1971; in Pennsylvania, the provision was accepted by the electorate and became effective on May 18, 1971. S. Witwer, *Introduction to the 1970 Illinois Constitution, in* ILL. ANN. STAT. Const. art. I (Smith-Hurd); PA. STAT. ANN. Const. art. 1 to 2 (1987 Supp.) (Purdon); Krasik, *A Review of the Implementation of the Pennsylvania Equal Rights Amendment*, 14 DUQUESNE L. REV. 683, 685 (1976).

Four other states having constitutional prohibitions dealing only with gender adopted them between November 1972 and January 1973. COLO. CONST. art. II, § 29; MD. CONST., Declaration of Rights, art. 46.; N.M. CONST., art. II, § 18; WASH. CONST. art. XXXI, § 1. However, at this point a substantial portion of the decade had already elapsed, and an unknown amount of the change experienced between 1970 and 1980 had occurred. Since the 1970 census cannot be employed as an indicator of conditions in the four states at the time their constitutional provisions were ratified, a comparison of data from the 1970 and 1980 censuses for these states cannot disclose the extent to which change in sex roles during the decade was subsequent to the provisions and may have resulted from them.

41. BUREAU OF THE CENSUS, U.S. DEP'T OF COMMERCE, 1980 CENSUS OF POPULATION. Vol. 1: CHARACTERISTICS OF THE POPULATION. Ch. D: DETAILED POPULATION CHARACTERISTICS. Part 40: PENNSYLVANIA—SECTION 2 C-1 (1983).

42. NAT'L CENTER FOR EDUC. STATISTICS, RESIDENCE AND MIGRATION OF COL-

LEGE STUDENTS: FALL 1968 ANALYTIC REPORT 28, 40 (1970); NAT'L CENTER FOR EDUC. STATISTICS, DIGEST OF EDUCATION STATISTICS: 1988 166 (1988).

43. College enrollment rates were calculated for Illinois residents from the following:

> BUREAU OF THE CENSUS, U.S. DEP'T OF COMMERCE. CENSUS OF POPULATION: 1950. Vol. II: CHARACTERISTICS OF THE POPULATION. Part 13: ILLINOIS tables 15, 63 (1952).
>
> BUREAU OF THE CENSUS, U.S. DEP'T OF COMMERCE. CENSUS OF POPULATION: 1960. Vol. I: CHARACTERISTICS OF THE POPULATION. Part 15: ILLINOIS tables 98, 101 (1963).
>
> BUREAU OF THE CENSUS, U.S. DEP'T OF COMMERCE. 1970 CENSUS OF POPULATION. Vol. I: CHARACTERISTICS OF THE POPULATION. Part 15: ILLINOIS—SECTION 2 tables 138, 146 (1973).
>
> BUREAU OF THE CENSUS, U.S. DEP'T OF COMMERCE. 1980 CENSUS OF POPULATION. Vol. 1: CHARACTERISTICS OF THE POPULATION. Ch. D: DETAILED POPULATION CHARACTERISTICS. Part 15: ILLINOIS—SECTION 1 tables 201, 203 (1983).

College enrollment rates were calculated for Pennsylvania residents from the following:

> BUREAU OF THE CENSUS, U.S. DEP'T OF COMMERCE. CENSUS OF POPULATION: 1950. Vol. II: CHARACTERISTICS OF THE POPULATION. Part 38: PENNSYLVANIA tables 15, 63 (1952).
>
> BUREAU OF THE CENSUS, U.S. DEP'T OF COMMERCE. CENSUS OF POPULATION: 1960. Vol. I: CHARACTERISTICS OF THE POPULATION. Part 40: PENNSYLVANIA tables 98, 101 (1963).
>
> BUREAU OF THE CENSUS, U.S. DEP'T OF COMMERCE. 1970 CENSUS OF POPULATION. Vol. I: CHARACTERISTICS OF THE POPULATION. Part 40: PENNSYLVANIA—SECTION 2 tables 138, 146 (1973).
>
> BUREAU OF THE CENSUS, U.S. DEP'T OF COMMERCE. 1980 CENSUS OF POPULATION. Vol. 1: CHARACTERISTICS OF THE POPULATION. Ch. D: DETAILED POPULATION CHARACTERISTICS. Part 40: PENNSYLVANIA—SECTION 1 tables 201, 203 (1983).

44. While 1.2 percentage points lower in both years, the state rate was 7.7% below the national rate in 1970 but 5.6% below in 1980.

45. BUREAU OF THE CENSUS, *supra* note 38, at 27, 425; BUREAU OF THE CENSUS, STATISTICAL ABSTRACT OF THE UNITED STATES: 1965 16, 334 (86th ed. 1965).

46. The proportion of 20- to 24-year-old persons in New Jersey who were enrolled in college was 13.1% among males and 3.9% among females in 1950, 13.8% among males and 5.8% among females in 1960, 24.8% among males and 13.7% among females in 1970, and 24.7% among males and 22.3% among females in 1980. These proportions were calculated from Bureau of the Census reports for New Jersey using the same-numbered tables cited in note 43 *supra* for Illinois and Pennsylvania.

47. Califano v. Webster, 430 U.S. 313, 317 (1977) (citations omitted).

48. Jasso & Rossi, *Distributive Justice and Earned Income*, 42 AM. SOC. REV. 639, 644 (1977). *See* J. KLUEGEL & E. SMITH, BELIEFS ABOUT INEQUALITY (1986).

49. *See* Bumpass & Rindfuss, *Children's Experience of Marital Disruption*, 85 AM. J. SOC. 49, 58 (1979); NAT'L CENTER FOR HEALTH STATISTICS, U.S. DEP'T OF HEALTH & HUMAN SERVICES, VITAL STATISTICS OF THE UNITED STATES, 1983. Vol. III: MARRIAGE AND DIVORCE (1987), at table 2–11.

50. HAGGSTROM, WAITE, KANOUSE, & BLASCHKE, CHANGES IN THE LIFESTYLES OF NEW PARENTS (1984); Felmlee, *A Dynamic Analysis of Women's Employment Exits*, 21 DEMOGRAPHY 171 (1984).

51. Cox, *Panel Estimates of the Effects of Career Interruptions on the Earnings of Women*, 22 ECON. INQUIRY 386 (1984); Haggstrom, Waite, Kanouse, & Blaschke, *supra* note 50, at 61; Nord, *supra* note 37.

52. *Cf.* P. Burstein, Labor Market Discrimination, Social Science, and the Law (paper presented at the 1988 meeting of the Law and Society Association).

53. *See* R. Bergstrom, Courting Danger: Injury Suits in New York City, 1870–1910 (paper presented at the 1988 meeting of the Law and Society Association).

54. Glenn & Taylor, *Education and Family Income: A Comparison of White Married Men and Women in the U.S.*, 63 SOCIAL FORCES 169 (1984).

55. Mirowsky, *The Psycho-Economics of Feeling Underpaid: Distributive Justice and the Earnings of Husbands and Wives*, 92 AM. J. SOC. 1404 (1987).

56. Schoen, Urton, Woodrow, & Baj, *Marriage and Divorce in Twentieth Century American Cohorts*, 22 DEMOGRAPHY 101 (1985).

57. Johnson & Skinner, *Labor Supply and Marital Separation*, 76 AM. ECON. REV. 455 (1986).

CHAPTER

4

Age

I would like to turn now to a second attribute that has been important to both social differentiation and legal doctrine. The attribute is age. Unfortunately, age is the subject of sociological research less often than is gender, and the analysis to be undertaken in this chapter is handicapped as a result. Age is nonetheless central to the organization of our society, and while presently attracting less attention than gender, it illuminates the macrosociological approach to legal thought developed in this book. We therefore consider it here.

Age serves in the United States to structure expectations for behavior and thus helps to order the social system. Different types of conduct are expected at different ages—e.g., persons who are 20 years old are not expected to act like persons who are 45 years old—and the resulting behavioral patterns are a significant factor in societal arrangements. The present chapter examines the role of age in one specific aspect of social life, namely, work. Use of the attribute is extensive in our work environment: Age patterns are found in the organization of occupations[1] and, as will be seen shortly, in the extent of labor force involvement. Age, consequently, has become a focus of legal doctrine and an important topic for analysis.

As characteristics involved in social classification, age and gender share similarities and exhibit differences. In terms of similarities, both possess a biological foundation that apparently affects behavior and in turn the social expectations for it. Not all of the behaviors that distinguish younger from older ages and males from females are immutable and permanent, of course, even when they have biological bases; biology seems in most instances to set limits on behavior rather than to dictate specific forms of conduct. However, biological factors undoubtedly create some differences by age and sex that social change cannot erase. It is likely therefore that age-based and sex-based behaviors will persist and that the two attributes will be important concerns of legal doctrine for the foreseeable future.

Turning to the distinctions that exist between age and gender—

distinctions that have promoted the dissimilar treatment of the two attributes in the legal system—we find that age and gender differ in the stability of their biological foundations and of their social definitions. With regard to the biological dimensions of the attributes, sex remains unchanged throughout the life of the individual except in rare instances; essentially all persons experience only one sex, and that is determined at conception. Age, on the other hand, alters with the passage of time, and the individual will encounter different ages as long as death does not intervene. The biological permanence of sex and impermanence of age has in turn affected legal doctrine: Partly because of this difference the U.S. Supreme Court has held that, in determining the constitutionality of public policy under the equal protection guarantee, a more stringent test must be satisfied in order to uphold sex-based classifications than to uphold age-based classifications.[2] Constitutional intolerance of government policy is greater when a classification appearing in policy involves a personal attribute that is fixed and unchanging, for such an attribute is more likely to be the subject of invidious stereotypes.

The second distinction between the two attributes concerns their social definitions: The manner in which gender is defined by our society has evidently shifted more than the manner in which age is defined. The differential has produced concrete manifestations. Specifically, since the alteration of a social system generates resistance that the system attempts to suppress by interpersonal pressure and legal doctrine, the pace of change is reflected in the frequency with which legally cognizable invidious discrimination is perceived to occur. Thus, the Equal Employment Opportunity Commission in the first half of the 1980s received twice as many complaints of sex discrimination as of age discrimination.[3] The incidence of complaints regarding the two types of discrimination stems from the greater shift prior to 1980 in social definitions of gender than of age. To illustrate the course of gender and age definitions over time, a crude indicator of change in each was developed for the period from 1950 to 1980. The indicators were selected because they deal with a salient aspect of American society, namely, participation in the labor force. The definition of sex was measured by the rate of labor force participation of women 25–64 years old. The definition of age was measured by the rate of labor force participation of men 45–64 years old. The amount of change in each definition was determined by the ratio of the rate in 1950 to the rate in 1980.

Two comments are in order with regard to the indicator adopted for age. First, the age range 45–64 was used for the indicator, because traditionally Americans in this portion of the life cycle are expected to have a commitment to work and to reach their peak in earnings, authority, and prestige. As a result, withdrawal from work at this age is likely to have important social concomitants and consequences. Second, the labor force participation rate of men but not of women was utilized for the indicator because of the need to exclude the effect of change in the female role. Men, I assumed, had experienced comparatively little sex role change and would provide a more accurate barometer of the degree to which the social meaning of age had been modified.

The labor force participation rate of women 25–64 years old was 35.1% in 1950 and 59.2% in 1980. The rate among men 45–64 years old was 91.9% in 1950 and 82.0% in 1980.[4] The ratio of the 1980 proportion to the 1950 proportion was thus 1.69 for sex and 0.89 for age. Since a ratio of 1.00 represents no change in labor force participation, the ratio that deviates the most from unity identifies the largest shift over time. Accordingly, if the indicators accurately reflect the dimensions for which they are being used, the definition of gender experienced substantially more alteration than the definition of age, and the difference is probably responsible for much of the discrepancy in the incidence of employment discrimination believed to have been directed at each of the two attributes during the early 1980s.

FACTORS AFFECTING THE SOCIAL DEFINITION OF AGE

While social definitions were transformed less for age than for sex, change occurred in the definition of age, and the sources of the change need to be identified. New views of discrimination emerge in response to the evolution of social structure and values; behavior that is socially acceptable in one historical context may not be in another because the organization and values of society have altered. The causes of societal shifts are thus central in a macrosociological analysis of legal doctrine since they affect the types of conduct that are deemed discriminatory.

Given the focus of the present chapter on age discrimination and the federal Age Discrimination in Employment Act (ADEA), an effort will be made here to identify the social forces that generated pressure for change in the definition of age prior to the Act and that presumably led to the adoption of the statute. While those forces have not been systematically investigated in sociological research and cannot be listed with certainty at the present time, two factors can be suggested. One involves the age distribution of Americans and shifts in that distribution; the other arises from the stock of knowledge possessed by society and the tempo at which the stock was expanding.

We begin with age structure and, in particular, with the trend in and level of the median age of the population. As a consequence of the elevated fertility that followed the second world war, median age decreased from 30.2 in 1950 to 29.4 in 1960 and reached a low of 27.9 in 1967,[5] the year in which the ADEA was approved. When the statute was enacted, therefore, median age was well below 30 and had fallen by more than two years in less than two decades; between the earlier and later portions of this period, moreover, the magnitude of the decline underwent a substantial enlargement.[6] The paradoxical result was that the ADEA emerged during an era when younger ages were receiving disproportionate attention. Illustrative of this attention was a constitutional amendment in 1971 that reduced the minimum age for voting in federal and state elections to eighteen.[7] Congress found in proposing the measure that, although attempts to approve it had been made for three decades, "[i]n recent years, we have achieved a nationwide political consensus favoring a lowering of the voting age to 18."[8] The extent of that consensus is indicated by the rapidity with which the amendment was accepted; less than four months were required for the requisite number of states to ratify it.[9] Significantly, the low point in median age that was attained in 1967 continued through 1971, and only afterward did the median begin to rise. Demographic conditions in the early 1970s were thus conducive to the amendment and undoubtedly facilitated its adoption.

But how did a more youthful population promote enactment of the ADEA, a statute banning age discrimination in employment against individuals who are at least 40 years old? The answer, I suspect, is that the increased focus on youth fostered disaffection among those who were older. It is unlikely to be simply coincidence that, while median age was decreasing during the 1950s and 1960s, political alienation in the United States was falling among persons who were less than 45 years old and rising among those who were 45 and over.[10] Moreover, the latter were persons who, because of their age, had assumed social and economic positions that were vital to the functioning of society. The commitment of middle-age and older citizens to the social system thus needed to be strengthened, and enactment of the ADEA followed. This argument is buttressed by evidence (to be presented later) that age discrimination did not appreciably affect rates of labor force participation in the United States. The ADEA accordingly seems to have been a reaction to the social neglect of older persons and their weakened identification with the social system, not to economic injury inflicted on them by age discrimination.[11]

A second factor influencing the definition of age prior to the middle of the 1960s was, I believe, the growth of knowledge. That growth worked through two processes. First, knowledge was evidently advancing by the middle of the twentieth century at a pace that generated significant obsolescence of skills within the lifetime of the individual, and the frequency with which existing skills were displaced by those of greater efficiency seems to have reached a threshold sufficient to create notice of it.[12] As a result, age became an index of some validity for the currency of the skills possessed by an individual and, in turn, a criterion that could be useful in determining the desirability of a person for employment. The economic system was not, in this view, generally characterized by hostility toward or a lack of concern for older persons; rather, to the extent that age was involved in employment policies and practices, the attribute was simply an indicator that increased the likelihood of selecting workers who were most likely to contribute to productivity and competitiveness.[13]

Growth in knowledge appears to have implicated age not only by causing skill obsolescence but also by generating skill specialization. Significantly, the pace of specialization was escalating rapidly during the period in which the ADEA was enacted. The number of occupations included in the decennial census rose from 252 in 1900 to 370 in 1940, an increase of 118 in four decades. However, the number jumped from 370 in 1940 to 470 in 1960, an increase of 100 occupations in just two decades, and then expanded by an additional 200 occupations between 1960 and 1970 (from 470 to 670).[14] Although empirical evidence is lacking, it is likely that employment policies and practices were profoundly affected by the tempo of specialization. In particular, the advance of specialization should have caused a reduction in the transferability of skills between jobs; an increase in the difficulty of assessing the suitability of individuals for new positions; and, as a consequence, a greater reliance by employers on readily identifiable indices having some validity in the measurement of skills. One index probably used was scores on standardized tests of aptitude and proficiency.[15] Another may have been age because of its correlation with the length of involvement in a particular endeavor and hence with specialization. Such indices could reasonably have been expected by employers to improve personnel selection procedures even though the indices would often be erroneous in individual cases.

Growth in the stock of knowledge thus seems to have promoted age limitations in employer policies and practices. Ironically, however, no substantial impact on rates of labor force participation is evident (a point that will be explored in depth shortly). Age limitations consequently either affected relatively few persons, or they affected large numbers in ways that did not implicate these rates, e.g., by reducing the movement of workers from one employer to another.[16] Regardless of which occurred, though, the existence of the policies was in conflict with the American emphasis on individualism, a cultural value stressing that the position of a person in the economy should be based on ability and motivation rather than on attributes over which the person can exercise no control.[17] Enactment of the ADEA was encouraged, in short, by a threat to an important ideal in our social system.[18]

In sum, it was in the context of changes in the age structure of the population and the occupational structure of the economy that the issue of age discrimination arose. Those changes made age a salient feature of the social landscape and produced legislation to deter its use in employment-related decisions. Specifically, the increasing representation of youth in the population promoted political alienation among persons at and beyond middle age. Skill obsolescence and occupational specialization, the result of advancing knowledge, caused employers to increase their reliance on easily identifiable criteria such as age to guide decisions regarding current and potential employees. Legislation to eliminate age from personnel policies and practices directed toward individuals at least 40 years old thus stemmed from two societal needs: the need to reduce an elevated level of alienation among persons who, because of their age, performed roles that were important to the operation of the social system; and the need to protect the cultural teaching that economic position should be determined by individual merit, a teaching that was threatened by the use of age in employment-related decisions.

AGE DISCRIMINATION IN EMPLOYMENT ACT

Twenty-three states had adopted legislation banning age discrimination before Congress approved the ADEA in December 1967.[19] The federal statute, which became law in June 1968, prohibited covered employers—i.e., those having a minimum of twenty-five employees during at least twenty weeks in a year—from using age to discriminate "against any individual with respect to his compensation, terms, conditions, or privileges of employment" and from using age in a manner that "would deprive or tend to deprive any individual of employment opportunities." Complementary proscriptions were applied to employment agencies and labor organizations. The protections of the Act initially extended to persons who were 40 through 64 years of age,[20] but the upper limit was increased to 69 years effective January 1979[21] and, except for a few occupations, eliminated altogether effective January 1987.[22]

But in prohibiting age discrimination, what exactly did the statute attack? The enactment of legislation presupposes the existence of widespread agreement regarding the nature of the object to which the legislation applies, and thus a definition of age discrimination should appear in the ADEA or court opinions construing it. However, the statute and its history fail to specify the elements of age discrimination, and court decisions to date have not done so either.[23] As a result, a legal definition appears not to be feasible at the present time; age discrimination under the ADEA must simply be considered those particular actions that courts and administrative agencies label as discriminatory.

An illustration of the ambiguity that characterizes the concept of age discrimination can be seen in a challenge under the ADEA to the early retirement plan of a company. The plan provided that an employee could elect to retire and receive $600 per month until age 62[24] when the sum of his/her age and tenure with the company was at least 75 years. However, if an employee 60 years old and an employee 50 years old were both eligible for the benefits and opted for them, payments would be made for only two years to the former but for twelve years to the latter. The monthly benefit would be the same for each of the two individuals, but a substantial discrepancy would exist between them in the total amount of money received. Notably, the total was determined by the age at which the payments commenced, and as that age increased, the total declined. The result was that advancing age reduced the economic value of the plan to the employees who were eligible for it.

Given the negative effect of age on total benefits, the manner in which the attribute operated under the plan arguably constituted age discrimination in the terms, conditions, or privileges of employment. The U.S. Court of Appeals for the Seventh Circuit, however, found no violation of the ADEA for three reasons. First, the amount of the monthly payment did not vary with age; the payment each month was unaffected by the age of recipients either at the time of retirement or subsequently. Second, the likelihood of eligibility for the payments increased with age, i.e., advancing age enhanced the ability of employees to qualify for the benefits. Third, the plan furthered the purposes of the Act by providing economic assistance to unemployed persons in the age range protected by the statute; the payments were advantageous to their recipients rather than injurious.[25] Moreover, although not explicitly mentioned by the court in its opinion, an older employee was eligible for benefits under the plan with fewer years of service to the company than a younger employee; to the extent the ADEA was concerned with alleviating economic problems caused by advancing age, the method for determining benefit eligibility was harmonious with the objective of the statute.

Language being what it is, every concept exhibits some degree of vagueness, and as the case described above illustrates, age discrimination is no exception. However, a credible argument can be made that the concept of age discrimination suffers from greater ambiguity than the concept of sex discrimination. The argument arises from the provision in the ADEA that age discrimination does not exist in a distinction made between individuals "where the differentiation is based on reasonable factors other than age."[26] Such a provision is unnecessary in a statutory ban against age discrimination, because the ban by its very nature is inapplicable to conduct and policies that do not discriminate on the basis of age. The existence of the provision thus presumably reflects uncertainty regarding the location of the line that demarcates age discrimination from nondiscrimination. Indeed, the Equal Employment Opportunity Commission has reached the conclusion that "[n]o precise and unequivocal determination can be made as to the scope of the phrase 'differentiation based on reasonable factors other than age.' Whether such differentiations exist must be decided on the basis of all the particular facts and circumstances surrounding each individual situation."[27] Notably, the Commission does not make such a statement regarding a similar provision that appears in a federal statute mandating equality between men and women in compensation for jobs that are substantially equivalent in skill, effort, responsibility, and working conditions.[28] The interpretation of sex discrimination, it seems, is clearer than the interpretation of age discrimination. Moreover, the provision has no counterpart in a federal statute, enacted just three years before the ADEA, that prohibits sex discrimination in employment and that is otherwise remarkably similar in wording to the ADEA.[29] The need to include the provision in the ADEA accordingly suggests that the concept of age discrimination is surrounded by greater uncertainty than the concept of sex discrimination.

In spite of the ambiguity characterizing the nature of the phenomenon with which it was dealing, Congress adopted the ADEA on the grounds that age discrimination was a frequent occurrence and had reached a problematic level. In its own words, Congress acted because:

> (1) in the face of rising productivity and affluence, older workers find themselves disadvantaged in their efforts to retain employment, and especially to regain employment when displaced from jobs;
> (2) the setting of arbitrary age limits regardless of potential for job performance has become a common practice . . . ;
> (3) the incidence of unemployment, especially long-term unemployment . . . , is, relative to the younger ages, high among older workers; their numbers are great and growing; and their employment problems grave. . . .[30]

In its belief that age discrimination was increasingly impairing the ability of older persons to participate successfully in the labor force, Congress was not alone. Twenty of the twenty-three states approving legislation against such discrimination prior to the ADEA did so between 1956 and 1965,[31] indicating a widespread perception during the 1950s and 1960s that age discrimination was pervasive. However, rates of labor force participation cast doubt on the contention that age discrimination had an appreciable effect on the job market, and we will thus consider that participation at length. Before doing so, however, some understanding of the concept of labor force participation is needed.

The labor force participation rate, a widely used measure of involvement in the economic system, is the proportion of the population in a given age, race, and/or sex category that is employed or unemployed. However, individuals who are not working are defined as unemployed and considered to be in the labor force only when they possess certain characteristics. Specifically, the unemployed are those who recently attempted to obtain a job, are waiting to return to a job from which they were laid off, or will be reporting to a new job within thirty days. Unemployed persons in the labor force are therefore those individuals who are involved in the economic system and exposed to the possibility of employment-related discrimination.

Table 4.1 presents age-specific rates of labor force participation since 1890 for male cohorts (of all races) born between 1831–1835 and 1941–1945 (panel A) and the changes in rates that each of these cohorts experienced as they aged (panel B).[32] Figures 4.1–4.3 graphically depict the rates in panel A and thus complement the table; to assist in using the figures, I have designated important years in the period covered and the point at which the ADEA was adopted. The table and figures are limited to men because their participation, unlike that of women, has been relatively unaffected by sex role change. The data are confined to men at least 40 years old because the ADEA does not apply to younger ages.

To aid the reader in understanding table 4.1, a brief discussion of its two panels may be helpful. Panel A shows labor force participation rates by cohort and age. The year in which a cohort reached a given age and experienced a specified rate appears in parentheses immediately above the rate. By reading across a row of the panel, the participation rates of a cohort can be found for different ages and years. For example, men born in 1831–1835 had a labor force participation rate of 92.3% when they were 55–59 years old (their age in 1890), a rate of 85.8% when they were 60–64 years old (in 1895), and a rate of 77.3% when they were 65–69 years old (in 1900). By reading down a column, the rates at a given age can be determined for different years. To illustrate, labor force participation among men who were 50–54 years of age was 93.9% in 1890, 93.4% in 1895, and 92.9% in 1900.

Panel B of the table presents *changes* in labor force participation rates and thus extends the analysis permitted by panel A. Specifically, panel B reports the number of percentage points by which participation changed in a cohort as the cohort passed from one age category to the next.

Table 4.1. Labor Force Participation Rates in the United States, by Birth Cohort

Panel A: Rates by Birth Cohort and Age
(Year in Which Each Cohort Reached Age Specified in Parentheses)

Birth cohort	*Cohort age* 40–44	45–49	50–54	55–59	60–64	65–69
1831–1835				(1890) 92.3	(1895) 85.8	(1900) 77.3
1836–1840			(1890) 93.9	(1895) 91.1	(1900) 83.9	(1905) 74.2
1841–1845		(1890) 95.7	(1895) 93.4	(1900) 90.1	(1905) 83.6	(1910) 71.2
1846–1850	(1890) 97.3	(1895) 95.3	(1900) 92.9	(1905) 89.8	(1910) 83.3	(1915) 71.7
1851–1855	(1895) 96.8	(1900) 94.9	(1905) 92.8	(1910) 89.5	(1915) 83.8	(1920) 72.2
1856–1860	(1900) 96.2	(1905) 94.8	(1910) 92.7	(1915) 89.9	(1920) 84.4	(1925) 72.2
1861–1865	(1905) 96.4	(1910) 94.7	(1915) 93.1	(1920) 90.3	(1925) 84.2	(1930) 72.3
1866–1870	(1910) 96.6	(1915) 95.1	(1920) 93.5	(1925) 90.5	(1930) 84.0	(1935) 67.0
1871–1875	(1915) 96.7	(1920) 95.5	(1925) 93.7	(1930) 90.6	(1935) 82.5	(1940) 61.7
1876–1880	(1920) 96.8	(1925) 95.6	(1930) 94.0	(1935) 90.1	(1940) 81.1	(1945) 69.0
1881–1885	(1925) 96.9	(1930) 95.7	(1935) 93.6	(1940) 89.6	(1945) 86.1	(1950) 62.9
1886–1890	(1930) 96.9	(1935) 95.2	(1940) 93.2	(1945) 92.9	(1950) 81.4	(1955) 55.8
1891–1895	(1935) 96.7	(1940) 94.8	(1945) 94.2	(1950) 88.5	(1955) 80.9	(1960) 45.9

and Age: All Men 40–69 Years Old

Panel B: Percentage Point Change in Rates from Age to Age

Birth cohort	35–39 to 40–44	40–44 to 45–49	45–49 to 50–54	50–54 to 55–59	55–59 to 60–64	60–64 to 65–69
1831–1835					(1890–1895) −6.5	(1895–1900) −8.5
1836–1840				(1890–1895) −2.8	(1895–1900) −7.2	(1900–1905) −9.7
1841–1845			(1890–1895) −2.3	(1895–1900) −3.3	(1900–1905) −6.5	(1905–1910) −12.4
1846–1850		(1890–1895) −2.0	(1895–1900) −2.4	(1900–1905) −3.1	(1905–1910) −6.5	(1910–1915) −11.6
1851–1855	(1890–1895) −0.6	(1895–1900) −1.9	(1900–1905) −2.1	(1905–1910) −3.3	(1910–1915 −5.7	(1915–1920) −11.6
1856–1860	(1895–1900) −0.8	(1900–1905) −1.4	(1905–1910) −2.1	(1910–1915) −2.8	(1915–1920) −5.5	(1920–1925) −12.2
1861–1865	(1900–1905) −0.1	(1905–1910) −1.7	(1910–1915) −1.6	(1915–1920) −2.8	(1920–1925) −6.1	(1925–1930) −11.9
1866–1870	(1905–1910) −0.2	(1910–1915) −1.5	(1915–1920) −1.6	(1920–1925) −3.0	(1925–1930) −6.5	(1930–1935) −17.0
1871–1875	(1910–1915) −0.3	(1915–1920) −1.2	(1920–1925) −1.8	(1925–1930) −3.1	(1930–1935) −8.1	(1935–1940) −20.8
1876–1880	(1915–1920) −0.3	(1920–1925) −1.2	(1925–1930) −1.6	(1930–1935) −3.9	(1935–1940) −9.0	(1940–1945) −12.1
1881–1885	(1920–1925) −0.3	(1925–1930) −1.2	(1930–1935) −2.1	(1935–1940) −4.0	(1940–1945) −3.5	(1945–1950) −23.2
1886–1890	(1925–1930) −0.4	(1930–1935) −1.7	(1935–1940) −2.0	(1940–1945) −0.3	(1945–1950) −11.5	(1950–1955) −25.6
1891–1895	(1930–1935) −0.7	(1935–1940) −1.9	(1940–1945) −0.6	(1945–1950) −5.7	(1950–1955) −7.6	(1955–1960) −35.0

Continued

Table 4.1. *(Continued)*

Panel A: Rates by Birth Cohort and Age (Year in Which Each Cohort Reached Age Specified in Parentheses)

Birth cohort	Cohort age 40–44	45–49	50–54	55–59	60–64	65–69
1896–1900	(1940) 96.5	(1945) 96.1	(1950) 93.0	(1955) 91.0	(1960) 79.6	(1965) 42.2
1901–1905	(1945) 96.4	(1950) 95.6	(1955) 94.3	(1960) 90.2	(1965) 76.8	(1970) 40.9
1906–1910	(1950) 96.2	(1955) 95.8	(1960) 93.4	(1965) 89.0	(1970) 74.0	(1975) 31.2
1911–1915	(1955) 96.7	(1960) 95.3	(1965) 93.8	(1970) 88.5	(1975) 64.8	(1980) 28.1
1916–1920	(1960) 96.3	(1965) 95.0	(1970) 92.1	(1975) 83.5	(1980) 60.4	(1985) 24.1
1921–1925	(1965) 95.9	(1970) 94.8	(1975) 89.2	(1980) 81.2	(1985) 55.1	
1926–1930	(1970) 95.5	(1975) 93.2	(1980) 88.6	(1985) 78.9		
1931–1935	(1975) 94.2	(1980) 92.6	(1985) 87.9			
1936–1940	(1980) 94.4	(1985) 92.6				
1941–1945	(1985) 94.0					

Looking at the first row of the panel, for example, we see that labor force participation among men born in 1831–1835 declined by 6.5 percentage points as the cohort aged from 55–59 to 60–64, a transition made between 1890 and 1895, and that it declined another 8.5 percentage points as the cohort aged from 60–64 to 65–69, a transition made between 1895 and 1900. Useful information is also gleaned from the columns of the panel. By reading down a column, it is possible to follow a particular age-to-age change in participation through different periods. Labor force

Panel B: Percentage Point Change in Rates from Age to Age

Birth cohort	*35–39 to 40–44*	*40–44 to 45–49*	*45–49 to 50–54*	*50–54 to 55–59*	*55–59 to 60–64*	*60–64 to 65–69*
1896–1900	(1935–1940) −1.0	(1940–1945) −0.4	(1945–1950) −3.1	(1950–1955) −2.0	(1955–1960) −11.4	(1960–1965) −37.4
1901–1905	(1940–1945) −1.2	(1945–1950) −0.8	(1950–1955) −1.3	(1955–1960) −4.1	(1960–1965) −13.4	(1965–1970) −35.9
1906–1910	(1945–1950) −1.0	(1950–1955) −0.4	(1955–1960) −2.4	(1960–1965) −4.4	(1965–1970) −15.0	(1970–1975) −42.8
1911–1915	(1950–1955) +0.2	(1955–1960) −1.4	(1960–1965) −1.5	(1965–1970) −5.3	(1970–1975) −23.7	(1975–1980) −36.7
1916–1920	(1955–1960) −0.6	(1960–1965) −1.3	(1965–1970) −2.9	(1970–1975) −8.6	(1975–1980) −23.1	(1980–1985) −36.3
1921–1925	(1960–1965) −0.7	(1965–1970) −1.1	(1970–1975) −5.6	(1975–1980) −8.0	(1980–1985) −26.1	
1926–1930	(1965–1970) −1.2	(1970–1975) −2.3	(1975–1980) −4.6	(1980–1985) −9.7		
1931–1935	(1970–1975) −2.3	(1975–1980) −1.6	(1980–1985) −4.7			
1936–1940	(1975–1980) −1.0	(1980–1985) −1.8				
1941–1945	(1980–1985) −1.1					

Source: J. Robinson, A Cohort Analysis of Trends in the Labor Force Participation of Men and Women in the United States: 1890 to 1985 table 4.1 (unpublished Ph.D. dissertation, University of Pennsylvania, 1988).

participation for the transition from age 55–59 to age 60–64 thus declined 6.5 percentage points between 1890 and 1895 and 7.2 percentage points between 1895 and 1900.

An argument has been made that age discrimination intensified from the last part of the nineteenth century to the end of the economic de-

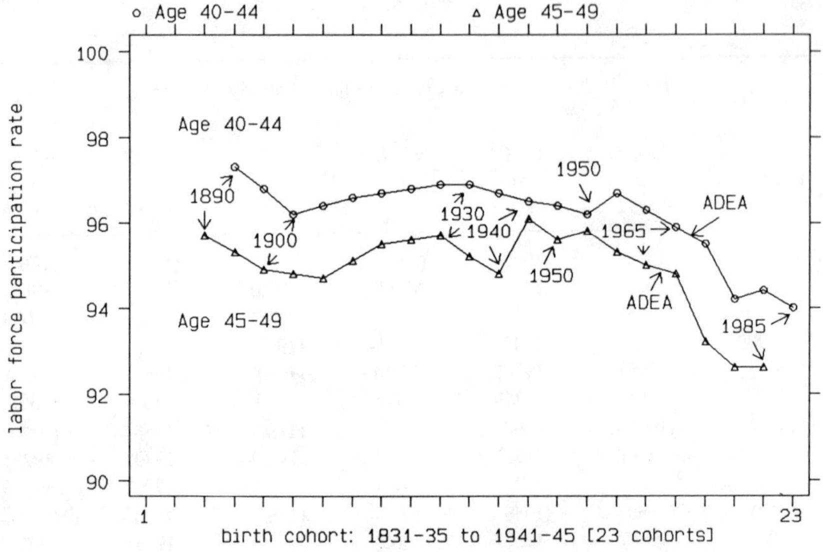

Figure 4.1 Labor force participation rate of men, ages 40–44 and 45–49.

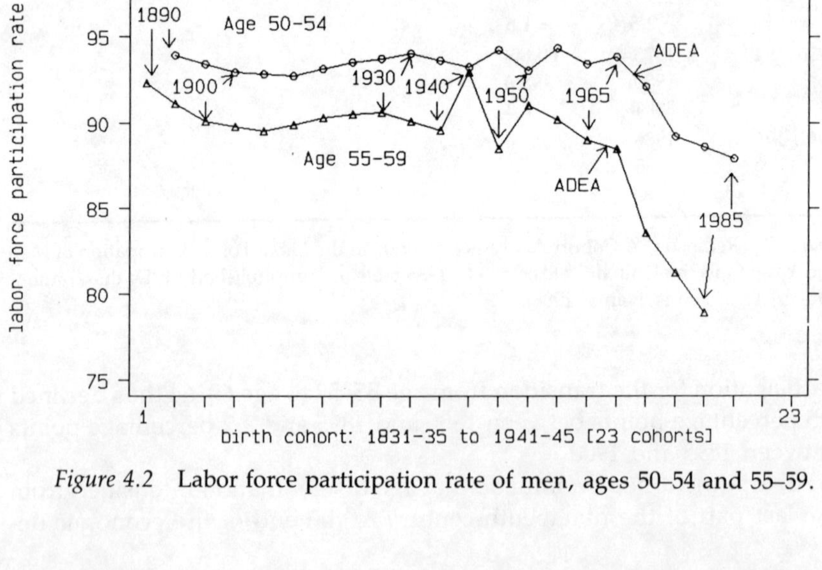

Figure 4.2 Labor force participation rate of men, ages 50–54 and 55–59.

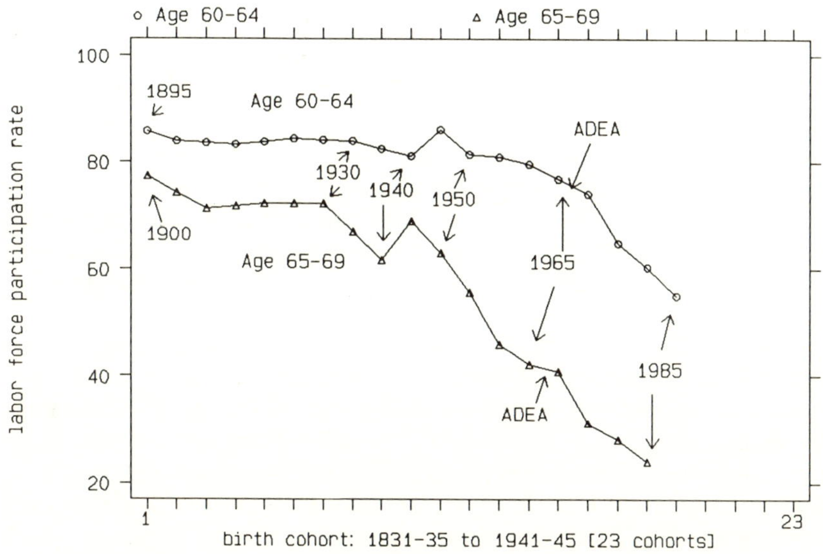

Figure 4.3 Labor force participation rate of men, ages 60–64 and 65–69.

pression of the 1930s,[33] but table 4.1 and the figures provide only limited support for the contention. Among men younger than 55, labor force participation rates and age-to-age changes in those rates fluctuated within a narrow range between 1890 and 1940. Among men 55–59 years of age, a marked decline in participation occurred between 1890 and 1900, but for the cohorts of 1836–1840 to 1871–1875 and the period until 1930, the pace at which men withdrew from the labor force did not vary much as they moved from age 50–54 to age 55–59 (see the column for this change in panel B of the table). The lower participation rate at age 55–59 in 1900 than in 1890 thus evidently resulted from increases in labor force withdrawals at an age younger than 55, increases from which the cohorts involved did not recover before reaching age 55–59. Unfortunately, the point in time at which the increases occurred cannot be determined.

Among men aged 60–64, an erosion is found in labor force participation between 1895 and 1900 and between 1930 and 1940. With regard to the 1895–1900 period, panel B of the table shows that, among men aging from 55–59 to 60–64, labor force withdrawals were only 0.7 percentage points larger between 1895 and 1900 than between 1890 and 1895. The abatement of 1.9 points in the participation rate of men 60–64 years old between 1895 and 1900 (see panel A) thus seems to have resulted primarily from an increase in withdrawals at an earlier age that continued to affect participation by the cohort of 1836–1840 as it grew older. With regard to the decline in the participation rate between 1930 and 1940, the change seems to have occurred during the depression, since the decline in the rate is closely matched by elevated increases in withdrawals among the cohorts that reached age 60–64 at this time (see panel B).

At age 65–69, participation fell appreciably from 1900 to 1910 and again from 1930 to 1940. Panel B of the table suggests that, except between 1900 and 1905, the declines can be attributed to an enlarged volume of labor force exits during these periods in the transition to 65–69 years of age and/or in the transition to 60–64 years of age.

Prior to the second world war, then, levels of and changes in labor force participation are consistent with the proposition that age discrimination intensified against men who were 60–69 years old. In addition, shifts in the magnitude of withdrawals from the labor force indicate that some increase in age discrimination against men 55–59 years old may have taken place in the 1930s. However, it is important to note that labor force participation is only a proxy for discrimination, and the degree to which labor force participation reflects discrimination may differ between groups and times. Accordingly, factors other than discrimination may explain variation in participation, and future research on groups experiencing declines in participation before World War II will need to consider these factors. For instance, one factor that reduced labor force participation among men aged 65 and older was the creation of retirement benefits by the federal government in the 1930s.[34] Another was the diminishing share of the economy devoted to agricultural occupations.[35] Farm employment in the United States fell rapidly between 1900 and 1940: from 39% of the civilian labor force in 1900 to 25% in 1920 and to 17% in 1940.[36]

In the period that began after the end of World War II in the latter half of 1945 and that continued to the enactment of the ADEA in late 1967—a period definable in table 4.1 and the figures as the fifteen years from 1950 to 1965—rates of and changes in labor force participation prior to age 55 display no clear deviations from historically established levels. At age 55–59, however, participation fell between 1955 and 1965, and panel B suggests that, among men reaching age 55–59 during this period, the volume of labor force withdrawals was larger than in earlier periods (other than those affected by the depression of the 1930s or World War II). Between 1955 and 1965, accordingly, a real decline in labor force participation seems to have occurred among men 55–59 years old.

Among men 60–69 years old, steady declines in participation rates are found between 1950 and 1965. Panel B indicates that substantially more men entering this age range withdrew from the labor force in the years from 1955 to 1965 than in earlier years (excluding those influenced by the depression and World War II). Prior to enactment of the ADEA, then, the erosion of participation levels among men 60–69 years old appears to have been due largely to an increased volume of exits from the labor force at this age and not to changes that affected the cohorts involved when they were younger.

In sum, labor force involvement waned among men age 55 and older during the decade preceding the ADEA. The question that must be answered, therefore, is the extent to which age discrimination contributed to the decline.[37] Since discrimination has not been measured directly, its role cannot be calculated precisely. Nonetheless, its impact is likely to have been small. In a complex social system such as that found in the United States, change has multiple causes, and the declines that occurred in labor force involvement prior to the mid-1960s were almost certainly not due exclusively to age discrimination. Other factors undoubtedly also contributed.

What were those factors? One probable influence was an augmented incidence of chronic health conditions among older men; the proportion of men 45–64 years of age who were limited in a major activity by a chronic disease or impairment rose steadily from 1960 onward.[38] In addition, labor force participation apparently declined because of growing affluence and the accumulating knowledge that was responsible for it. Increasing wealth seems to have permitted more frequent early retirement during this period by providing income from personal assets and pensions.[39] Technological advance, the result of an enlarged stockpile of knowledge, is likely to have progressively impaired the skills of older workers and, given the limited number of years remaining in the productive life of persons age 55 and older, made retraining economically impractical.[40] Unfortunately, the impact of each factor cannot be determined, but if the influence of each on labor force participation by men age 55 and older was only equal to that of age discrimination, the contribution of discrimination was minimal. For men 55–59 years old, the disadvantage in participation rates and age-to-age changes in these rates was only 1 or 2 percentage points during the years immediately preceding the ADEA compared to earlier periods (other than those affected by the depression and World War II). For men 60–64 years old—the last age before our society has expected retirement and provided full retirement benefits—the disadvantage was no more than 8 percentage points. If an equal contribution was made by each of the four factors discussed—increasing physical disability, augmented affluence, expanding knowledge, and age discrimination—the disappearance of discriminatory practices would have eliminated approximately one-half of a percentage point from the decline in labor force participation among men 55–59 years old and a maximum of 2 percentage points from the decline among men 60–64 years old.[41]

To recapitulate, we have seen that rates of labor force participation provide no evidence of increasing age discrimination against men younger than 55 between the late nineteenth century and the enactment of the ADEA in 1967. In believing that such discrimination was a growing problem for this age group, Congress appears to have been simply wrong. As to men 55 years of age and older, their labor force experience suggests that age discrimination increased to a negligible extent at age 55–59 and to only a small extent at age 60–64.

We now come to the period that followed enactment of the ADEA and to the question of the impact of the statute. Did men in the age range covered by the Act measurably benefit from the legislation? Logically, if age discrimination had no more than a minor effect on labor force involvement, a statute banning such discrimination would not have an appreciable impact. It should not be surprising, therefore, that table 4.1 and the figures suggest the ADEA failed to alter labor force participation. Among men who were less than 65 years old—the only group covered by the Act from its inception—participation rates generally fell after the effective date of the statute (i.e., from 1970 to 1985) and reached lows that had not been attained previously. At the same time, panel B discloses that age-to-age declines in participation were generally as large in magnitude after the statute was enacted as they were before (excluding periods affected by the depression and the second world war), and frequently they were much larger.[42] A multiple regression analysis (presented in the chapter appendix) of annual data on labor force participation and employment in two age groups—45–54 and 55–64—also suggests that the ADEA did not improve the position of men in the economy.

Trends in labor force participation accordingly provide little support for the assertion that the ADEA curtailed a factor that was markedly depressing the involvement of older men in the economy. Similarly, no appreciable impact on labor force participation is likely as a result of raising or eliminating the maximum age for protection under the ADEA.[43] The extent of labor force involvement, it seems, is not a function of a statute banning discrimination but, rather, of large-scale social forces.

CONCLUSION

The evidence reviewed in this and preceding chapters strongly suggests that the social system in the United States is relatively impervious to influence by legislation and litigation. As a component of the system, legal doctrine appears to be a dependent variable, affected by social circumstances but not appreciably affecting them. The evidence is thus contrary to popular notions regarding law and will be lamented by many. However, the inability of law to modify social patterns can also be considered a societal asset. For a social system to be molded by legal doctrine, two conditions are presumably necessary: societal homogeneity and centralized control. These conditions, however, appear to endanger the ability of a society to respond effectively to pressures for significant change. To be capable of adapting to consequential alterations in its environment, a social system would seem to require the same attributes that allow a biological ecosystem to survive severe stress created by an external source, viz., diversity and complexity.[44] The ineffectiveness of law as an instrument for social change may thus be a concomitant of the heterogeneity and decentralization created by relatively high population density[45] and of a greater resilience conferred on society by that density. From a macrosociological perspective, in short, the marginal social impact of law may be understood as neither aberrant nor deplorable but, rather, an inherent and advantageous aspect of our social system.

APPENDIX

To assess the impact of the ADEA, separate logit models were estimated (with weighted least squares) for the annual rate of labor force participation and the annual rate of employment. The analysis covered civilian, noninstitutionalized men of all races who were 45–54 years old and 55–64 years old. The data began with 1949, the base year for the rise in affluence that followed World War II, and ended with 1979, the last year of the initial economic recovery from the marked increase in energy costs that took place in the mid-1970s.[46] By extending to 1979, the data included twelve calendar years after the ADEA was adopted and eleven calendar years after the statute went into operation.

Prior to studying the impact of the ADEA, regression models estimated the influence on labor force participation and employment of five factors other than the Act. Specifically, the models included a dummy variable for age group (45–54 versus 55–64) and a dummy variable that distinguished the period of growing affluence after the second world war (1949–1973) from the period in the 1970s affected by elevated energy prices (1974–1979). The models also contained year as a continuous variable in order to capture trends that influenced labor force participation and employment; the gross national product in constant (1982) dollars in order to measure the robustness of the economy; and the average annual yield on three-month Treasury bills in order to gauge the cost of credit. To assess the impact of the cost of credit, the yield on Treasury bills was lagged one year.

Using the criteria of parsimony, goodness-of-fit, and the statistical significance of individual variables, one model appeared to be the most appropriate for both labor force participation and employment. The model was comprised of three variables: the gross national product; the dummy for 1949–1973 versus 1974–1979; and the dummy for age group. These variables were included in and controlled by the regression models studying the effect of the ADEA.

The impact of the ADEA was assessed with dummy variables for each year from 1949 to 1979 other than the reference year. Rather than rely on a single regression equation for this purpose, I estimated a set of regression equations and systematically varied the reference year, an approach that allowed year-to-year change in labor force participation and employment to be portrayed clearly. Change was measured in terms of odds ratios, not regression coefficients, and the ratios are for the specified year relative to the year that preceded it. A ratio that deviates from unity and is statistically significant indicates that change has occurred in the odds of labor force participation or employment compared to the year before: A ratio larger than 1.000 signifies a rise in the odds of labor force participation/employment over the preceding year, while a ratio less than 1.000 signifies a decline.

Let us first consider the regression results for labor force participation. The odds ratios for each year are shown below along with their t values and probabilities under the null hypothesis. (Results for the three control variables are not presented.) Without the year dummies in the equations (i.e., with only age group, gross national product, and the period dummy for 1949–1973 versus 1974–1979), the adjusted R^2 was .988 and the square root of the mean square error was .078; with the year dummies in the equations, the two measures were .997 and .038, respectively (N = 62).

Year	*Odds ratio*	*t*	*Probability*	*Year*	*Odds ratio*	*t*	*Probability*
1950	1.021	0.464	.646	1965	0.949	1.198	.240
1951	1.077	1.644	.111	1966	0.997	0.061	.952
1952	1.066	1.378	.179	1967	0.996	0.106	.916
1953	1.083	1.698	.100	1968	0.990	0.245	.808
1954	1.040	0.808	.426	1969	0.948	1.384	.177
1955	0.993	0.160	.874	1970	0.957	1.200	.239
1956	1.064	1.309	.201	1971	0.960	1.123	.270
1957	0.938	1.375	.179	1972	0.926	2.109	.043
1958	1.010	0.210	.835	1973	0.942	1.722	.095
1959	0.997	0.062	.951	1974	1.083	2.575	.015
1960	0.963	0.858	.398	1975	0.923	2.575	.015
1961	1.041	0.936	.357	1976	0.981	0.642	.526
1962	0.991	0.216	.831	1977	1.016	0.517	.609
1963	1.056	1.346	.188	1978	1.045	1.501	.144
1964	1.026	0.653	.519	1979	1.017	0.583	.564

The period of interest is 1968 and subsequent years, because 1968 is the earliest that enforcement of the ADEA could have increased labor force participation among men. Do the data provide any reason to believe that such an effect occurred? The answer, clearly, is negative. If the statute benefited men, we should find statistically significant odds ratios that exceed 1.000 over a number of years, particularly those immediately following implementation of the law, but no such pattern appears. Indeed, using .100 as the criterion for rejecting the null hypothesis, a significant odds ratio larger than 1.000 emerges just once (in 1974) and it occurs so long after the ADEA was implemented that it cannot reasonably be attributed to the Act. Moreover, the ratio is an isolated event, representing just a one-year improvement in labor force participation, and it is both preceded and followed by a decline in participation. The odds of labor force participation at this time thus seem to have been in a state of change, and their improvement in 1974 cannot be credited to the ADEA. Finally, the ratios for 1969, 1970, and 1971, though not significant, may suggest that labor force involvement experienced a gradual, multiyear decline after the statute went into operation.

Labor force participation, however, is arguably less important for assessing the impact of the ADEA than employment. The Act is directed at employment, and its influence on labor force participation is necessarily indirect. What influence did the statute have on employment? Presented below are the odds ratios for the year dummies from the employment models together with the t values and probabilities of the ratios under the null hypothesis. For these models (N = 62), the adjusted R^2 was .958 without the year dummies and .978 with them; the square root of the mean square error was .116 without the year dummies and .085 with them.

Year	*Odds ratio*	*t*	*Probability*	*Year*	*Odds ratio*	*t*	*Probability*
1950	1.041	0.422	.676	1965	1.004	0.041	.967
1951	1.249	2.294	.029	1966	1.030	0.305	.762
1952	1.077	0.716	.480	1967	0.992	0.089	.930
1953	1.041	0.386	.702	1968	1.007	0.077	.939
1954	0.841	1.673	.105	1969	0.949	0.581	.566
1955	1.050	0.506	.616	1970	0.895	1.307	.201
1956	1.109	1.040	.307	1971	0.913	1.088	.285
1957	0.936	0.670	.508	1972	0.945	0.679	.502
1958	0.830	1.951	.060	1973	0.971	0.366	.717
1959	1.090	0.970	.340	1974	1.120	1.502	.144
1960	0.972	0.309	.760	1975	0.829	2.614	.014
1961	0.940	0.702	.488	1976	0.994	0.089	.930
1962	1.075	0.850	.402	1977	1.034	0.477	.637
1963	1.055	0.627	.535	1978	1.046	0.644	.524
1964	1.049	0.566	.575	1979	1.002	0.033	.974

The regression results furnish no evidence that the ADEA assisted a substantial number of men to obtain and/or retain jobs. If the Act had worked as intended, there should have been a number of statistically significant odds ratios exceeding 1.000 during the 1968–1979 period. None, however, are found.

NOTES

1. Kaufman & Spilerman, *The Age Structures of Occupations and Jobs*, 87 AM. J. SOC. 827 (1982).

2. *Compare* Massachusetts Board of Retirement v. Murgia, 427 U.S. 307, 313–314 (1976) *with* Frontiero v. Richardson, 411 U.S. 677, 686 (1973) *and* Craig v. Boren, 429 U.S. 190 (1976).

3. EQUAL EMPLOYMENT OPPORTUNITY COMMISSION, ANNUAL REPORT (16th ed. 1982, 17th ed. 1983, 18th ed. 1984, 19th ed. no date). During fiscal years 1981–1984, the Commission received 208,326 complaints of sex discrimination or gender-based unequal pay but only 96,575 complaints of age discrimination. The disparity cannot be explained by the difference between the number of women who are in the labor force and the number of persons in the labor force who are in the age range covered by the federal statute banning age discrimination. *See* BUREAU OF LABOR STATISTICS, U.S. DEP'T OF LABOR, BULL. 2340, HANDBOOK OF LABOR STATISTICS 13, 15 (1989).

4. Calculated from BUREAU OF LABOR STATISTICS, *supra* note 3, at tables 3 and 4.

5. 1 BUREAU OF THE CENSUS, U.S. DEP'T OF COMMERCE, HISTORICAL STATISTICS OF THE UNITED STATES: COLONIAL TIMES TO 1970 19 (1975); Bureau of the Census, U.S. Dep't of Commerce, *Estimates of the Population of the United States, by Age, Sex, and Race: 1980 to 1986*, CURRENT POPULATION REP. Series P-25, No. 1000 (1987), at table B.

6. The mean annual reduction in median age was .08 years between 1950 and 1960 and .21 years between 1960 and 1967.

7. Twenty-Sixth Amendment to the Constitution, 85 Stat. 829.

8. S. REP. No. 92–26, 92nd Cong., 1st Sess., *reprinted in* 1971 U.S. CODE CONG. & ADMIN. NEWS 931, 934, 937.

9. The proposed amendment was approved by the Senate on March 10, 1971, and by the House of Representatives 13 days later. Its ratification by the necessary number of states and its incorporation into the Constitution was certified on July 5, 1971.

10. Agnello, *Aging and the Sense of Political Powerlessness*, 37 PUB. OPINION Q. 251 (1973).

11. *See* Shapiro & Sandell, *Age Discrimination in Wages and Displaced Older Men*, 52 SO. ECON. J. 90 (1985).

12. One test of this argument would be adult education courses—i.e., courses pursued on a part-time basis, whether or not taken for credit or for a degree. While data on such courses prior to 1969 apparently do not exist, be-

tween 1969 and 1984 the proportion of persons 35–54 years old who enrolled in adult education courses rose from 1 in 10 to 1 in 6 and the number of job-related courses more than doubled. CENTER FOR EDUC. STATISTICS, U.S. DEP'T OF EDUC., TRENDS IN ADULT EDUCATION, 1969–1984 6, 8 (n.d.). Presumably, the increases did not originate in 1969 but were an extension of change that began earlier.

13. A study in five metropolitan areas of 540 employers that had more than 50 employees was conducted by the U.S. Department of Labor in 1965. Although concluding that age limits in hiring were frequent, the study noted:

> We have found no evidence of prejudice based on dislike or intolerance of the older worker. The issue of discrimination revolves around the nature of the work and its rewards, in relation to the ability or presumed ability of people at various ages, rather than around the people as such. This issue thus differs greatly from the primary one involved in discrimination on the basis of race, color, religion, or national origin, which is basically unrelated to ability to perform work.

U.S. DEP'T OF LABOR, THE OLDER AMERICAN WORKER—AGE DISCRIMINATION IN EMPLOYMENT 6 (1965).

14. Williams, *The Changing U.S. Labor Force and Occupational Differentiation by Sex*, 16 DEMOGRAPHY 73, 79 (1979).

15. Such tests had become so important in the employment context by the mid-1960s that their use was explicitly permitted by Congress in Title VII of the Civil Rights Act of 1964, which prohibited employment discrimination based on race, religion, sex, and national origin. Pub. L. 88–352, § 703(h), 78 Stat. 257 (1964) (codified at 42 U.S.C. § 2000e-2(h) (1982)).

16. The latter is suggested by Baron, Jennings, & Dobbin, *Mission Control? The Development of Personnel Systems in U.S. Industry*, 53 AM. SOC. REV. 497, 511 (1988).

17. J. KLUEGEL & E. SMITH, BELIEFS ABOUT INEQUALITY (1986).

18. Political support for the ADEA was apparently motivated more by the desire to provide opportunities for individuals to demonstrate their talents than by the desire to protect economic security. Persons in the age range encompassed by the statute are less likely than those who are younger to desire government policies that assure economic security. Heaton, *Objective Status and Class Consciousness*, 68 SOCIAL SCI. Q. 611 (1987); Hasenfeld & Rafferty, *The Determinants of Public Attitudes Toward the Welfare State*, 67 SOCIAL FORCES 1027 (1989). Presumably, they are also less likely to need and seek such policies. If so, the ADEA would seem to have been aimed chiefly at preserving the value of individualism.

19. *Age Discrimination in Employment: Hearings Before the Subcommittee on Labor of the Senate Committee on Labor and Public Welfare*, 90th Cong., 1st Sess. 119–44 (1967).

20. Pub. L. 90–202, 81 Stat. 602 (1967) (codified at 29 U.S.C. § 621 et seq. (1982)).

21. Pub. L. 95–256, 92 Stat. 189 (1978).

22. Pub. L. 99–592, 100 Stat. 3342 (1986).

23. *See* Eglit, *The Age Discrimination in Employment Act's Forgotten Affirmative*

Defense: The Reasonable Factors Other Than Age Exception, 66 Boston Univ. L. Rev. 155, 180–85 (1986).

24. The 62nd birthday was presumably selected for cessation of the payment because it was the age at which the individual could receive Social Security benefits.

25. Dorsch v. L. B. Foster Company, 782 F.2d 1421 (7th Cir. 1986). The Seventh Circuit encompasses Illinois, Indiana, and Wisconsin.

26. Pub. L. 90–202 § 4(f)(1), 81 Stat. 603 (1967).

27. 29 C.F.R. § 1625.7(b) (1987).

28. The statute, known as the Equal Pay Act, exempts compensation disparities that are "based on any other factor other than sex." Pub. L. 88–38, 77 Stat. 56. The statute was adopted in June 1963.

29. The statute, which was enacted in July 1964, was Title VII of the Civil Rights Act of 1964. Pub. L. 88–352, 78 Stat. 253 (1964).

30. Pub. L. 90–202 § 2(a), 81 Stat. 602 (1967) (codified at 29 U.S.C. § 621 (1982)).

31. *Age Discrimination in Employment*, *supra* note 19.

32. The labor force participation rates in table 4.1 include the total male population and thus are based on institutionalized as well as noninstitutionalized men. Rates for 1940 and later years are derived from the Current Population Survey; rates before 1940 are estimated from the decennial census. Data from the census were adjusted in order to make them comparable to data from the Current Population Survey. The procedures used to develop the labor force participation rates in table 4.1 are described in chapter 2 of J. Robinson, A Cohort Analysis of Trends in the Labor Force Participation of Men and Women in the United States: 1890 to 1985 (unpublished Ph.D. dissertation, University of Pennsylvania, 1988).

33. Specifically, the argument is that age discrimination became more prevalent in the United States between 1885 and 1940. However, support for the argument is not based primarily on systematically gathered longitudinal data covering the nation as a whole. W. Graebner, A History of Retirement 18–53 (1980). Some use is made of labor force participation rates, but the rates are only for men who were over 65 years of age. W. Achenbaum, Old Age in the New Land 74 (1978). Significantly, a survey in 1935 suggests that, during the preceding eight years, a maximum hiring age existed in only one out of eight or nine firms. Baron, Dobbin, & Jennings, *War and Peace: The Evolution of Modern Personnel Administration in U.S. Industry*, 92 Am. J. Soc. 350, 377 (1986). If age discrimination intensified between 1885 and 1940, its extent was nonetheless minimal at the latter time.

34. Gratton, *The Labor Force Participation of Older Men: 1890–1950*, 20 J. Social Hist. 689 (1987).

35. Pampel & Weiss, *Economic Development, Pension Policies, and the Labor Force Participation of Aged Males: A Cross-National, Longitudinal Approach*, 89 Am. J. Soc. 350 (1983).

36. Calculated from Bureau of the Census, U.S. Dep't of Commerce, Historical Statistics of the United States: Colonial Times to 1970. Part 1 (1975), at 126.

37. I define age discrimination as any age-based distinction in the context of employment that (1) promotes economic efficiency no more than marginally or (2) promotes economic efficiency to a degree that could be attained as easily by less disruptive means.

38. Verbrugge, *Longer Life but Worsening Health? Trends in Health and Mortality of Middle-Aged and Older Persons*, 62 MILBANK MEMORIAL FUND Q./HEALTH & SOC'Y 475, 484 (1984). *See generally* Hayward, Hardy, & Grady, *Labor Force Withdrawal Patterns among Older Men in the United States*, 70 SOCIAL SCI. Q. 425 (1989).

39. As financial resources improve, retirement becomes more frequent since most persons want to retire. Morgan, *Antecedents and Consequences of Retirement*, *in* 9 FIVE THOUSAND AMERICAN FAMILIES—PATTERNS OF ECONOMIC PROGRESS: ANALYSES OF THE FIRST TWELVE YEARS OF THE PANEL STUDY OF INCOME DYNAMICS 207 (M. Hill, D. Hill, & J. Morgan eds., 1981); Lorence, *Age Differences in Work Involvement*, 14 WORK & OCCUPATIONS 533 (1987).

Nonearned income from sources other than pensions apparently promotes retirement before as well as after age 65. Hanoch & Honig, *Retirement Wages, and Labor Supply of the Elderly*, 1 J. LABOR ECON. 131, 135–37 (1983). Between 1950 and 1965, the purchasing power of per capita personal income from interest, dividends, and rents—i.e., from personal assets rather than from earnings or transfer payments—rose by 72%. Calculated from BUREAU OF THE CENSUS, U.S. DEP'T OF COMMERCE, SOCIAL INDICATORS III: SELECTED DATA ON SOCIAL CONDITIONS AND TRENDS IN THE UNITED STATES table 9/7 (1980). The age distribution of the recipients of such income is not available, but presumably the recipients were disproportionately concentrated among persons of middle and older age because of the considerable time required to accumulate assets. *Cf.* Hurd, *Research on the Elderly: Economic Status, Retirement, and Consumption and Saving*, 28 J. ECON. LITERATURE 565, 570 (1990). Substantial income of this type has been frequent among retirees in recent years; among married couples who first received retirement benefits from the Social Security Administration between June 1980 and May 1981, one out of four derived at least $400 a month from personal assets. Maxfield & Reno, *Distribution of Income Sources of Recent Retirees: Findings from the New Beneficiary Survey*, 48 SOCIAL SECURITY BULL. 7, 12 (Jan. 1985). While undoubtedly found less often during the 1950s and 1960s, such income probably fostered retirement prior to age 65 even then.

The augmentation of wealth in the United States also seems to have allowed an increasing number of retirement plans in the private sector to provide benefits prior to age 65. U.S. DEP'T OF LABOR, THE OLDER AMERICAN WORKER—AGE DISCRIMINATION IN EMPLOYMENT: RESEARCH MATERIALS 25 (1965); Sherman, *Reported Reasons Retired Workers Left Their Last Job: Findings from the New Beneficiary Study*, 48 SOCIAL SECURITY BULL. 22, 25 (March 1985); Mitchell & Luzadis, *Changes in Pension Incentives Through Time*, 42 INDUS. & LABOR REL. REV. 100 (1988). Eligibility for a pension from an employer promotes the election of early retirement benefits from the Social Security Administration. Bould, *Factors Influencing the Choice of Social Security Early Retirement Benefits*, 5 POPULATION RES. & POL'Y REV. 217 (1986). Those benefits can commence at age 62, and it was in 1961 that men were given access to them. Pub. L. 87–64 § 102(a), 75 Stat. 131.

40. *See* Pampel & Weiss, *supra* note 35.

41. In 1965, a survey in five metropolitan areas of 540 firms exceeding 50 employees reported that one out of four firms had a policy disqualifying job applicants who were beyond a certain age from at least one type of position and that another one out of four firms had some age limits in practice. U.S. DEP'T OF LABOR, THE OLDER AMERICAN WORKER—AGE DISCRIMINATION IN EMPLOYMENT: RESEARCH MATERIALS 7–8 (1965). The survey suggests, therefore, that age discrimination was pervasive in the mid-1960s and that its elimination would have had a marked impact on rates of labor force involvement. However, evidence is lacking on the proportion of men in the affected age range who were outside the labor force or unemployed and whose status would have changed if age barriers did not exist. In addition, the findings of the survey may not be applicable to employers in general for two reasons. First, firms in the survey were not selected with a probability sampling technique. *Id.* at 19. The survey results may therefore not be generalizable even to firms of the type studied, viz., firms in metropolitan settings that have large numbers of employees. Second, firms with more than 50 workers in the 1960s employed substantially less than one-half, and possibly no more than one-third, of all persons holding a job at that time. Granovetter, *Small Is Bountiful: Labor Markets and Establishment Size*, 49 AM. SOC. REV. 323, 327–28 (1984). Small firms thus accounted for most employment, and they may have differed markedly from large firms in hiring policies and practices with regard to age. U.S. DEP'T OF LABOR, *supra*, at 5.

42. Table 4.1 includes men of all races, but the same conclusions apply to white men. Robinson, *supra* note 32, at table 4.5.

43. Burkhauser & Quinn, *Is Mandatory Retirement Overrated? Evidence from the 1970s*, 18 J. HUM. RESOURCES 337 (1983); Lawlor, *The Impact of Age Discrimination Legislation on the Labor Force Participation of Aged Men: A Time-Series Analysis*, 10 EVALUATION REV. 794 (1986).

44. Bates, *The Human Ecosystem, in* RESOURCES AND MAN 21 (Committee on Resources and Man, National Academy of Sciences—National Research Council 1969).

45. Wilson, *Community Population Size and Social Heterogeneity: An Empirical Test*, 91 AM. J. SOC. 1154 (1986); Stephan & McMullin, *The Historical Distribution of County Seats in the United States: A Review, Critique, and Test of Time-Minimization Theory*, 46 AM. SOC. REV. 907 (1981).

46. BUREAU OF ECONOMIC ANALYSIS, U.S. DEP'T OF COMMERCE, THE NATIONAL INCOME AND PRODUCT ACCOUNTS OF THE UNITED STATES, 1929–82: STATISTICAL TABLES table 1.2 (1986).

CHAPTER

5

Contraception and Abortion

Chapters 3 and 4, in illustrating my thesis, focused on personal characteristics involved in the structure of social relationships and the organization of society. The characteristics were selected both because they are salient in our social system and because they could be studied with a sizable body of quantitative data. The topic of the present chapter was chosen for the same reasons. However, while chapters 3 and 4 examined attributes of the individual, our concern here will be with a form of human activity—namely, procreation—and the jurisprudential theme that emerged for it in the 1960s and 1970s. The central tenet of the theme was that control over procreation among adults should rest with the persons directly involved; a corollary proposition was that government policies aimed at seriously curtailing or burdening such control are unacceptable. The defining element of the theme was thus the principle of reproductive freedom.

For investigating the social nature of legal doctrine, the theme of reproductive freedom has a number of attractions beyond the widespread public interest that exists in it. Perhaps the most important is that longitudinal data are available both to identify the societal environment for procreation that preceded the theme and to determine the effect of the theme on behavior. In addition, a relatively small number of discrete legal events—viz., a handful of U.S. Supreme Court decisions construing the Constitution—largely delineate the theme. Though extensive, legislation manifesting the theme has been of secondary importance: The principle of reproductive freedom appeared in statutes only after the Supreme Court incorporated it into constitutional law,[1] and legislation that adopted the principle was overshadowed by constitutional jurisprudence that did so.[2]

THE CASES

Let me begin with a brief review of the cases in which reproductive freedom was employed as a constitutional principle by the U.S. Supreme Court. The first decision,[3] *Griswold v. Connecticut,* was rendered in 1965 and stemmed from the conviction of the executive director and medical director of a birth control clinic for providing married persons with information and products to avoid pregnancy. The conviction was based on a state statute that made it illegal either personally to use items designed to prevent conception or to assist others to use them. In reviewing the conviction, the Supreme Court held the statute unconstitutional on the ground that the law intruded unnecessarily into the marital relationship. The Constitution was violated, according to the majority opinion, because the statute, "in forbidding the *use* of contraceptives rather than regulating their manufacture or sale, seeks to achieve its goals by means having a maximum destructive impact upon that [marital] relationship."[4] Marriage and the intimacy that occurs within it, the Court emphasized, are traditional and essential features of our social system, and the Constitution protects them with a right of privacy that severely circumscribes the regulatory powers of government.

Seven years passed before the Supreme Court again employed the principle of reproductive freedom in constitutional law. In *Eisenstadt v. Baird* (decided in 1972), the Court dealt with a state statute that prohibited the distribution to unmarried persons of products intended to prevent conception and designated the sources (physicians and pharmacists) that could legally provide these products to married persons. Given the provisions of the statute, the issue in the case was only whether government was permitted by the equal protection guarantee to distinguish on the basis of marital status when it regulated access to contraceptives by adults; the issue was not whether contraception per se was constitutionally protected or whether unmarried couples have a right to use contraceptives. However, in holding that government must treat unmarried and married persons alike when specifying the conditions under which contraceptives are to be legally available to adults, the Court endorsed a doctrine that was broader than the issue it decided. "If the right of privacy means anything," the majority argued, "it is the right of the *individual,* married or single, to be free from unwarranted governmental intrusion into matters so fundamentally affecting a person as the decision whether to bear or beget a child."[5] Indeed, several years after *Eisenstadt* avoided the question of whether government possesses the power to outlaw contraception entirely, the Court acknowledged that the Constitution imposes strict limits on statutes and regulations that severely curtail the availability or use of contraceptives.[6] In the view of the Justices, governmental measures seriously affecting the control of procreation, whether by unmarried or married individuals, would be constitutional only if those measures directly advanced a compelling public interest—a test that is rarely satisfied.

Perhaps the best-known decision of the Supreme Court on the subject of reproduction is its 1973 ruling on abortion—*Roe v. Wade*.[7] In deciding the case, the Court concluded that a right of privacy is created by the Constitution—in particular, by the assurance of personal liberty in the due process guarantee—and that the right protects women who wish to terminate a pregnancy. In outlining the scope of the right, furthermore, the Court acknowledged just two interests that can justify the regulation of abortion by government—protecting the health of pregnant women and preserving the life of potentially viable fetuses—and deemed only the latter interest sufficient to justify the prohibition of abortion. Government can impose no restrictions on the abortion procedure (other than to require that a licensed physician perform it) while the fetus is not viable and the maternal mortality rate from abortion is less than that from childbirth. It is only after the risk of maternal death from abortion equals or exceeds the risk of death from childbirth—a period found by the Justices to start roughly at the end of the twelfth week of pregnancy—that restrictions on abortion are permissible, but until fetal viability the restrictions must be confined to protecting maternal health and the procedure cannot be banned.

In a 1992 decision, four of the nine Justices—one short of a majority—argued that the Supreme Court should overrule *Roe* and repudiate its constitutional precepts.[8] Even if the decision is overruled, however, it and the cases elaborating on it will remain socially significant developments and merit serious study. One of the cases that extended *Roe* seems particularly relevant to the thesis that I have advanced. In 1976, the Court in *Planned Parenthood of Central Missouri v. Danforth* held unconstitutional a state statute that required a married woman to obtain the approval of her husband before terminating a pregnancy during the first twelve weeks of gestation. In the view of the Court, the right of privacy that allows a woman to have an abortion is possessed by her as an individual and its scope is not affected by the presence of a marital relationship:

> [W]hen the wife and the husband disagree on this decision, the view of only one of the two marriage partners can prevail. Inasmuch as it is the woman who physically bears the child and who is more directly and immediately affected by the pregnancy, as between the two, the balance weighs in her favor.[9]

As the preceding discussion suggests, the theme of reproductive freedom has been applied primarily to birth control methods and government restrictions on those methods. But the theme did not protect just adults from such restrictions; it was used to shield minors as well. In 1977, the Supreme Court held in *Carey v. Population Services International* that minors who are less than sixteen years old possess a right of privacy that not only prevents government from completely denying them contraceptives but bars government from requiring them to secure nonprescription contraceptives from a physician—at least when proof is lacking that the restrictions deter minors from sexual activity.[10] The constitutional rights of minors may not be as fully developed as those of adults, but they are not entirely absent either.[11]

While the theme of reproductive freedom has been used most often for contraception and abortion, the Supreme Court has on occasion employed it for a different type of reproductive issue. Contraception and abortion prevent conception and the birth of children. They are, accordingly, means by which women can avoid the physical hazards of pregnancy and both men and women can escape the economic and psychological costs of child rearing. But to what extent does the principle of reproductive freedom protect those who desire to have children? Case law on the question is sparse, but one decision of the Supreme Court offers some guidance. In 1974 the Court held unconstitutional the policies of public school districts under which pregnant teachers were required to take an unpaid leave of absence starting at least four months prior to their expected delivery date. The policy of one district that denied reemployment to a teacher as long as her child was less than three months old was also invalidated. Since the school districts had not shown that the policies promoted their concededly legitimate interests in maintaining continuity of classroom instruction and employing teachers who are physically capable of performing their instructional duties, the policies were viewed as arbitrary and held to violate the constitutional guarantee of due process. In the view of the Court, the Constitution does not permit government to adopt an inflexible rule that forces all pregnant women to leave employment at a designated point that is substantially in advance of childbirth; a requirement that pregnant women terminate their employment at a fixed time shortly before their expected delivery might be permissible, but one that unnecessarily disadvantages women for having children is not. Moreover, when a woman who has given birth is disqualified from reemployment until her child reaches a specified age, public policy suffers from an unwarranted degree of rigidity. In dealing with reproduction, the Court stressed, government must act with maximum sensitivity to the abilities, circumstances, and wishes of the individual.[12]

THE DATA

Since birth control methods have been the primary concern of the theme of reproductive freedom, the cases dealing with their regulation should be related to trends over time in the use of contraception and abortion. Especially valuable to the assessment of the context and impact of the cases would be data on the use of contraception and abortion by both married and unmarried women at numerous points in a period that commenced well before and continued substantially after the theme developed. Unfortunately, such data do not exist for contraception,[13] and estimates of the frequency of abortion begin only a few years before *Roe v. Wade* was decided. However, birth rates (the number of births per thousand women of a given age) are available on an annual basis for an extended period both prior and subsequent to the appearance of the theme, and shifts in these rates provide an indirect measure of changes in contraception and abortion use. As such, birth rates provide a basis for assessing the context and impact of law: All else being equal, a court decision (or statute) that removes a major legal impediment to contraception or abortion and permits a sizable unmet need for either to be satisfied will cause a decline in birth rates that have been constant, a slowing or decrease in rates that have been rising, and a (faster) drop in rates that have been falling. The tempo of natality, then, can be expected to respond to changes in the prevalence and efficacy of birth control practices, and alterations in that tempo afford the opportunity to ascertain the degree to which law affected the use of family planning methods.

The data on which I base my analysis are birth rates measured in terms of three factors jointly: the age of the mother at the time the birth occurred, the year (i.e., period) when the birth took place, and the year or range of years in which the mother was born (i.e., the cohort of the mother).[14] Birth rates were thus cross-classified by age, period, and cohort simultaneously. Two sets of age-period-cohort data were employed; both identified the exact year (period) in which the birth occurred, but one specified the age and cohort of the mother in single years while the other specified the age and cohort of the mother in five-year categories.[15] Though five-year categories provide less precision than single years, the data set with those categories was needed because it distinguished childbearing within marriage from childbearing outside marriage. Marital status is central to three of the Supreme Court decisions on which I will focus (viz., *Griswold, Eisenstadt*, and *Danforth*), but the data set that reported age and cohort in single years did not differentiate fertility by whether the mother was married or unmarried.

Age-period-cohort data offer unique advantages for evaluating the context in which Supreme Court decisions arose and the impact that these decisions had. The three variables are global in nature, and each captures an array of factors that influence childbearing: Age measures variation in the biological ability to bear children and in the social pressures to have them at particular points in the life cycle; period measures variation in the broad social-economic conditions that constrain or facilitate childbearing; and cohort measures variation in the content of socialization and in the age-sex structure of the population. Age, period, and cohort, in short, "are proxies for underlying causal networks that affect aggregate age specific fertility,"[16] and a statistical control for the three variables can eliminate the influence of a wide range of factors that affect birth rates without the need to acquire and deal with data on each factor individually. Dummy variables for the years in the period studied can then be employed to assess the setting and impact of a Supreme Court decision.[17] In the statistical analysis undertaken here, the relationships of age, period, cohort, and the dummies to birth rates were estimated with weighted least-squares logit regression.

Data sets that use age, period, and cohort are not without their problems, however. Two should be mentioned. First, while age, period, and cohort provide a framework that is *conceptually* valuable for deciphering the causes of birth rates, the manner in which each of the three variables is related *statistically* to birth rates must be established. It is possible that one or more of the variables may not be associated with fertility in some situations; that relationships that exist may be nonlinear rather than linear; and that there may be one or more interactions between age, period, and/or cohort that affect childbearing. As a consequence, I tested the set of birth rates that I proposed to use for an analysis of a case with a regression equation that included age, period, and cohort; with regression equations in which each variable was replaced by its square (one at a time); with regression equations containing the three unsquared variables and each possible interaction term (one at a time); and with regression equations containing the three (unsquared) variables and all possible combinations of interaction terms.[18] One model was chosen for use with each case; the choice was determined by parsimony, goodness of fit, the absence of collinearity, and the statistical significance of individual variables. If two or more models were comparable in terms of these criteria, preference was given to a model containing age. The dummies for year were then added to the selected model.

A second problem, however, characterizes data cross-classified by age, period, and cohort. Because the values of any two of the variables determine (i.e., identify) the value of the third, a statistical procedure such as multiple regression cannot use all three variables simultaneously unless some constraint is placed on the values of one of them, i.e., unless the interdependence of the three is eliminated. In the terminology of the social sciences, interdependence among the three variables creates an "identification problem" the solution of which requires an "identifying restriction." Selection of an appropriate identifying restriction involves logical considerations and empirical knowledge regarding the effects of age, period, and cohort on the phenomenon of interest. The empirical knowledge employed, however, must be derived from a source other than the data set being used.[19]

In the data analyses that follow, one of four restrictions was adopted to solve the identification problem. Cohort was restricted for the cases dealing with contraception, but the restriction differed according to whether minors or adults were involved. For the one case involving minors—viz., *Carey v. Population Services International*—identical coding was used for females born between 1938 and 1949 since, while minors, members of these cohorts did not differ in their rates of premarital intercourse and thus in their need for contraceptives.[20] For the two cases involving adults, identical coding was applied to women born between 1939 and 1945.[21] On purely logical grounds, the cohorts of 1939–1945 can be expected to share numerous attributes because their members were born in a unique and clearly delineated historical era: the era marked by the second world war, which extended from the invasion of Poland by Germany in 1939 to the armistice in 1945. Not surprisingly, the era shaped the marriage behavior of the parents of the cohorts,[22] and it evidently also affected the values transmitted to their children. Thus, for the decision that involved unmarried adults—viz., *Eisenstadt v. Baird*—the cohorts of 1939–1945 apparently had similar rates of premarital sexual intercourse as adults[23] and hence a similar need for contraception. For the decision that involved married adults—viz., *Griswold v. Connecticut*—the cohorts held the same attitudes toward and expectations for marriage (as indicated by their relatively stable median age at first marriage[24]) and possessed a common set of values with regard to childbearing (as indicated by the age-specific rates at which they had first births[25]). Adult women born between 1939 and 1945, as a consequence, can be treated as equivalent in analyzing birth rates for *Eisenstadt* and *Griswold*.

While cohort was restricted for cases dealing with contraception, period was restricted for the two cases dealing with abortion. The restriction on period, however, was not the same for the two cases. For *Roe v. Wade*, the years 1981 through 1988 were coded identically because 1981 marked the post-*Roe* peak in both the abortion rate (the number of abortions per thousand women in their childbearing years) and the abortion ratio (the number of abortions per hundred pregnancies that ended in either an abortion or live birth).[26] Since the incidence of abortion did not rise from 1981 to 1988, the impact of *Roe* was evidently constant. For *Planned Parenthood of Central Missouri v. Danforth*, 1985 and 1986 were coded identically because married women aborted pregnancies at the same rate in both years.[27]

A PREFACE TO THE DATA ANALYSIS

Before proceeding to the data analysis, three matters should be mentioned. First, I omit the decision of the Supreme Court on mandatory maternity leave. The effect of such leave on fertility is indirect, and birth rates are therefore a dubious measure to assess the decision of the Court. In addition, while the five cases I will examine involved important issues regarding birth control and were potentially relevant to a large segment of the American population, the ruling on mandatory maternity leave affected relatively few women. When the Court invalidated mandatory maternity leave requirements for government workers in the mid-1970s, only about one out of eight women of childbearing age was employed by government.[28] The number who were subject to a mandatory maternity leave policy would of course have been smaller.

The second matter to be addressed is important to both methodology and theory: All of the Supreme Court decisions we are studying deal with *state* legislation, but the data being used are birth rates for the United States as a whole. Are data for the entire country appropriate when just a minority of states possess a statute comparable to legislation the Court has declared unconstitutional? *Griswold* is illustrative: At the time the case was decided, only one out of three states imposed severe restrictions on access to contraceptives.[29] In these circumstances, is it justifiable to use national data to investigate Supreme Court decisions?

In answering the question, we should keep in mind that a legal doctrine emanating from the Supreme Court (or from Congress) applies without geographic restriction throughout the United States. If we were to focus on just the states with a statute invalidated by a ruling of the Court, we would neglect the society-wide character of the law with which this chapter is concerned and of the needs and values that produced that law. Indeed, the very purpose of federal law is to impose the requirements and standards of the nation uniformly across the country[30]—a principle that the Constitution makes explicit in providing that "[t]his Constitution, and the Laws of the United States which shall be made in Pursuance thereof . . . shall be the supreme law of the Land."[31] National data are accordingly essential for investigating the theme of reproductive freedom in Supreme Court jurisprudence.

Finally, let me mention that the analysis of birth rates presented in the following section was limited to women who reached childbearing age after the second world war—i.e., women who were born no earlier than 1932 and who thus had their fourteenth birthday no earlier than 1946. The limitation was adopted because the postwar era in the United States differed sharply from the era that preceded it in terms of affluence, sex roles, and the stability of the relationship (marriage) within which births typically occur. Since the postwar period seems to have created a unique setting for fertility, it is the focus of my analysis.

THE CONTRACEPTION CASES

To organize the discussion, I will first consider the cases dealing with contraception and then examine the cases dealing with abortion. Table 5.1 presents the odds ratios for the year dummies, together with their *t* values and probabilities under the null hypothesis, for the three Supreme Court decisions on contraception. The odds ratios were obtained from regression equations that varied in terms of the reference year; each ratio reported in the table is for the year that chronologically followed the reference. Every ratio shown is thus a measure of the increase or decrease in the odds of fertility during the year specified relative to the year before. Whether a ratio represents an actual change or a random fluctuation in natality can be judged from the column labeled *Probability*, which specifies the likelihood that the odds of fertility in a particular year differed only by chance from the odds of fertility in the prior year. I will attribute an odds ratio to a factor other than chance—i.e., deem an odds ratio to be statistically significant—where its probability is .100 or less. However, change may also be suggested by ratios that are not individually significant but that are consistently above or below 1.000 in a multiyear interval.

I begin with *Griswold v. Connecticut*. Since the case invalidated a statute as applied to married couples, the birth rates that I employed were those for married women. The rates were for adult women, because few minors were married at the time the case was decided.[32] In excluding married females who were younger than 18, however, it was also necessary to exclude married females 18 and 19 years old, because the data set that I used reported age in five-year categories and ages 18 and 19 were combined with ages 15–17. Furthermore, the analysis was limited to women who were in the age groups 20–24 and 25–29. Among married women who were born in 1932 or later, birth rates by marital status were available starting only in 1956 for women who were 20–24 years old, and between 1956 and the year in which *Griswold* was decided (1965), the sole groups in the data set were ages 20–24 and 25–29. Given that a baseline existed just for married women in their twenties, the analysis was confined to them (with the two age groups represented by a dummy variable).

In considering the cases in this section, it is important to keep in mind that changes in contraceptive practice will not substantially alter fertility for eight or nine months. As a consequence, a revision of law regarding contraception that occurs in the last eight or nine months of a year (i.e., in April or later) cannot alter birth rates during that year. Since *Griswold* was announced in June 1965, childbearing in 1965 was the result of contraceptive behavior that had already taken place, and a fertility effect of the ruling would have appeared in 1966 or later. In gauging the context and impact of *Griswold* with the dummies, therefore, the social factors that produced the decision are measured by natality in 1965 and earlier years, and the impact of the decision is measured by natality in 1966 and subsequent years.

The results of the regression analysis for *Griswold* (shown in the top panel of table 5.1) are relatively straightforward. Prior to the time the decision was capable of altering fertility, the odds ratios for the year dummies are not statistically significant with one exception. The exception is 1965: In that year, the odds of childbearing were 87.8% of (12.2% lower than) the odds in 1964 independent of the effects of age and period (the variables that, together with the interaction of age and period, were controlled in the regression equations for *Griswold*). This was, however, just a one-year change, and the 1957–1965 time span should be viewed as a whole. Doing so leads to the conclusion that legal barriers were not creating an appreciable unmet need for contraceptives among married couples before the Court announced its ruling in *Griswold*; shifts in age and period and the fertility influences associated with them may have produced such a need, but law did not contribute to the problem. Two aspects of the data warrant the conclusion that law at the time did not often frustrate attempts by married couples to obtain the contraceptives they wanted. First, the odds ratios move from greater than 1.000 to less than 1.000 between 1957 and 1965, a movement that may signify a decline in the unmet need for contraceptives. Second, and of greater importance, if legal restrictions were preventing a large number of married couples from securing contraceptives, the appearance of *Griswold* should have depressed fertility, but it did not—a finding to which we now turn.

As already mentioned, *Griswold* was able to affect natality starting in 1966. In that year, a statistically significant reduction is observed in the birth rate, but it is no larger than the reduction found in 1965 and is thus unlikely to have been a product of the ruling. The odds ratios for the next four years, moreover, are not significant. A significant decrease occurs in 1971 (and in 1972), but this is fully six years after *Griswold* had the potential to influence childbearing. If law alters social behavior, its impact should emerge in substantially less time. The Supreme Court, in short, apparently had no material influence on marital fertility—a result that should not be surprising given the widespread use of contraceptives by married couples in the mid-1960s.[33]

Table 5.1. Odds Ratios for Year Dummies: *Griswold v. Connecticut, Eisenstadt v. Baird,* and *Carey v. Population Services International*

Year	*Odds ratio*	*t*	*Probability*	*Year*	*Odds ratio*	*t*	*Probability*
			Griswold v. Connecticut (*Births to married women 20–29 years old*)				
1957	1.076	1.583	.125	1973	0.975	0.717	.480
1958	1.009	0.198	.845	1974	1.054	1.497	.146
1959	1.014	0.302	.765	1975	1.020	0.557	.582
1960	1.041	0.901	.376	1976	1.039	1.089	.286
1961	0.978	0.560	.581	1977	1.116	3.155	.004
1962	0.976	0.744	.463	1978	1.026	0.735	.469
1963	0.963	1.191	.244	1979	1.091	2.532	.018
1964	0.966	1.092	.285	1980	1.054	1.546	.134
1965	0.878	4.009	.000	1981	1.029	0.843	.407
1966	0.933	2.090	.047	1982	1.042	1.216	.235
1967	0.948	1.614	.119	1983	1.008	0.228	.821
1968	0.991	0.266	.792	1984	1.028	0.803	.430
1969	1.029	0.881	.386	1985	1.038	1.068	.295
1970	1.022	0.701	.490	1986	1.005	0.150	.882
1971	0.909	3.024	.006	1987	1.030	0.840	.409
1972	0.854	4.884	.000	1988	1.047	1.275	.214
			Eisenstadt v. Baird (*Births to unmarried women 20–34 years old*)				
1957	1.029	0.131	.896	1973	0.954	0.233	.817
1958	1.031	0.146	.885	1974	0.979	0.104	.918
1959	1.063	0.309	.759	1975	1.037	0.171	.865
1960	1.000	0.002	.998	1976	1.016	0.070	.945
1961	1.077	0.430	.670	1977	1.076	0.308	.760
1962	1.011	0.068	.946	1978	1.051	0.199	.843
1963	1.024	0.127	.900	1979	1.079	0.293	.770
1964	1.024	0.216	.830	1980	1.124	0.436	.665
1965	1.024	0.218	.828	1981	1.012	0.044	.965
1966	1.004	0.030	.976	1982	1.026	0.090	.929
1967	0.942	0.435	.665	1983	1.025	0.081	.936
1968	0.959	0.287	.776	1984	1.044	0.138	.891
1969	1.009	0.055	.957	1985	1.093	0.276	.784
1970	1.028	0.170	.866	1986	1.072	0.207	.837
1971	0.923	0.447	.657	1987	1.076	0.213	.833
1972	0.929	0.396	.694	1988	1.083	0.225	.823
			Carey v. Population Services International (*First births to females 14–17 years old*)				
1950	0.997	0.023	.981	1953	1.029	0.251	.802
1951	1.069	0.580	.563	1954	1.023	0.195	.845
1952	0.982	0.162	.871	1955	0.977	0.189	.850

(*continued*)

Table 5.1. (Continued)

Year	Odds ratio	t	Probability	Year	Odds ratio	t	Probability
1956	1.063	0.571	.569	1973	0.990	0.113	.910
1957	1.030	0.287	.774	1974	0.965	0.404	.687
1958	0.956	0.443	.658	1975	0.969	0.360	.720
1959	0.988	0.124	.902	1976	0.950	0.576	.566
1960	0.975	0.255	.799	1977	0.996	0.045	.964
1961	0.987	0.133	.895	1978	0.956	0.492	.624
1962	0.954	0.460	.646	1979	1.013	0.136	.892
1963	0.988	0.117	.907	1980	1.018	0.189	.851
1964	0.981	0.200	.842	1981	0.970	0.323	.747
1965	0.982	0.188	.851	1982	1.016	0.159	.874
1966	1.000	0.003	.997	1983	0.998	0.020	.984
1967	0.993	0.075	.940	1984	0.982	0.174	.862
1968	1.019	0.204	.839	1985	1.017	0.162	.872
1969	1.030	0.326	.745	1986	1.005	0.053	.957
1970	1.091	0.989	.325	1987	1.022	0.211	.833
1971	0.990	0.115	.908	1988	1.041	0.395	.694
1972	1.039	0.452	.652				

Notes: The following variables were controlled in the regression equations containing the year dummies:

Griswold v. Connecticut: age (measured as a dummy variable), period, and an interaction term for age and period.

Eisenstadt v. Baird: age (measured as a three-category scale), cohort, period, an interaction term for age and cohort, an interaction term for age and period, and an interaction term for cohort and period.

Carey v. Population Services International: age (measured in single years), cohort, and period. The same independent variables were used for first births and for second births.

For *Griswold,* the addition of the year dummies to the control variables listed above changed the adjusted R^2 from .845 to .993 and the square root of the mean square error from .156 to .034. The number of observations was 61. For *Eisenstadt,* the addition of the year dummies to the control variables changed the adjusted R^2 from .852 to .953 and the square root of the mean square error from .095 to .053. The number of observations was 84. For *Carey,* the addition of the year dummies to the control variables changed (for first births) the adjusted R^2 from .954 to .949 and the square root of the mean square error from .131 to .138. The number of observations was 160.

The next Supreme Court decision on contraception is *Eisenstadt v. Baird*. For *Eisenstadt* as for *Griswold,* the time series begins with 1956, the first year that birth rates are available by marital status for adult women who were born in 1932 or later. Since *Eisenstadt* focused on access to contraceptives by unmarried individuals, the birth rates analyzed were for unmarried women. However, the decision did not clearly apply to unmarried minors, and the analysis was thus limited to birth rates among unmarried women 20–34 years of age (in three five-year age groups from 20–24 to 30–34). Unmarried women 18 and 19 years old could not be included because the data set employed an age category for females younger than 20 that merged ages 18–19 and ages 15–17. In addition, unmarried women in the age category 35–39 had to be excluded since women in the data set did not bear children out of wedlock at this age for a sufficient number of years prior to the decision to establish a baseline.

The odds ratios for the year dummies (in the middle panel of table 5.1) provide a simple and consistent picture of the reproductive behavior of unmarried adult women. From 1957 to 1988, the ratios are close to 1.000 and carry probabilities that are far from the level necessary to find yearly fluctuations in natality; otherwise stated, had fertility-related factors linked to age, cohort, and period remained constant, yearly changes would not have occurred in the childbearing of unmarried women 20–34 years old. What are the implications of this finding for the context and impact of *Eisenstadt*? The decision, having appeared in late March 1972, could have influenced fertility in 1973 and subsequent years. There is, however, no evidence of an effect. Instead, the data suggest, the decision did not alter childbearing among unmarried adults, implying that the decision did not improve access by those adults to contraceptives. And if access to contraception was unaffected by *Eisenstadt,* law was presumably not preventing a large number of single persons from obtaining birth control products before the Court issued its ruling. The unmet need of unmarried adults for means of preventing pregnancy was, then, a consequence of forces outside, not inside, the legal system.[34]

The last ruling on contraception to be examined is *Carey v. Population Services International.* The data set I employ for *Carey,* however, differs from that used for *Griswold* and *Eisenstadt.* The differences are twofold. First, the data set for *Carey* specifies birth rates by single years of age of the mother rather than in five-year age categories. Since *Carey* was concerned with minors, ages 14, 15, 16, and 17 were included in the analysis.[35] Second, the data set used here identifies birth order. Given the relative frequency of the different birth orders among adolescent females, however, regression equations were estimated for just first and second births.[36] For both birth orders, the control variables in the equations were age, cohort, and period.

The bottom panel of table 5.1 presents the odds ratios for first births. The most important observation emerging from the panel is that none of the year dummies have ratios that are statistically significant at a level approaching .100; indeed, the smallest probability for a ratio is .325. The probabilities of the ratios from 1978 onward are particularly noteworthy because 1978 was the earliest that *Carey* (which was announced in June

1977) could have affected births. However, the probabilities starting in 1978 were not less than .624. (Though not shown, the findings for second births are remarkably similar to those for first births: In the ten years from 1978 through 1987, the odds ratios for second births had probabilities of .660 or higher.) Thus, the unmet need of minors for contraceptives seems not to have been reduced by *Carey*, which implies that an appreciable unmet need was not created by law prior to the decision.

To take stock, what generally does table 5.1 tell us about the social milieu that preceded and followed *Griswold, Eisenstadt,* and *Carey*? The regression results provide no support for the argument that, in holding government-imposed restrictions on contraceptives to be unconstitutional, the U.S. Supreme Court had a major and enduring influence on the extent to which Americans employed pregnancy prevention methods. Birth rates should have exhibited a pattern of decline or deceleration after the three decisions if the statutes invalidated had been keeping a large number of persons from obtaining contraceptives, but such a pattern did not materialize. A fertility response failed to occur, it can be logically inferred, because statutes that were in force at the time of the rulings were not denying contraceptives to a large number of persons. The unmet need for methods to prevent conception, whatever it may have been, was thus produced by impediments of a nonlegal nature.

But if constitutional law did not measurably affect the contraceptive behavior of Americans and solve a pressing social problem, what societal function did it serve? Presumably, the legal doctrine found in *Griswold, Eisenstadt,* and *Carey* would not have appeared and been retained unless there were distinct social benefits. Since the doctrine did not reduce the unmet demand for methods to avert pregnancy, in what manner did it advance the public welfare? The answer must be speculative, of course, but a likely possibility is that the constitutional jurisprudence in the three decisions provided a formal mechanism by which the social system extended recognition to the use of contraceptive methods and deemed their use to be acceptable. In so doing, alienation from the system was reduced and system equilibrium was increased.

THE ABORTION CASES

While Supreme Court rulings on the subject of contraception have been accompanied by relatively little controversy, constitutional law regarding abortion has produced intense debate. The different public reaction to the two issues is probably attributable to the fact that social values strongly supported the constitutional doctrines adopted for contraception[37] but not for abortion. With regard to the latter, fewer than half of all adults favored the legalization of abortion during the first trimester of pregnancy when *Roe v. Wade* invalidated statutes severely restricting access to the procedure in the first and second trimesters;[38] even a decade and a half later, three out of five adults felt that abortion was "morally wrong" and that a woman should not be entitled legally to end a pregnancy, regardless of her reason for wanting to do so.[39] A large segment of the American public has thus not endorsed the unconditional availability of abortion or believed that governmental measures restricting abortion necessarily violate a constitutional right to terminate a pregnancy. As a result, abortion has been a divisive issue for politicians and a frequent topic for legal scholars. One observer, writing in the early 1980s, described the situation succinctly:

> No other case, not even *Brown v. Board of Education,* caused such a loud and sustained public outcry. Even now, a decade after the decision, the abortion controversy shows no sign of abating. Political pressure remains strong for a constitutional amendment to end legalized abortion. Nor has the debate been confined to the political arena. There have been literally hundreds of law review articles about *Roe v. Wade* and its progeny.[40]

The duration and intensity of the controversy surrounding *Roe* suggests that the case transformed American society and altered the course of history. But did the decision in fact represent a radical innovation in the American social system, or was it merely an extension of change that was already occurring in social behavior and needs? The question lies at the heart of the thesis I have advanced.

Contrary to popular belief regarding the social importance of *Roe,* there is no persuasive evidence that the decision materially affected the prevalence of abortion in the United States. Indeed, the most sophisticated study to date suggests that *Roe* changed little. Using the course of natality as a measure of variation in the frequency of abortion, the study applied the statistical technique ARIMA to (1) the number of births each year from 1909 to 1980 and (2) the number of births each month from 1960 to 1979. Notably, neither of the two data sets indicated that the action of the Court affected the frequency of childbearing. In the words of the investigator, "[i]ntervention analysis of the effects of the 1973 Supreme Court decision was not able to identify any independent impact of the nationwide legalization of abortion upon aggregate U.S. fertility."[41] The study, however, suffered from three limitations. First, it failed to consider whether *Roe* might have affected some birth orders but not others; its sole concern was with whether total fertility behaved differently after the Court issued its ruling than before. Second, the study did not expressly control for variation in factors that might have influenced childbearing and obscured an effect of the decision, e.g., the cohort and age of the mother. Finally, the study was based on births to mothers of all ages, including those younger than 18, but *Roe* explicitly refrained from deciding whether a minor was entitled constitutionally to an abortion on the same terms as an adult.[42] Births to adolescent females should therefore be omitted when investigating *Roe*. The data analysis I report below avoids these limitations.

In assessing the context and impact of *Roe*, it should be kept in mind that the Court required abortion to be legally available before but not after the fetus had become viable (unless a pregnancy involving a viable fetus threatened the life or health of the woman). While *Roe* is unlikely to have changed the proportion of pregnancies that were terminated after the fetus was viable—i.e., pregnancies in their final three months—it allowed the abortion of pregnancies that were four (or more) months away from the end of gestation, and the decision therefore had the potential to effect a major change in birth rates very soon after it appeared. Since *Roe* was announced in late January 1973 and could have reduced births starting in May, it had the ability to influence childbearing well before the middle of 1973. The impact on natality should have been greater in 1974, but some impact should be found in 1973—at least if the ruling was as socially significant as is widely believed. As a result, 1973 is the first year included in the assessment of whether *Roe v. Wade* lessened the unmet demand for abortion. Conversely, 1972 ends the time for ascertaining whether legal restrictions invalidated by the decision were producing a substantial unmet demand for the procedure.

With this background, we turn to the results of the regression analyses. Equations were estimated for the fertility of women 18–39 years old (measured in single years) during the period 1950–1988. Each of the first five birth orders was examined separately. The odds ratios, *t* values, and probability levels for the year dummies are reported in table 5.2.

It will be helpful to divide the discussion of table 5.2 into the period before *Roe* was capable of affecting fertility and the period after. With regard to the former, declines in natality (evidenced by statistically significant odds ratios of less than 1.000) are found for all birth orders in 1971 and/or 1972 and for third through fifth births in some years of the last half of the 1960s. By contrast, a pattern of significant odds ratios larger than 1.000 is absent. If changes had not occurred in age, cohort, and period, accordingly, fertility prior to *Roe* would have been for the most part stable, with some instances of decline.

Was the course of natality altered by *Roe*? Did the decision ease access to abortion and allow substantially more women to terminate pregnancies? For first, second, and third births, the answer is unquestionably

Table 5.2. Odds Ratios for Year Dummies: *Roe v. Wade*

Year	*Odds ratio*	*t*	*Probability*	*Year*	*Odds ratio*	*t*	*Probability*
			First births				
1951	1.292	2.105	.032	1970	1.002	0.040	.968
1952	1.108	1.214	.225	1971	0.900	2.684	.007
1953	1.108	1.458	.145	1972	0.885	3.049	.002
1954	1.095	1.480	.140	1973	0.935	1.637	.102
1955	1.043	0.759	.448	1974	0.998	0.050	.960
1956	1.073	1.367	.172	1975	0.970	0.752	.453
1957	1.033	0.668	.505	1976	0.982	0.463	.643
1958	0.976	0.515	.607	1977	1.030	0.762	.447
1959	0.992	0.170	.865	1978	0.990	0.272	.786
1960	0.988	0.271	.786	1979	1.037	0.968	.334
1961	0.993	0.160	.873	1980	1.031	0.851	.395
1962	0.979	0.484	.628	1981	0.979	0.583	.560
1963	1.000	0.005	.996	1982	0.999	0.020	.984
1964	1.012	0.282	.778	1983	0.984	0.496	.620
1965	0.910	2.080	.038	1984	0.987	0.410	.682
1966	1.000	0.005	.996	1985	1.012	0.377	.706
1967	0.951	1.179	.239	1986	0.984	0.392	.695
1968	1.005	0.130	.896	1987	0.994	0.142	.887
1969	0.980	0.485	.628	1988	1.005	0.134	.894
			Second births				
1951	1.254	0.878	.380	1970	1.002	0.033	.973
1952	1.189	1.014	.311	1971	0.928	1.266	.206
1953	1.162	1.150	.251	1972	0.899	1.769	.077
1954	1.113	1.001	.317	1973	0.957	0.720	.472
1955	1.090	0.945	.345	1974	1.003	0.056	.956
1956	1.079	0.938	.348	1975	0.963	0.643	.521
1957	1.050	0.670	.503	1976	0.985	0.258	.797
1958	1.013	0.190	.850	1977	1.029	0.503	.615
1959	1.014	0.219	.826	1978	0.967	0.606	.545
1960	0.989	0.182	.856	1979	1.023	0.420	.675
1961	0.976	0.399	.690	1980	0.999	0.025	.980
1962	0.970	0.511	.610	1981	0.981	0.360	.719
1963	0.976	0.402	.688	1982	1.024	0.499	.618
1964	0.967	0.560	.576	1983	0.989	0.235	.814
1965	0.921	1.376	.169	1984	1.001	0.030	.976
1966	0.952	0.818	.414	1985	1.020	0.425	.671
1967	0.965	0.543	.588	1986	0.970	0.524	.600
1968	0.959	0.663	.508	1987	0.994	0.113	.910
1969	1.005	0.081	.936	1988	1.005	0.087	.931

(*continued*)

Table 5.2. (Continued)

Year	Odds ratio	t	Probability	Year	Odds ratio	t	Probability
			Third births				
1951	1.420	0.783	.434	1970	0.988	0.176	.860
1952	1.278	0.924	.356	1971	0.894	1.682	.093
1953	1.176	0.861	.390	1972	0.825	2.763	.006
1954	1.176	1.125	.261	1973	0.907	1.352	.177
1955	1.108	0.880	.379	1974	0.964	0.505	.614
1956	1.111	1.075	.283	1975	0.983	0.238	.812
1957	1.080	0.903	.367	1976	1.010	0.138	.890
1958	1.038	0.486	.627	1977	1.054	0.759	.448
1959	1.050	0.697	.486	1978	0.986	0.209	.834
1960	1.037	0.560	.576	1979	1.031	0.463	.644
1961	1.009	0.152	.879	1980	1.007	0.103	.918
1962	0.987	0.213	.832	1981	0.988	0.192	.847
1963	0.973	0.478	.633	1982	1.005	0.085	.933
1964	0.967	0.583	.560	1983	0.976	0.425	.671
1965	0.900	1.790	.074	1984	0.983	0.301	.764
1966	0.834	2.592	.010	1985	1.012	0.212	.832
1967	0.902	1.456	.146	1986	0.990	0.150	.881
1968	0.915	1.263	.207	1987	1.015	0.219	.827
1969	0.993	0.101	.920	1988	1.021	0.322	.748
			Fourth births				
1951	1.802	0.708	.479	1970	0.932	0.912	.362
1952	1.489	0.934	.351	1971	0.862	1.945	.052
1953	1.295	0.949	.343	1972	0.790	2.999	.003
1954	1.249	1.145	.253	1973	0.840	2.107	.036
1955	1.168	1.053	.293	1974	0.897	1.270	.204
1956	1.143	1.132	.258	1975	0.931	0.829	.407
1957	1.104	1.006	.315	1976	0.958	0.490	.624
1958	1.075	0.848	.397	1977	1.013	0.148	.882
1959	1.083	1.064	.288	1978	0.976	0.285	.776
1960	1.063	0.907	.365	1979	1.013	0.154	.877
1961	1.055	0.865	.388	1980	0.994	0.072	.943
1962	1.015	0.246	.806	1981	0.980	0.256	.798
1963	0.997	0.057	.955	1982	0.995	0.075	.940
1964	0.983	0.304	.762	1983	0.971	0.435	.664
1965	0.911	1.653	.099	1984	0.967	0.492	.623
1966	0.895	1.881	.061	1985	0.997	0.047	.963
1967	0.838	2.202	.028	1986	1.008	0.096	.923
1968	0.857	1.930	.054	1987	1.028	0.340	.734
1969	0.940	0.793	.428	1988	1.043	0.545	.586

(continued)

Table 5.2. (Continued)

Year	Odds ratio	t	Probability	Year	Odds ratio	t	Probability
			Fifth births				
1951	[a]			1970	0.940	0.993	.321
1952	[a]			1971	0.881	2.039	.042
1953	1.424	0.806	.421	1972	0.795	3.474	.000
1954	1.383	1.267	.206	1973	0.842	2.415	.016
1955	1.256	1.315	.189	1974	0.875	1.767	.078
1956	1.194	1.365	.173	1975	0.938	0.813	.417
1957	1.173	1.551	.121	1976	0.969	0.390	.697
1958	1.115	1.282	.201	1977	0.999	0.017	.987
1959	1.103	1.336	.182	1978	0.983	0.206	.836
1960	1.100	1.485	.138	1979	1.017	0.210	.834
1961	1.103	1.703	.089	1980	1.017	0.209	.834
1962	1.056	1.028	.304	1981	0.999	0.011	.991
1963	1.027	0.534	.594	1982	0.979	0.297	.766
1964	1.006	0.129	.897	1983	0.976	0.343	.732
1965	0.926	1.574	.116	1984	0.947	0.757	.449
1966	0.913	1.802	.072	1985	1.002	0.023	.981
1967	0.950	0.982	.326	1986	1.011	0.120	.904
1968	0.850	2.574	.010	1987	1.041	0.475	.635
1969	0.956	0.706	.481	1988	1.052	0.618	.537

[a] Dropped due to collinearity.

Notes: For each birth order, the following variables were controlled in the regression equations containing the year dummies: age, cohort, period, an interaction term for age and cohort, and an interaction term for age and period. For first births, the addition of the year dummies to the control variables changed the adjusted R^2 from .956 to .966 and the square root of the mean square error from .134 to .117. For second births, the addition of the year dummies to the control variables changed the adjusted R^2 from .882 to .902 and the square root of the mean square error from .189 to .172. For third births, the addition of the year dummies to the control variables changed the adjusted R^2 from .868 to .908 and the square root of the mean square error from .232 to .195. For fourth births, the addition of the year dummies to the control variables changed the adjusted R^2 from .893 to .927 and the square root of the mean square error from .258 to .214. For fifth births, the addition of the year dummies to the control variables changed the adjusted R^2 from .921 to .952 and the square root of the mean square error from .244 to .189. The number of observations was 627 for birth orders one through four and 550 for fifth births.

negative; the odds ratios from 1973 onward are not statistically significant. Whatever shifts occurred in the unadjusted rates of first, second, and third births were, then, produced by changes in age, cohort, and/or period, not by *Roe.*

Turning to higher birth orders, we find that fourth births decreased in 1973 and that fifth births decreased in both 1973 and 1974. These reductions, if due to *Roe,* were surprisingly brief in duration, but it is unlikely they were caused by the decision because declines of comparable magnitude were registered in 1971 and 1972 as well as in a number of earlier years. The postdecision reductions thus seem to be merely a continuation of an existing movement toward fewer fourth and fifth births at the time of the ruling.

To summarize, the data in table 5.2 indicate that, among adult women, natality was not affected by *Roe v. Wade* and that law did not appreciably influence the prevalence of abortion. The finding suggests that neither constitutional adjudication nor the legislation to which it applied was critical in determining whether unwanted pregnancies were terminated and that whatever barriers to abortion existed before *Roe* were not eliminated by the decision. Undoubtedly, the constitutional doctrine adopted in *Roe* allowed some women to procure abortions that they would have been denied if the decision had not materialized, but the number of such women was small.[43] In spite of the emotional nature and remarkable persistence of the debate over *Roe*, therefore, the ruling seems to be more appropriately viewed as a response to social conditions than an important influence on them.

Changes in birth rates are not, however, the only data on which we can draw to assess the context and impact of constitutional law on abortion. Table 5.3 presents the most accurate estimates available of the total number of abortions legally performed in the United States each year from 1963 to 1985. Before considering the estimates, however, two aspects of the table require comment. First, since data do not exist on the marital status of abortion patients until the 1970s, the table includes abortions on both married and unmarried women. As a result, the table is useful for *Roe v. Wade* but not for *Planned Parenthood of Central Missouri v. Danforth*. Second, caution must be exercised in using the estimates for *Roe*. Because of data limitations, abortion patients of all ages—minors as well as adults—had to be included in the table even though *Roe* did not apply to minors. Fortunately, available information on the age distribution of abortion patients during the 1970s indicates that little change occurred in the proportion of all abortions that involved adult women. The proportion rose, but the magnitude of the rise was small.[44] Since the fraction of all abortions for which adult women were responsible seems to have been largely constant, the table portrays *relative change* in the number of abortions obtained by adults with reasonable precision. Nonetheless, in reviewing table 5.3, it should be kept in mind that the number of abortions on adults each year is overstated, that the overstatement evidently declines somewhat over time, and that the change that took place in adult abortions is measured more accurately in later years than in earlier years.

Table 5.3 shows a steady rise in abortion frequency starting in the middle-to-late 1960s and continuing until 1981. *Roe v. Wade* clearly did

Table 5.3. Number of Legal Abortions in the United States, 1963–1985

Year	Number of abortions performed	Increase over prior year: Number	Increase over prior year: Percentage
1963	5,000	—	—
1964	9,000	4,000	80
1965	7,000	−2,000	−22
1966	6,000	−1,000	−14
1967	9,000	3,000	50
1968	18,000	9,000	100
1969	22,670	4,670	26
1970	193,491	170,821	754
1971	485,816	292,325	151
1972	586,760	100,944	21
1973	744,600	157,840	27
1974	898,600	154,000	21
1975	1,034,200	135,600	15
1976	1,179,300	145,100	14
1977	1,316,700	137,400	12
1978	1,409,600	92,900	7
1979	1,497,700	88,100	6
1980	1,553,900	56,200	4
1981	1,577,300	23,400	2
1982	1,573,900	−3,400	[a]
1983	1,575,000	1,100	[a]
1984	1,577,200	2,200	[a]
1985	1,588,600	11,400	1

[a] Less than 0.5%.

Sources: Data for 1963–1968 are estimates of the number of abortions performed in hospitals and appear in Tietze, *United States: Therapeutic Abortions, 1963 to 1968,* Stud. Fam. Plan. No. 59, at 5, 7 Nov. 1970.

Data for 1969–1972 are from CENTERS FOR DISEASE CONTROL, U.S. DEP'T OF HEALTH & HUMAN SERVICES, ABORTION SURVEILLANCE: ANNUAL SUMMARY 1981 24 (1985).

Data for 1973–1985 are from the Alan Guttmacher Institute and appear in Henshaw et al., *Abortion Services in the United States, 1984 and 1985,* 19 FAM. PLAN. PERSP. 63, 64 (1987). Data prior to 1973 are not provided by the Institute.

Note: The Centers for Disease Control report the following number of abortions for 1973–1985:

Year	Number	Year	Number
1973	615,831	1979	1,251,921
1974	763,476	1980	1,297,606
1975	854,853	1981	1,300,760
1976	988,267	1982	1,303,980
1977	1,079,430	1983	1,268,987
1978	1,157,776	1984	1,333,521
		1985	1,328,570

CENTERS FOR DISEASE CONTROL, U.S. DEP'T OF HEALTH & HUMAN SERVICES, ABORTION SURVEILLANCE: ANNUAL SUMMARY 1981 24 (1985); Ellerbrock et al., *Abortion Surveillance, 1982–1983,* 36 MORBIDITY & MORTALITY WEEKLY REP., No. 1SS, at 11SS, 12SS (Feb. 1987); Koonin et al., *Abortion Surveillance, United States, 1988,* 40 MORBIDITY & MORTALITY WEEKLY REP. No. SS-1 at 15, 22 (July 1991); Nat'l Center for Chronic Disease Prevention and Health Promotion, Centers for Disease Control, *Abortion Surveillance: Preliminary Analysis—United States, 1989,* 40 MORBIDITY & MORTALITY WEEKLY REP. No. 47, at 817, 818 (Nov. 29, 1991).

not initiate the rise since, having been decided in 1973, it appeared only after large increments in abortion were registered. Moreover, there is no indication that *Roe* contributed significantly to the increases that are found in subsequent years. Two aspects of the table are important to this conclusion. First, the average increment was larger both numerically and proportionally in the years prior to the decision than in the years after. According to the Centers for Disease Control—which provide the most accurate estimates available for the 1969–1972 period—the number of abortions rose from 22,670 in 1969 to 586,760 in 1972. According to the Alan Guttmacher Institute—which seems generally regarded as a more definitive source but which does not report abortion levels prior to 1973—the number expanded from 744,600 in 1973 to 1,179,300 in 1976. However, while pregnancy terminations were more frequent after *Roe* than before, the mean annual increase was substantially larger between 1969 and 1972 than between 1973 and 1976 (roughly 188,000 versus 145,000).[45] Phrased differently, the use of abortion continued to grow in the years following *Roe,* but the pace of growth was clearly slower, suggesting that access to and reliance on the procedure was unaffected by the decision. The same conclusion arises from an examination of the abortion *rate,* the number of abortions per thousand women of child-bearing age (15–44 years old), which climbed from 0.5 in 1969 to 13.2 in 1972 and from 16.3 in 1973 to 24.2 in 1976.[46] The mean annual increase in the abortion rate was 4.2 points in the three years before *Roe* but only 2.6 points in the three years after.

Whether measured in absolute numbers or in rates, then, pregnancy terminations expanded more rapidly in the period prior to *Roe* than in the period after. However, a second aspect of table 5.3 should also be considered, namely, change in the incidence of abortion between 1972 and subsequent years. If the decision abruptly altered the social fabric, as many seem to believe, the number of abortions should have grown more in 1973 than in earlier years. The table, however, discloses that the 1972–1973 increment was less than two of the three increments that preceded it. Specifically, the increment from 1972 to 1973 was smaller than either the increment from 1969 to 1970 or the increment from 1970 to 1971. Only the increment between 1971 and 1972 indicates that *Roe* allowed greater access to abortion, but this is scant evidence for the argument that the decision was a watershed event in American history since each of the prior two increments (1969–1970 and 1970–1971) was larger—indeed, each was larger than any subsequent year-to-year change. Clearly, *Roe* was not needed for abortions to increase by the number they did between 1972 and 1973; bigger year-to-year increases had occurred in the period immediately preceding the decision. Moreover, there is no evidence that *Roe* had a delayed impact. The possibility of a two-year delay seems precluded by the fact that the number of abortions rose by more than 393,000 from 1970 to 1972 but by only about 312,000 from 1972 to 1974. The increase was thus greater in the two-year period that preceded *Roe* than in the two-year period that spanned its adoption and implementation. A similar conclusion is reached if we consider a three-year lag. Abortion use grew substantially more between 1969 and 1972 than between 1972 and 1975 (roughly 564,000 versus 447,000).

The conclusion arising from the discussion above—that *Roe* did not markedly affect abortion use—is reinforced by the near certainty that the preceding discussion exaggerates the magnitude of the change from 1972 to the years that follow the action of the Court. The reason is that the data appearing in the body of table 5.3 for 1969–1972 and for 1973–1985 are derived from different sources. The data for 1969–1972 were developed by the Centers for Disease Control, which has consistently reported fewer abortions than the source employed for the period beginning in 1973, the Alan Guttmacher Institute. (The abortion frequencies of the Centers for Disease Control for 1973–1985 appear in the note beneath the table.) The discussion above thus moves from a low-estimate data source for the period ending in 1972 to a high-estimate source for the period starting in 1973. In so doing, it overstates the change in abortion levels that arises from a comparison of 1972 and later years using the data in the body of the table.

In view of the shift in sources and the differences between them, the number of abortions reported for 1973 and subsequent years by the Centers for Disease Control can also be employed to calculate year-to-year changes. When that is done, abortion levels are found to have expanded by approximately 29,000 or 5% in 1973, a numerical and proportional increase that was less than in any of the preceding three years. Reliance on data from the Centers for Disease Control thus provides no reason to believe the Supreme Court had an impact on the prevalence of abortion.[47] Further, there is no evidence from those data of a delayed effect. Over both two-year and three-year time spans, the rise in abortion numbers was more than twice as large during the period that ended in 1972 than during the period that began in 1972.

It appears, in short, that abortion levels were not measurably influenced by *Roe*. On the other hand, in the years preceding the decision the use of abortion may have increased because many state legislatures expanded the permissible grounds for the procedure. Sixteen states liberalized their abortion statutes between 1967 and 1972,[48] and a credible argument can be made that statutory change was responsible for the rising volume of abortion during this period. If the argument is correct, legal doctrine and its alteration affected social patterns. However, another explanation is possible, namely, that a growing demand for and use of abortion generated the wave of statutory revision.[49]

The second explanation must be considered at some length not only because it is more complex than the first but also because it leads to a profoundly different conclusion regarding the nature of law. The explanation—which follows from my thesis—presumes that a society provides arrangements to satisfy the needs of its members; that, in this process, means not condoned by its legal system may temporarily be employed; but that legal doctrine conforms to social practices and values within a relatively short time. According to the second explanation, then, an increasing demand for abortion was largely accommodated after a relatively brief period and the demand was generally being met before statutes were changed. Abortions were obtained illegally when pregnancies could not be terminated legally, and the revision of legal doctrine simply recognized the existence of a new social reality.[50] Law, in this perspective, is a manifestation of social predispositions rather than a significant influence on conduct.

Since the two explanations of the pre-*Roe* increase in abortion—that law affects social patterns and that it reflects them—involve markedly different views of the role of law in society, it is unfortunate that little rigorous research has been conducted on the states that adopted liberalized abortion statutes in the last half of the 1960s and the early 1970s. The most thorough investigation of the subject to date examined time series data on natality in two states: California, which modified its statutory restrictions on pregnancy termination as of 1968, and New York, which did so as of 1970. Using monthly data on total births, the study concluded that easing legal requirements for abortion did not discernibly affect childbearing in California but that it reduced childbearing in New York by about 6%.[51] However, the legislation was enacted during a period when both desired family size and unwanted births were declining in the United States. A national survey conducted in 1970 found that

> American couples have changed their reproductive behavior radically over the course of the past five years, adjusting their fertility goals sharply downward, and increasing substantially their ability to stop childbearing at the wanted level. All parts of the population have shared in these developments, particularly those whose performance previously deviated most from the national averages.[52]

The shift in reproductive intentions seems to have commenced shortly before states revised their statutes on abortion.[53] Perhaps more importantly, the shift was preceded, as well as accompanied, by rapid growth in the use of the contraceptive pill, which was approved for public distribution in 1960.[54] The liberalization of state abortion statutes thus occurred after substantial gains had been made in fertility control and intended family size began to fall. However, the changes were probably not uniform across all birth orders; in all likelihood, the changes were decidedly larger for higher-order births than for lower-order births. Total births, then, may mask important differences in the course of fertility during the 1960s and 1970s, and research on state legislation that relaxed restrictions on abortion should, where possible, examine childbearing by birth order.

With these considerations, we turn to the first jurisdiction that by legislation appreciably eased statutory restrictions on abortion prior to *Roe v. Wade*. The state was Colorado, which liberalized its abortion policy in April 1967.[55] To study the environment for and the effect of the legislation, weighted least-squares logit models were estimated for the annual number of births in Colorado to women 20–44 years old (in five-year age groups) weighted by the number of state residents.[56] Births to females younger than 20 were not included because it was not possible to determine whether such births occurred under age 18 or at age 18–19. (Births to mothers less than 20 years old were reported in a single category encompassing ages 15–19.) Births to minors and adults needed to be distinguished, however, since the legislation treated females younger than 18 differently than females who had reached their 18th birthday.

Regression models for first, second, third, fourth, and fifth births were estimated with fertility measured in terms of the age of the mother at the time of the birth, the year (cohort) in which the mother was born, and the year (period) in which the birth occurred. The analysis covered the years 1950 through 1980; to solve the identification problem, 1979 and 1980 were coded identically, since the abortion rate in Colorado was the same in both years.[57] The results of the regression equations appear in table 5.4.

With respect to the year dummies, 1966 will end the period for describing the fertility context of the new law and 1967 will begin the period for describing its impact. The statute did not confine abortion to the early stages of gestation in the case of adults but allowed the termination of pregnancies that at any point appeared likely to jeopardize seriously the mental or physical health of the woman or that appeared likely to result in a child with a major physical or mental defect. Since the law was in force as of April 1967 and permitted abortions well into pregnancy, it had the ability to reduce births in the state to some extent during 1967. Although the full impact of the statute would not be expected until 1968, 1967 cannot be omitted in assessing the effect.

Turning to table 5.4, we see virtually no statistically significant odds ratios for first, second, third, or fourth births either before or after the new law. Otherwise stated, had age, cohort, and period not changed

Table 5.4. Odds Ratios for Year Dummies: Colorado Abortion Statute

Year	*Odds ratio*	*t*	*Probability*	*Year*	*Odds ratio*	*t*	*Probability*
			First births				
1951	1.048	0.332	.741	1966	1.087	0.530	.597
1952	0.969	0.226	.821	1967	1.119	0.749	.455
1953	0.890	0.817	.416	1968	1.182	1.190	.236
1954	1.013	0.090	.929	1969	1.071	0.523	.602
1955	0.961	0.279	.781	1970	1.069	0.527	.599
1956	0.952	0.345	.730	1971	0.930	0.594	.553
1957	0.944	0.400	.690	1972	0.941	0.488	.626
1958	0.990	0.066	.947	1973	0.986	0.113	.911
1959	0.955	0.318	.751	1974	1.035	0.280	.780
1960	0.990	0.072	.943	1975	1.047	0.381	.704
1961	0.973	0.191	.849	1976	1.052	0.434	.665
1962	0.965	0.246	.806	1977	1.064	0.548	.585
1963	0.946	0.387	.699	1978	1.041	0.365	.715
1964	1.085	0.527	.599	1979	1.090	0.809	.420
1965	0.920	0.535	.593	1980	0.966	0.346	.730
			Second births				
1951	1.029	0.229	.820	1966	1.002	0.012	.991
1952	0.983	0.133	.895	1967	1.106	0.701	.485
1953	0.993	0.052	.958	1968	1.034	0.239	.811
1954	0.964	0.295	.769	1969	1.107	0.752	.453
1955	0.983	0.141	.888	1970	1.050	0.375	.709
1956	0.995	0.042	.967	1971	1.031	0.241	.810
1957	0.943	0.475	.636	1972	0.951	0.403	.688
1958	0.987	0.106	.916	1973	1.042	0.334	.739
1959	1.002	0.014	.989	1974	1.041	0.333	.740
1960	0.957	0.346	.730	1975	1.032	0.268	.789
1961	1.012	0.093	.926	1976	1.042	0.355	.723
1962	0.943	0.462	.645	1977	1.044	0.378	.706
1963	1.007	0.053	.958	1978	1.012	0.104	.918
1964	1.016	0.116	.908	1979	1.043	0.385	.701
1965	0.916	0.621	.536	1980	1.085	0.768	.444
			Third births				
1951	1.136	1.230	.221	1963	0.990	0.112	.911
1952	1.118	1.131	.260	1964	0.923	0.867	.388
1953	1.033	0.347	.729	1965	0.913	0.879	.381
1954	1.007	0.075	.941	1966	0.897	0.996	.321
1955	1.053	0.563	.575	1967	0.977	0.203	.839
1956	1.024	0.268	.789	1968	1.006	0.054	.957
1957	1.026	0.295	.769	1969	1.090	0.774	.440
1958	1.052	0.577	.565	1970	0.987	0.122	.903
1959	1.003	0.029	.977	1971	0.928	0.682	.497
1960	1.030	0.336	.738	1972	0.892	0.999	.320
1961	1.043	0.478	.633	1973	0.964	0.306	.760
1962	0.989	0.128	.899	1974	1.010	0.084	.933

(*continued*)

Table 5.4. *(Continued)*

Year	Odds ratio	*t*	Probability	Year	Odds ratio	*t*	Probability
1975	1.116	0.934	.352	1978	1.046	0.418	.677
1976	1.053	0.455	.650	1979	1.073	0.679	.498
1977	1.065	0.568	.571	1980	1.222	1.995	.048
			Fourth births				
1951	1.134	1.372	.173	1966	0.827	2.192	.030
1952	1.120	1.293	.198	1967	0.900	1.133	.259
1953	1.112	1.278	.204	1968	0.940	0.650	.517
1954	1.069	0.838	.403	1969	1.036	0.371	.711
1955	1.097	1.204	.231	1970	0.974	0.270	.788
1956	1.083	1.087	.279	1971	0.873	1.379	.171
1957	1.009	0.127	.899	1972	0.892	1.102	.273
1958	1.166	2.148	.034	1973	0.865	1.308	.193
1959	1.027	0.383	.702	1974	0.931	0.612	.541
1960	1.094	1.289	.200	1975	1.063	0.517	.606
1961	1.048	0.690	.491	1976	1.051	0.423	.673
1962	1.010	0.145	.885	1977	1.134	1.097	.275
1963	1.034	0.474	.637	1978	0.974	0.232	.817
1964	0.988	0.170	.865	1979	1.067	0.586	.559
1965	0.950	0.687	.494	1980	1.426	3.348	.001
			Fifth births				
1951	1.162	1.492	.138	1966	0.846	1.867	.064
1952	1.146	1.440	.153	1967	0.871	1.442	.152
1953	1.150	1.570	.119	1968	0.914	0.896	.372
1954	1.044	0.507	.613	1969	1.034	0.330	.742
1955	1.125	1.421	.158	1970	0.903	0.997	.321
1956	1.051	0.619	.537	1971	0.803	2.009	.047
1957	1.134	1.644	.103	1972	0.936	0.565	.573
1958	1.038	0.502	.616	1973	0.794	1.829	.070
1959	1.045	0.586	.559	1974	0.958	0.318	.751
1960	1.180	2.285	.024	1975	1.060	0.425	.672
1961	1.045	0.629	.530	1976	0.943	0.419	.676
1962	1.065	0.891	.375	1977	1.085	0.583	.561
1963	1.059	0.802	.424	1978	1.056	0.397	.692
1964	1.001	0.012	.991	1979	1.108	0.772	.442
1965	0.828	2.273	.025	1980	1.432	2.800	.006

Notes: For each birth order, the regression equations controlled cohort, period, and the square of age. For first births, the addition of the year dummies to the control variables changed the adjusted R^2 from .917 to .934 and the square root of the mean square error from .231 to .206. For second births, the addition of the year dummies to the control variables changed the adjusted R^2 from .908 to .920 and the square root of the mean square error from .211 to .197. For third births, the addition of the year dummies to the control variables changed the adjusted R^2 from .907 to .941 and the square root of the mean square error from .200 to .159. For fourth births, the addition of the year dummies to the control variables changed the adjusted R^2 from .860 to .963 and the square root of the mean square error from .264 to .137. For fifth births, the addition of the year dummies to the control variables changed the adjusted R^2 from .810 to .961 and the square root of the mean square error from .324 to .147. The number of observations was 155 for each birth order.

over the three decades studied, childbearing at these birth orders would have remained at essentially the same level. For family sizes of four or less, then, there is no reason to believe that the revised law removed a major barrier confronting Colorado residents who wanted to abort a pregnancy. And if the new law did not expand access to abortion for the first four birth orders, the restrictive statute that preceded it is unlikely to have been the source of a substantial unsatisfied demand for abortion.

Arguably, fifth births have a greater potential than lower-order births to be affected by liberalized statutory requirements for abortion. At the time the requirements were being modified by states, relatively few Americans endorsed a family size of five or more,[58] and less-restrictive abortion laws should logically have permitted many mothers of four children to avoid having a fifth. Table 5.4, however, does not provide evidence of such an effect in Colorado. In the poststatute period, an odds ratio for fifth births that is less than 1.000 and that is statistically significant is not found until 1971; another appears in 1973. However, the longer is the interval between the enactment of legislation and the occurrence of a change, the less plausible is the argument that the legislation was responsible for the change. If the odds of having a fifth birth did not decline until the new abortion law had been in operation for four years, as table 5.4 suggests, the decline is unlikely to have been a product of the law. Moreover, fifth births had significant odds ratios of less than 1.000 in the two years preceding the statute (1965 and 1966); that the decline in fifth births ended as a change was made in the legal requirements for abortion indicates that the change did not affect the odds of such births.

By way of summary, the regression equations furnish no evidence that, in liberalizing its abortion statute, Colorado materially influenced the frequency with which births occurred in the state or, by inference, the frequency with which pregnancies were surgically terminated. And if the new statute did not measurably enlarge the number of abortions, the law it replaced was not the source of an appreciable unmet need for the procedure. Instead, the reproductive behavior of Colorado residents appears to have determined, but not to have been determined by, the content of their state statute on abortion, and revision of the statute presumably served only to acknowledge and accept changes that had taken place in this behavior.

In concluding the present section, I would like to return to *Planned Parenthood of Central Missouri v. Danforth* and its holding that a married woman cannot be required by law to secure the consent of her husband for an abortion during the first twelve weeks of gestation. To assess the context and impact of the case, we can take advantage of annual data on abortions obtained by married women from 1973 through 1983. Of all

Table 5.5. Proportion of Pregnancies Aborted by Married Women, 1973–1983

Year	*Proportion (%)*	*Percentage point change from year before*
1973	7.0	—
1974	8.3	+1.3
1975	9.6	+1.3
1976	9.5	−0.1
1977	9.8	+0.3
1978	10.4	+0.6
1979	9.9	−0.5
1980	9.8	−0.1
1981	9.2	−0.6
1982	9.5	+0.3
1983	9.3	−0.2

pregnancies experienced by married women, the proportion aborted each year is shown in table 5.5.[59] The change in the proportion from one year to the next is given in the last column.

The data indicate that the percentage of pregnancies terminated by married women was increasing before *Danforth* was decided in 1976 and that the increases were not enlarged by the decision. The argument that the Court allowed a substantial number of married women to obtain abortions is not plausible even though the proportion of pregnancies aborted was higher in the years immediately after the ruling (i.e., in 1977 and 1978) than previously. As the last column shows, the proportion jumped 1.3 percentage points in each of the two years prior to the decision (i.e., 1974 and 1975), but in the year after the ruling (1977), the proportion rose just 0.3 percentage points. While the increment was greater the next year (0.6 percentage points in 1978), it was still only half as large as the increments found in the two years before the decision (1974 and 1975). Moreover, in the year of the decision (1976), the proportion did not rise—as it should have if the Court eliminated a major obstacle to abortion for married women. The higher proportion of pregnancies aborted by married women after the ruling thus appears to have been merely an extension of change already underway and must be attributed to the forces responsible for that change, not to the Court. This conclusion is buttressed by other evidence: An analysis of birth rates also suggests that *Danforth* did not alter the reproductive behavior of married women.[60]

CONCLUSION

The material reviewed in the present chapter indicates that the constitutional principle of reproductive freedom conforms to the thesis advanced in this book: The principle was a response to social patterns and needs rather than an important influence on them. Law—constitutional and statutory—did not materially affect birth control practices but reflected and endorsed the evolution of social life. Reproductive freedom as a theme in constitutional law was thus an expression of ideals needed to accept fundamental changes in society—changes that accompanied alterations in age, period, and/or cohort—and in closing the chapter, I will attempt to identify some of these changes. Unfortunately, theory on the antecedents of legal doctrine is poorly developed, and the discussion to follow is necessarily incomplete and tentative. Nevertheless, it seems likely that the aspects of the social milieu outlined below contributed to the adoption of the principle of reproductive freedom in constitutional jurisprudence.

The social conditions with which I deal are of two types: those that were common to all of the cases I have considered and those that were specific to particular cases. Among the former was the ideology of individual autonomy: The ability of the individual to analyze and reason was valued increasingly in the United States over the several decades that preceded the adoption of the principle of reproductive freedom by the Supreme Court.[61] Individual autonomy by its very nature conflicts with governmental restrictions, and the conflict was particularly sharp for restrictions on methods of birth control because, if the course of fertility is an accurate barometer, incentives to reduce family size were becoming stronger in the years before the principle was endorsed by the Court.[62]

Turning to case-specific social conditions, the Supreme Court initially employed the theme of reproductive freedom in 1965 to hold that married couples possess a constitutional right to use contraceptives. Notably, the Court did so shortly after the mean age at first marriage ended a lengthy decline. When the Court acted, moreover, the proportion of women and men who ever married was rising and approaching an historic peak.[63] The decision thus occurred in an era in which marriage was emphasized, and in giving priority to the marital relationship over government regulation, it presumably resulted in part from that emphasis.

The principle of reproductive freedom was next used by the Supreme Court in two cases, decided less than a year apart, that appeared in the first half of the 1970s. Two features of the decisions indicate that they were produced in large measure by the same social conditions: their contemporaneous timing and their common conclusion that unmarried individuals possess a constitutionally protected interest in methods of birth control. In *Eisenstadt,* government was barred from distinguishing unmarried persons from married persons in regulations involving the distribution of contraceptives; in *Roe,* unmarried women were found to be entitled to terminate pregnancies by abortion. *Roe,* of course, encompassed all adult women regardless of marital status, but married and unmarried women are conceptually distinct and might have been treated differently. That unmarried women were found to have a constitutional right to abortion is, I believe, important and must be explained.

What generated constitutional concerns with the accessibility of birth control methods to unmarried persons in the first part of the 1970s? One factor that undoubtedly played a role was the rapid rise in premarital sexual activity during the period that preceded the two decisions. The proportion of white women who first experienced premarital intercourse at age 19, for example, was 11% in the last half of the 1950s and early 1960s, 16% in the middle-to-late 1960s, and 27% in the late 1960s and early 1970s.[64] Equally important, out-of-wedlock births as a percentage of total childbearing had reached a peak in the first part of the 1970s[65] primarily because of declines in both fertility within marriage and the proportion of women who were married.[66] The two rulings of the Court thus occurred in the context of markedly more noticeable rates of pregnancy exposure and pregnancy outside marriage, and that they did so is almost certainly not accident. The regression analyses reported in this chapter indicate that the use of family planning methods by unmarried adults was not seriously hindered by the statutes the Supreme Court invalidated in *Eisenstadt* and *Roe,* but that use was not frequent enough given dominant social values with regard to out-of-wedlock childbearing. As a consequence, constitutional doctrine was changed, and society formally recognized the problem of nonmarital sexual activity and procreation.

Other features of the social milieu were also probably at work in the two decisions. It is unlikely to be simply coincidence that young adults became a substantially larger segment of the population in the decade preceding the two decisions. Persons who were 18–24 years old, for example, were 8.9% of the population in 1960 but 12.0% in 1970,[67] a rise of one-third in just ten years. The increasingly youthful age structure, combined with the greater propensity to engage in premarital intercourse, rapidly expanded the number of young adults who were sexually active outside marriage. That number was boosted further by a growing estrangement from marriage: The proportion of women 18–24 years of age who were unmarried increased from 42% in 1960 to 51% in 1970.[68] The regression results in the present chapter suggest that, prior to *Eisenstadt* and *Roe,* law was not creating a substantial unmet need for birth control methods among unmarried adults, but changes in the age structure, sexual behavior, and marital status of the population made fertility prevention for those adults a more salient aspect of the social order and intensified pressure on society to acknowledge and promote such prevention. The Supreme Court seems to have responded to that pressure in its constitutional jurisprudence.

Two cases remain for consideration, but their social settings require only a brief discussion. At the time the Supreme Court ruled in *Planned Parenthood of Central Missouri v. Danforth* that a married woman must be allowed to abort a first-trimester pregnancy even if her husband refuses to approve, the institution of marriage had been seriously weakened, and the Court presumably was responding in part to this situation. In the mid-1970s, when the case was decided, the proportion of marriages dissolved by women born between 1890 and 1950 had become generally higher with each successive cohort.[69] At the time *Carey v. Population Services International* held that minors must be allowed to obtain contraceptives, the incidence of premarital intercourse among adolescents was clearly rising.[70] Social patterns among minors thus favored, and presumably helped to produce, supporting legal doctrine.

The present chapter and the two that preceded it have considered legal doctrine on three topics—gender, age, and methods of controlling procreation—and reviewed the evidence on these topics that is relevant to the thesis I outlined. The evidence is supplemented by the large body of research cited in chapter 2 that finds statutes and court decisions directed at social problems do not work as intended. Ample support accordingly exists for the argument that law is a response to social needs and patterns but not a significant determinant of them. In view of that support, I proceed to chapter 6 and a different task—prediction.

NOTES

1. Blackshield, *Constitutionalism and Comstockery,* 14 KANSAS L. REV. 403, 410 (1966).

2. Reproductive freedom as a constitutional principle applicable to Americans generally appeared in a case decided by the Court in 1965. Griswold v. Connecticut, 381 U.S. 479 (1965). The principle emerged in legislation at the federal level in 1970, when Congress attempted to increase the control that individuals exercised over reproduction by enacting the Family Planning Services and Population Research Act. Pub. L. 91–572, 84 Stat. 1504 (1970). State statutes advancing the theme of reproductive freedom were adopted between 1967 and 1972 when 16 states increased access to legal abortion by legislation. Knecht, *A Survey of the Present Statutory and Case Law on Abortion: The Contradictions and the Problems,* 1972 UNIV. ILLINOIS L. FORUM 177, 179. *Roe v. Wade,*

holding restrictive abortion statutes unconstitutional, was announced by the U.S. Supreme Court in January 1973. Roe v. Wade, 410 U.S. 113 (1973).

3. Because World War II and the economic depression that preceded it appear to have altered fundamentally the nature of American society, I have chosen to concentrate on the period that followed the war. As a result, I am omitting consideration of Skinner v. Oklahoma, 316 U.S. 535 (1942). It should be noted, however, that *Skinner* dealt with the constitutionality of a statute authorizing the sterilization of persons convicted of specified crimes and that the decision thus affected a relatively small number of people; the cases considered in this chapter determined the constitutionality of statutes having far wider applicability.

4. Griswold v. Connecticut, 381 U.S. 479, 485 (1965).

5. Eisenstadt v. Baird, 405 U.S. 438, 453 (1972).

6. Carey v. Population Services International, 431 U.S. 678, 685–86 (1977).

7. 410 U.S. 113 (1973).

8. Planned Parenthood of Southeastern Pennsylvania v. Casey, 112 S.Ct. 2791, 2855 (1992) (Rehnquist, White, Scalia, & Thomas, JJ., concurring in part & dissenting in part).

9. Planned Parenthood of Central Missouri v. Danforth, 428 U.S. 52, 71 (1976). Under the statute, a woman did not need the consent of her husband to end a pregnancy that jeopardized her life.

10. Carey v. Population Services International, *supra* note 6, at 691–99, 702–03.

11. I will not deal with constitutional jurisprudence on the right of a minor to obtain an abortion. I omit that jurisprudence partly because the conditions under which a minor was constitutionally entitled to abort a pregnancy were ambiguous for a period of several years and the point at which constitutional law on the issue was settled cannot be clearly identified. Moreover, when the rights of a minor to an abortion were established, the Court permitted substantial government regulation. Planned Parenthood of Central Missouri v. Danforth, *supra* note 9, at 73–76; Bellotti v. Baird, 443 U.S. 622 (1979); City of Akron v. Akron Center for Reproductive Health, 462 U.S. 416 (1983); Planned Parenthood Assoc. of Kansas City v. Ashcroft, 462 U.S. 476 (1983). The degree to which the principle of reproductive freedom applies to minors is thus debatable.

12. Cleveland Bd. of Educ. v. LaFleur, 414 U.S. 632 (1974). *See also* Turner v. Dep't of Employment Security, 423 U.S. 44 (1975).

13. *See* Goldscheider & Mosher, *Religious Affiliation and Contraceptive Usage: Changing American Patterns, 1955–82,* 19 STUD. IN FAM. PLAN. 48 (1988); Mosher & Bachrach, *First Premarital Contraceptive Use: United States, 1960–82,* 18 STUD. IN FAM. PLAN. 83 (1987).

14. Data were obtained from the annual volumes of *Vital Statistics of the United States* and from S. VENTURA, TRENDS AND DIFFERENTIALS IN BIRTHS TO UNMARRIED WOMEN: UNITED STATES, 1970–76 (Vital and Health Statistics Series 21, No. 36, 1980) (DHHS Publication No. (PHS) 80–1914).

The central birth rate is used as the measure of childbearing. A "central" rate is the number of events of a certain type (here, births) that occur during a year divided by the number of persons in the relevant population in the middle of that year. H. SHRYOCK, J. SIEGEL, & E. STOCKWELL, THE METHODS AND MATERIALS OF DEMOGRAPHY 228 (condensed ed. 1976).

The rate, it should be noted, was analyzed with a statistical test (multiple regression) that required data on both the numerator and denominator of the rate—i.e., the number of births to women of a given age and the number of women of that age. However, just one of the two numbers was reported in the published figures that I utilized. The number that was missing had to be estimated from the number that was furnished and from the birth rate; the birth rate was consistently available and is adjusted for the underregistration of births and the underenumeration of women.

15. The age categories in the latter data set were 15–19, 20–24, 25–29, 30–34, and 35–39. Cohort was calculated by subtracting the oldest age in these categories from period; the measure of cohort was thus the first year in a five-year range.

16. F. Willekens & N. Baydar, Age-Period-Cohort Models for Forecasting Fertility 42 (Netherlands Interuniversity Demographic Institute Working Paper No. 45, 1984) (available from the Netherlands Interdisciplinary Demographic Institute, P.O. Box 11650, 2502 AR The Hague, The Netherlands).

17. *See* Buttner & Lutz, *Estimating Fertility Responses to Policy Measures in the German Democratic Republic,* 16 POPULATION & DEV. REV. 539 (1990).

The data analyses reported in this chapter utilized one dummy variable for each calendar year in a time series except the reference year. A dummy variable indicates whether different intercepts exist for the two conditions it represents. R. PINDYCK & D. RUBINFELD, ECONOMETRIC MODELS AND ECONOMIC FORECASTS 104–06 (3rd ed. 1991). The analyses thus ascertained whether the *level* of the birth rate differed over time.

18. Age was measured by a dummy variable in analyzing birth rates for *Griswold v. Connecticut* and hence could not be meaningfully squared.

Interaction terms were formed by multiplication of the component variables. Where a component variable had an identifying restriction (discussed *infra*), the restriction was utilized in the interaction.

19. Glenn, *A Flawed Approach to Solving the Identification Problem in the Estimation of Mobility Effect Models: A Comment on Brody and McRae,* 67 SOCIAL FORCES 789 (1989).

20. Hofferth, Kahn, & Baldwin, *Premarital Sexual Activity Among U.S. Teenage Women Over the Past Three Decades,* 19 FAM. PLAN. PERSP. 46, 53 (1987).

21. For the cases concerned with the access of adults to contraceptives, the data set measured the cohort of the mother in five-year overlapping groups. See *supra* note 15. Only cohorts *all* of whose members were born between 1939 and 1945 were subject to the identifying restriction. Cohorts that encompassed years earlier than 1939 or later than 1945 were not included in the restriction even though some of their members may have been born in the 1939–1945 period.

In the case concerned with the access of minors to contraceptives, the data set specified the exact year in which the mother was born.

22. Cooney & Hogan, *Marriage in an Institutionalized Life Course: First Marriage Among American Men in the Twentieth Century,* 53 J. MARR. & FAM. 178 (1991).

23. Hofferth, Kahn & Baldwin, *supra* note 20, at 49.

24. Bureau of the Census, U.S. Dep't of Commerce, *Marital Status and Living Arrangements: March 1990,* CURRENT POPULATION REP. Series P-20, No. 450, at 1 (1991).

25. Adult women born in the five-year cohorts of 1935–1939 and 1940–1944 were very similar at each age of the childbearing cycle in the rates at which they had first births, but their rates at each age differed noticeably from those of women in subsequent five-year cohorts. Bureau of the Census, U.S. Dep't of Commerce, *Fertility of American Women: June 1981,* CURRENT POPULATION REP. Series P-20, No. 378, at 42 (1983). While first-birth rates are not reported for the same cohorts used in my analysis, the pattern of rates suggests the presence of uniform values regarding procreation among women who were born during the years that preceded and encompassed World War II.

26. Henshaw & Van Vort, *Abortion Services in the United States, 1987 and 1988,* 22 FAM. PLAN. PERSP. 102, 103 (1990).

27. Henshaw, Koonin, & Smith, *Characteristics of U.S. Women Having Abortions, 1987,* 23 FAM. PLAN. PERSP. 75, 76 (1991).

28. In the mid-1970s, approximately three out of five women 20–34 years of age were in the labor force. Bureau of the Census, U.S. Dep't of Commerce, *A Statistical Portrait of Women in the United States: 1978,* CURRENT POPULATION REP. Series P-23, No. 100, at 46 (1980). Among women who were employed outside of agriculture, roughly one out of five worked for government. Calculated from BUREAU OF LABOR STATISTICS, U.S. DEP'T OF LABOR, BULL. 2217, HANDBOOK OF LABOR STATISTICS 183 (1985). Multiplying the two proportions ($3/5 \times 1/5 = 3/25 = 12/100$) indicates that just 12 out of every 100 (1 out of 8) women who were of prime childbearing age held a government job.

29. Smith, *The History and Future of the Legal Battle Over Birth Control,* 49 CORNELL L. Q. 275, 277–79 (1964).

Spousal consent requirements for abortion present a similar situation: At the time *Planned Parenthood of Central Missouri v. Danforth* appeared, only about one-third of the states required a married woman to obtain the consent of her husband in order to abort a pregnancy. Moss, *Abortion Statutes After Danforth: An Examination,* 15 J. FAMILY L. 537, 556–58 (1977).

30. Martin v. Hunter's Lessee, 14 U.S. (1 Wheat.) 304 (1816).

31. U.S. CONST. art. VI, cl. 2. See also Dodge v. Woolsey, 59 U.S. (18 How.) 331, 347–51 (1856).

32. Among females less than 18 years old, the proportion that had ever been married was only 6.8% in 1960 and 2.7% in 1970. Bureau of the Census, U.S. Dep't of Commerce, *Marital Status and Living Arrangements: March 1985,* Series P-20, No. 410, table A-2 (1986).

33. Among currently married women 15–44 years old in 1965, approximately half were relying on a contraceptive method (including sterilization) that was in principle subject to effective government regulation; an additional one-fourth were not using contraception because they were sterile (for reasons unrelated to reproduction), postpartum, pregnant, or attempting to conceive. Only one out of four married women—those who used a pregnancy prevention method (e.g., rhythm, withdrawal, douche) that was beyond the ability of government to regulate or who, without explanation, used no method—may have been unable

to obtain contraceptives because of legal barriers. However, the behavior of this group also may have stemmed from nonlegal factors such as social pressure and personal preference. Calculated from W. Mosher & C. Westoff, *Trends in Contraceptive Practice: United States, 1965–76,* Vital & Health Statistics, Series P-23, No. 10, table A and table 7 (1982) (DHHS Publication No. (PHS) 82–1986).

34. Different identifying restrictions were employed for *Eisenstadt* and for *Roe v. Wade,* but a plausible argument can be made that the restriction for *Eisenstadt* is justified for *Roe*: Specifically, since the incidence of premarital intercourse was similar in the cohorts of 1939–1945, the need to terminate out-of-wedlock conceptions was presumably constant across these cohorts. If the argument is correct and the restriction on the cohorts of 1939–1945 is warranted for abortion, the results of the present analysis apply to *Roe* because *Roe* could have affected fertility in the same year (1973) as *Eisenstadt* and because unmarried women, who are the focus of the analysis, produced the vast majority of abortions. Of all abortions performed on women 15–44 years old in 1973, 7 out of 10 were performed on unmarried women. The proportion rose gradually and reached 8 out of 10 in 1983. (The proportion for adult women is unavailable.) S. Henshaw & J. Van Vort, Abortion Services in the United States, Each State & Metropolitan Area, 1984–1985 table 3 (1988). See also Trent & Powell-Griner, *Differences in Race, Marital Status, and Education Among Women Obtaining Abortions,* 69 Social Forces 1121 (1991).

35. The data analyzed, it should be noted, include both married and unmarried females. The analysis ideally should focus on the birth rates of just those minors who are unmarried, because state law often provides that a married minor possesses the rights of an adult. H. Clark, The Law of Domestic Relations in the United States 309 (2d ed. 1988). Unfortunately, birth rates are not reported for unmarried females who are minors; data on the fertility of unmarried females younger than 20 are available only for an age category (viz., 15–19) that includes both minors and adults. Nonetheless, birth rates among all females 14–17 years old can be used to study pregnancies among those who are unmarried because few females marry before their 18th birthday. In 1960, just 6.8% of all females less than 18 years old had been married; in 1970 and 1980, the proportions were 2.7 and 3.0%, respectively. Bureau of the Census, *supra* note 32.

36. In the data set I employed—which covers childbearing between 1949 and 1988 among females younger than 18 in post-1931 cohorts—the mean number of births per thousand females was 26.7 for first births, 6.4 for second births, 0.9 for third births, and 0.09 for fourth births. No fifth births were reported.

37. R. Niemi, J. Mueller, & T. Smith, Trends in Public Opinion 191 (1989).

38. Marshall, *The Supreme Court as an Opinion Leader,* 15 Am. Politics Q. 147, 164 (1987).

39. Los Angeles Times Poll No. 176, at questions 64 and 68. Available from the Los Angeles Times, Times Mirror Square, Los Angeles, CA 90053.

40. Chemerinsky, *Rationalizing the Abortion Debate: Legal Rhetoric and the Abortion Controversy,* 31 Buffalo L. Rev. 107 (1982).

41. Hogan, *An Intervention Analysis of the Effects of Legalized Abortion Upon U.S. Fertility,* 3 Population Res. & Pol'y Rev. 201, 214–15 (1984).

42. 410 U.S. at 165 note 67.

43. Let me state that I personally believe abortion should be lawful and widely available from competent medical personnel. My contention is only that the legality of abortion is not an important determinant of its incidence—or, for that matter, of its safety. With regard to safety, an estimated 1500 women would have died from pregnancy-related causes between 1970 and 1980 if the legal grounds for abortion had not been expanded by state statutes and by *Roe v. Wade*. Tietze, *The Public Health Effects of Legal Abortion in the United States*, 16 FAM. PLAN. PERSP. 26 (1984). However, the estimate is a function of the number of abortions legally performed, and as table 5.3 shows, there were almost 11 million such abortions during 1970–1980. The ratio of legal abortions to deaths averted is therefore greater than 7000 to 1. Given the large number of legal abortions that were needed to avert one death from an illegal abortion, unlawful pregnancy terminations were rarely fatal. *See also* J. LEGGE, ABORTION POLICY 129–40 (1985).

44. HENSHAW & VAN VORT, *supra* note 34, table 1.

45. Data from the Centers for Disease Control show a mean annual increment of approximately 124,000 between 1973 and 1976. This is even less than the increase indicated by the Alan Guttmacher Institute.

46. For both periods, the abortion rate applies to the resident population of the United States. For 1969–1972, the rate was calculated using the number of abortions appearing in table 5.3 in the text and estimates of the resident population reported in the following sources: for 1970–1972, Bureau of the Census, U.S. Dep't of Commerce, *Preliminary Estimates of the Population of the United States, by Age, Sex, and Race: 1970 to 1981*, CURRENT POPULATION REP. Series P-25, No. 917, table 2 (1982); for 1969, Bureau of the Census, U.S. Dep't of Commerce, *Estimates of the Population of the United States, by Age, Sex, and Race: April 1, 1960 to July 1, 1973*, CURRENT POPULATION REP. Series P-25, No. 519, table 2 (1974). Abortion rates for 1973 through 1976 were taken from Henshaw, Forrest, & Van Vort, *Abortion Services in the United States, 1984 and 1985*, 19 FAM. PLAN. PERSP. 63, 64 (1987).

47. The pattern for the abortion rate is the same as that for abortion numbers. My calculations show the rate to be 0.5 in 1969, 4.5 in 1970, 11.1 in 1971, 13.2 in 1972, and 13.5 in 1973 using the number of abortions reported by the Centers for Disease Control; the rate was 16.3 in 1973 according to the Alan Guttmacher Institute. The rate thus increased less in 1973 than in two of the preceding three years when AGI data are used for 1973 and less in 1973 than in all of the preceding three years when CDC data are employed.

48. Knecht, *supra* note 2, at 179.

Colorado was the first jurisdiction substantially to relax statutory restrictions on abortion. Its legislation took effect on April 25, 1967. 1967 Colo. Sess. Laws ch. 190; COLO. CONST. art. V, § 19. California—the first state with a sizable population to adopt a liberalized abortion statute—implemented its policy on January 1, 1968. 1967 Cal. Stat. ch. 327; CAL. CONST. art. 4, § 8. Other populous states that eased restrictions on abortion by statute prior to *Roe* (and the dates their statutes became law) were: Maryland: June 1968. 1968 Md. Laws ch. 470; MD. CONST. art. XVI, § 2. Washington: May 1970. 1970 Wash. Laws Ex. Sess. ch. 3; WASH. CONST. art. 2, §

1(c). New York: July 1970. N.Y. Penal Law § 125.05 (3) (McKinney 1987). Virginia: July 1970. 1970 Va. Acts ch. 508; VA. CONST. art. IV, § 13.

49. *See* Granberg & Granberg, *Social Bases of Support and Opposition to Legalized Abortion,* in PERSPECTIVES ON ABORTION 191, 193 (P. Sachdev ed., 1985). *See also* Orcutt & Bayer, *Student Protest and Sex-Role Attitude Change, 1967–1971: A Log-Linear Analysis of Longitudinal Data,* 4 SEX ROLES 267 (1978); Burstein, *Public Opinion, Demonstrations, and the Passage of Antidiscrimination Legislation,* 43 PUB. OPINION Q. 157 (1979).

Between 1940 and the mid-1950s, declines occurred both in the rate at which pregnant women died from abortion and in the rate at which they died from other causes associated with pregnancy and childbirth. During the last half of the 1950s, however, the death rate from abortion increased even though the maternal mortality rate from other causes generally fell. Cates et al., *Trends in National Abortion Mortality, United States, 1940–1974: Implications for Prevention of Future Abortion Deaths,* 11 ADVANCES IN PLANNED PARENTHOOD 106, 108 (fig. 2) (1976). The increasing incidence of mortality due to abortion in the latter part of the 1950s may indicate that the number of illegal pregnancy terminations was rising at this time.

During most of the 1960s, there was a decline in the rate of abortion-related mortality among pregnant women. *Id.* However, the decrease may have stemmed from the willingness of a growing number of physicians to perform illegal abortions rather than from a drop in the frequency of the procedure. Tietze, *The Effect of Legalization of Abortion on Population Growth and Public Health,* 7 FAM. PLAN. PERSP. 123 (1975).

50. This proposition is supported by qualitative evidence (i.e., narratives and impressions obtained from interviews) on the development of abortion law in California. K. LUKER, ABORTION AND THE POLITICS OF MOTHERHOOD 66–91 (1984).

51. Hogan, *supra* note 41. New York is estimated to have experienced 19,700 fewer births in 1971 than in 1970 as a result of its revised abortion policy. *Id.* at 212. Approximately 319,000 children were born in the state in 1970. NAT'L CENTER FOR HEALTH STATISTICS, U.S. DEP'T OF HEALTH, EDUC. & WELFARE, VITAL STATISTICS OF THE UNITED STATES: 1970. Vol. I: NATALITY table 1–48 (1975). The former divided by the latter (19,700/319,000) is .062 or 6.2%.

The New York statute seems to have had an enduring and much more substantial impact on births to black females under 20 years of age who resided in New York City. T. JOYCE & N. MOCAN, THE IMPACT OF A BAN ON LEGALIZED ABORTION ON ADOLESCENT CHILDBEARING IN NEW YORK CITY (National Bureau of Economic Research Working Paper No. 3002, 1989).

In a study of a panel of young women over a seven-year period (1979–1986), the restrictiveness of state statutes regulating abortion was found to have no effect on the probability that a first premarital pregnancy would be aborted. Lundberg & Plotnick, *Effects of State Welfare, Abortion and Family Planning Policies on Premarital Childbearing Among White Adolescents,* 22 FAM. PLAN. PERSP. 246 (1990) (hereinafter Lundberg & Plotnick). The lack of an effect appeared among both Whites and Blacks. S. Lundberg & R. Plotnick, Adolescent Premarital

Childbearing: Do Opportunity Costs Matter? (University of Washington Institute for Economic Research Paper No. 90–23, 1990). However, the study also reported that the presence of a restrictive state statute regulating the advertisement, sale, or licensing of contraception (as measured by a dummy variable) increased the probability of a first premarital pregnancy among white women. *Id.* tables 2 and 3. Unfortunately, the regression equation did not include any indicators of state-level characteristics for Whites, though it did for Blacks (who were unaffected by the presence of a restriction). Specifically, the regression equation for Blacks included a dummy variable for residence in the South. If my thesis is to be tested rigorously, the role of macrolevel characteristics must be examined. Indeed, the investigators caution that such characteristics might have been responsible for the relationship they found between restrictive state statutes on contraception and the likelihood of a first premarital pregnancy among white women. *Id.* at 22–23; Lundberg & Plotnick, *supra* at 251.

52. Ryder & Westoff, *Wanted and Unwanted Fertility in the United States: 1965 and 1970, in* DEMOGRAPHIC AND SOCIAL ASPECTS OF POPULATION GROWTH 467, 484 (C. Westoff & R. Parke, Jr., eds., 1972). The decline in unwanted births continued through the 1970s. Westoff, *The Decline in Unwanted Fertility, 1971–1976,* 13 FAM. PLAN. PERSP. 70 (1981); Williams, *Determinants of Unintended Childbearing Among Ever-Married Women in the United States: 1973–1988,* 23 FAM. PLAN. PERSP. 212, 214 (1991).

The preceding studies were confined to married women, but such women accounted for at least 87% of all births annually during the last half of the 1960s and the early 1970s. VENTURA, *supra* note 14, table 6.

53. Bureau of the Census, U.S. Dep't of Commerce, *Fertility Histories and Birth Expectations of American Women: June 1971,* CURRENT POPULATION REP., Series P-20, No. 263, at 7, 8 (1974).

54. L. WESTOFF & C. WESTOFF, FROM NOW TO ZERO 88, 91 (1971); Mosher & Bachrach, *Contraceptive Use: United States, 1982,* Series 23, No. 12, at 15 (1986) (DHHS Publication No. (PHS) 86–1988).

55. 1967 Colo. Sess. Laws ch. 190.

56. Estimates of the size of the Colorado population were obtained from *Current Population Reports* Series P-25. The regression equations used the total resident population rather than the number of persons (or women) in their childbearing years, because state-level population estimates were not available for the categories of maternal age in which births were reported.

57. HENSHAW & VAN VORT, *supra* note 34, at 109.

58. Blake, *Income and Reproductive Motivation,* 21 POPULATION STUD. 185, 190–93 (1967).

59. HENSHAW & VAN VORT, *supra* note 34. All pregnancies, regardless of the length of gestation, are included, but they can be used to evaluate the impact of *Danforth* because abortions performed in the first 12 weeks of gestation comprised at least 85% of all abortions each year. Calculated from *id.* at table 4. While the latter percentage is not reported by marital status, there is no reason to believe that it differs markedly between married and unmarried women.

60. The analysis of birth rates used the same data set employed for *Griswold*

except that all married women 20–39 years old were included. In assessing the impact of the decision, the regression model controlled age, cohort, and the interaction of age and cohort, and covered the period 1956–1988. The adjusted R^2 was .937 and the square root of the mean square error was .172 with only the control variables in the regression equations, and .964 and .130, respectively, with both the control variables and the year dummies in the equations ($N = 102$).

Since *Danforth* appeared in July 1976 and did not alter legal doctrine for pregnancies that were in their last six months, 1977 was the first year the decision could have influenced births. However, the odds ratios from 1977 through 1988 had probabilities of not less than .351 and, in any event, exceeded 1.000. They therefore provide no evidence that the decision permitted an appreciable number of married women to terminate pregnancies that otherwise would have been carried to term.

In addition, births to adult married women did not change prior to the decision. The odds ratios for 1956–1976 uniformly failed to reach the .100 significance level.

61. Alwin, *From Obedience to Autonomy: Changes in Traits Desired in Children, 1924–1978,* 52 PUB. OPINION Q. 33 (1988); Alwin, *Trends in Parental Socialization Values: Detroit, 1958–1983,* 90 AM. J. SOC. 359 (1984).

62. NAT'L CENTER FOR HEALTH STATISTICS, U.S. DEP'T OF HEALTH & HUMAN SERVICES, VITAL STATISTICS OF THE UNITED STATES: 1986. Vol. I: NATALITY table 1–1 (1988).

63. Schoen, Urton, Woodrow, & Baj, *Marriage and Divorce in Twentieth Century American Cohorts,* 22 DEMOGRAPHY 101, 107, 110 (1985).

64. Hofferth, Kahn, & Baldwin, *supra* note 20, at 50.

65. VENTURA, *supra* note 14, table 6; O'Connell & Moore, *The Legitimacy Status of First Births to U.S. Women Aged 15–24, 1939–1978,* 12 FAM. PLAN. PERSP. 16, 18, 19 (1980).

66. Smith & Cutright, *Thinking About Change in Illegitimacy Ratios: United States, 1963–1983,* 25 DEMOGRAPHY 235, 242–43 (1988).

67. Calculated from Bureau of the Census, U.S. Dep't of Commerce, *Estimates of the Population of the United States, by Age, Sex, and Race: April 1, 1960 to July 1, 1973,* CURRENT POPULATION REP. Series P-25, No. 519, table 1 (1974).

68. Calculated from: BUREAU OF THE CENSUS, U.S. DEP'T OF COMMERCE. CENSUS OF POPULATION: 1960. Vol. I: CHARACTERISTICS OF THE POPULATION. Part 1: UNITED STATES SUMMARY table 176 (1963). BUREAU OF THE CENSUS, U.S. DEP'T OF COMMERCE. 1970 CENSUS OF POPULATION. Vol. I: CHARACTERISTICS OF THE POPULATION—SECTION 2. Part 1: UNITED STATES SUMMARY table 203 (1973).

The proportion of males 18–24 years old who were unmarried was 66% in 1960 and 68% in 1970. *Id.*

69. Schoen, Urton, Woodrow, & Baj, *supra* note 63, at 110, 113.

70. Hofferth, Kahn, & Baldwin, *supra* note 20, at 49; I RISKING THE FUTURE—ADOLESCENT SEXUALITY, PREGNANCY, AND CHILDBEARING 42 (C. Hayes ed., 1987).

CHAPTER

6

Euthanasia

While research conducted over the course of the preceding decade makes possible a better understanding of how law and the social system are related, a theory that permits us to understand the relationship in detail has yet to be developed. Unquestionably, as research expands our body of knowledge, the quality of theory will improve. However, a relatively comprehensive, accurate theory will not necessarily predict the nature and behavior of law in the future; rather, it may only allow us to identify the links between law and society in the past. A theory will not provide correct predictions regarding a phenomenon where, for example, past change in the phenomenon resulted from factors that no longer operate and further change will result from factors that the theory has not recognized. In that situation, theory will provide insight and comprehension, but it will not foretell the future.

While disagreement may exist over whether a theory should be able to predict, distinct advantages accrue from prediction. Indeed, the major practical benefits of a theory are likely to be determined by the degree to which it generates accurate predictions—or, more exactly, predictions that are correct substantially more often than the forecasts from random guesses or an alternative theory. The value of the theoretical framework advanced in the preceding pages will accordingly increase to the extent it allows us to anticipate the future.

This chapter will attempt to predict how law will treat one issue in the years to come. The issue is euthanasia or, more technically, active euthanasia—acts that are designed to quickly terminate the life and end the suffering of persons who are afflicted with severe, stressful physical conditions. Euthanasia, popularly known as mercy killing, became the focus of nationwide public attention in the United States most recently in June 1990 when a physician in Michigan connected an individual with Alzheimer's disease to a device that allowed her to end her life painlessly and swiftly.[1] Predicting future legal doctrine on euthanasia is an appropriate undertaking for this chapter because excellent data are available on the views of Americans concerning the subject. Analysis of the data strongly suggests that the currently universal refusal of law to accept euthanasia[2] is more likely than not to be replaced by legal doctrine that provides individuals with the option to have their death initiated under prescribed conditions. While it is not possible to predict the timing of the change in different jurisdictions, physician-assisted death brought on at the request and with the consent of a mentally competent, terminally ill patient will probably come to be generally authorized by the legal system in the next two decades. The issue thus warrants the close attention of researchers who are interested in the evolution of law.

In the present chapter, I will focus on the social science evidence that leads me to believe that prohibitions on euthanasia will be lifted in the foreseeable future by statute and/or court decision. In doing so, I hope to furnish additional support for my view that the factors responsible for fundamental change in legal doctrine cannot be investigated effectively with the techniques of conventional legal scholarship. That scholarship is concerned with the logical and conceptual aspects of legal issues, and it is unable to measure phenomena in a precise fashion. Major doctrinal shifts in law, however, are the result of broad societal-level forces that must be treated quantitatively, and those forces therefore need to be investigated with the research methods of the social sciences.

I divide my discussion into two parts. In the next section, I consider the societal forces that seem likely to alter formal legal doctrine on the intentional application of medical technology to end the lives of individuals who wish to die at a time of their own choosing. Because of the nature of the evidence available, the bulk of my attention in this part of the discussion will be devoted to the social values of Americans regarding euthanasia, and I will explore in depth a unique data set on these values. In the section that follows, I will focus on the ability of law to influence the frequency of euthanasia. If law is a mirror of social practices and preferences rather than a significant determinant of them, as my thesis contends, making euthanasia legal should have little impact on its incidence. As a test of the thesis, I will examine a statute enacted by the state of Pennsylvania that imposed criminal penalties for assisting another person to end his/her life, and I will attempt to determine whether the statute reduced suicide among the elderly. Legalization of euthanasia is not likely to increase substantially the number of assisted deaths if statutes that prohibit such assistance have not appreciably influenced the frequency of suicide in old age.

SOCIETAL FORCES PROMOTING EUTHANASIA

Two societal-level forces can be expected to foster acceptance of euthanasia by the legal system. The first is economic pressure: Medical care is consuming a growing share of the wealth of the nation. Specifically, expenditures for health care in the United States tripled over the past half-century as a percentage of the gross national product per capita, rising from 4.0% in 1940 to 12.2% in 1990.[3] Clearly, the increase cannot continue indefinitely, and as spending for health care reaches its upper limit, expenditures will probably be curtailed for expensive medical procedures that provide only brief benefits and/or help relatively few individuals. Indeed, the pressure on affluence from outlays for medical care has already led one state to attempt to deny public funds for some types of costly medical procedures,[4] and such policies are likely to become common in the coming decades as affluence is limited by the forces that now threaten it—particularly population growth and environmental degradation.[5]

How will economic pressure from rising medical care prices affect the legal status of euthanasia? The pressure will lead, I think, to the general elimination of expenditures for expensive medical services for individuals who have terminal physical conditions. The heavy burden that such persons place on the financing of health care is suggested by data from Medicare: Approximately 29% of all Medicare expenditures during the course of a year are devoted to the 5% of beneficiaries who are in their last twelve months of life.[6] Even with no change in the percentage of expenditures claimed by persons whose lives will soon end, the total amount of money spent on them will increase under present policy because the group with the highest mortality rates—i.e., the elderly—comprise a growing share of the population.[7] Economic pressure can thus be expected to lead to limitations on health care spending for individuals who are terminally ill, and as this occurs, it is probable that the law will provide such individuals with the option of euthanasia.

The second factor that is likely to rework law and lead to the legalization of euthanasia is social values. Legal doctrine appears to conform generally to dominant values,[8] and at least since the 1970s, a majority of Americans have supported the legalization of euthanasia.[9] In the pages to follow, accordingly, attitudes toward euthanasia will be studied at some length with data from the General Social Survey of the National Opinion Research Center. The Survey annually interviews a national probability sample of English-speaking, noninstitutionalized persons 18 years of age and older, and it included a question on euthanasia starting in 1977. The question is particularly useful because it required respondents to state whether euthanasia should be legal. Specifically, respondents were asked: "When a person has a disease that cannot be cured, do you think doctors should be allowed by law to end the patient's life by some painless means if the patient and his family request it?"

My exploration of social values begins with a regression analysis of responses to the above question in order to identify the socially salient demographic variables that are associated with attitudes toward euthanasia. Demographic attributes are often the basis of the political divisions involved in debates on and the development of public policy, and information regarding the attributes that are linked to attitudes toward euthanasia will reveal the groups that form these divisions and the manner in which their attitudes differ. This in turn will allow us to determine whether the groups have experienced an increase or decrease over time in their approval of physician-assisted death and whether the attitudes of the public as a whole conceal crosscurrents. If all of the groups have become more approving of euthanasia between the late 1970s and early 1990s (the period for which data on attitudes are available from the General Social Survey), legalization of the practice is more likely than if some of the groups exhibit a declining level of approval.[10]

A number of studies have already utilized the General Social Survey to ascertain whether a relationship exists between some of the demographic variables that I will consider and attitudes toward euthanasia. Each of the studies, however, possesses a potentially serious methodological defect that casts doubt on the conclusions that were reached. One study failed to control for multiple factors when assessing the effect of the demographic variables included in its analysis.[11] Three studies relied upon multiple regression but apparently used ordinary least-squares regression even though the dependent variable (attitudes) was scaled as a dichotomy (approve/disapprove).[12] In so doing, the studies employed an inappropriate statistical procedure. Least-squares regression can produce erroneous results when a dependent variable is measured as a dichotomy unless the data for that variable are analyzed in a nonlinear form[13]—a form the three studies did not employ. A final study used path analysis but applied it to a three-category scale of attitudes that was created from the responses to two separate questions on euthanasia.[14] Unfortunately, there was no evidence to support the implicit assumption of the study—an assumption required by its statistical analysis—that the intervals between the three categories of its scale were equal in size. The second question that formed the scale, which was asked only if the first question was not answered in the affirmative, infrequently produced views that differed from those obtained from the first item. The two questions therefore seem largely to have duplicated one another, and their joint use is unlikely to have created a scale with between-category intervals of identical magnitude.

To improve on the preceding studies, the present investigation will employ a probit model (with maximum likelihood estimation), a form of multiple regression suitable for a dependent variable that is measured as a dichotomy.[15] Moreover, since my goal is to identify the demographic factors that have a *durable* relationship to attitudes regarding euthanasia, the data from the General Social Survey will be analyzed for nine separate years: 1977, 1978, 1982, 1983, 1985, 1986, 1988, 1989, and 1990.[16] Unlike the studies cited above, which examined data from the Survey for only a single year or for a combination of two adjacent years, I will estimate regression coefficients for each of the nine years. Doing so will also update these studies, all of which are based on the surveys carried out in 1977 and/or 1978.

The demographic factors selected as the independent variables were those that intuitively appeared to me to be salient features of American social life. Table 6.1 lists the variables and describes the dummies created for them. Dummies were used even when continuous scales could have been employed, because debates on government policy are characterized by social divisions and dummies by their very nature measure divisions. The dummies were thus developed to determine the splits that characterize the public with respect to the issue of legalizing euthanasia. The categories for each dummy were those that Americans generally seem to have adopted; in terms of age, the categories were based on the findings of empirical research.[17]

In reviewing the demographic variables chosen for the regression analysis, it is important to keep in mind that different measures were often available for a given variable; that only one of the measures was incorporated into the analysis; and that the measure employed was the one I believed to be the most salient in our society. Thus, occupational prestige of the respondent was used instead of occupational category (from the classification system of the Bureau of the Census) or the type of work performed.[18] Income was assessed in terms of the total income of the respondent and his/her family rather than in terms of the earned income of the respondent alone. Education was captured by the highest degree possessed by a respondent instead of the number of years of schooling that he or she had completed.[19] Marital status was considered in terms of whether the respondent was currently married, currently widowed, currently divorced, currently separated, or never married, not in terms of whether he or she had ever been married. Finally, religion was assessed by respondents' self-expressed preference rather than by the content of religious belief or the frequency of church attendance, and four groups were distinguished: Protestant, Catholic, Jewish, and None.

Because my purpose is to identify the social divisions that exist with regard to views on euthanasia rather than to obtain precise estimates of the effects of the variables, table 6.2 presents the results of the probit analysis in simplified form. Specifically, a plus is used for a positive coefficient, and a minus for a negative coefficient, that had a probability under the null hypothesis of .10 or less; a zero is used for a coefficient

Table 6.1. Variables and Measures in Probit Models

Variable	*Mnemonic(s)*	*Measure*
Attitude toward euthanasia	LETDIE	Approve of euthanasia = 1; disapprove of euthanasia = 0
Age	YOUNGAGE OLDAGE	Age 18–45 = 1; age 46+ = 0 Age 66+ = 1; age 18–65 = 0 Reference group: age 46–65.
Education (highest degree received)	GRAD BACH ASSOC HISCHOOL	Graduate degree = 1; other = 0 Bachelor's degree = 1; other = 0 Junior college degree = 1; other = 0 High school diploma = 1; other = 0 Reference group: persons with less than a high school diploma
Income (total family income)	LOINC HIINC	In each year, the distribution of family income was divided as evenly as possible into thirds. LOINC was 1 for the bottom third and 0 for all others; HIINC was 1 for the top third and 0 for all others; the middle third served as the reference group
Marital status (at time of interview)	MARRIED WIDOWED DIVORCED SEPARATED	Married = 1; other = 0 Widowed = 1; other = 0 Divorced = 1; other = 0 Separated = 1; other = 0 Reference group: never-married persons
Prestige of occupation	LOPRES HIPRES	Low prestige (scores up to 29) = 1; other = 0 High prestige (scores 50 and above) = 1; other = 0 Reference group: prestige scores 30–49
Race	BLACK	Black = 1; White = 0
Region of residence	NOEAST	Northeast (New England and Middle Atlantic states) = 1; other = 0
	MIDWEST	Midwest (West North Central and East North Central states) = 1; other = 0
	WEST	West (Pacific and Mountain states) = 1; other = 0 Reference group: persons who reside in the South, i.e., in West South Central, East South Central, and South Atlantic states
Religious preference	PROT	Protestant = 1; Catholic, Jewish, None = 0
	CATH JEW	Catholic = 1; Protestant, Jewish, None = 0 Jewish = 1; Protestant, Catholic, None = 0 Reference group: persons who state that their religious preference is "None"
Sex	MALE	Male = 1; female = 0

that had a probability under the null hypothesis of more than .10. A plus and minus thus indicate the presence of a relationship and the nature of a social division in attitudes toward legalizing euthanasia. A zero, on the other hand, indicates that a relationship was not found and that a social division was not present.

Table 6.2 discloses that one variable—race—was related to attitudes in eight of the nine years and that the relationship was uniform in direction, with Blacks less willing than Whites to endorse euthanasia. The data also suggest that another variable was linked to attitudes—namely, age. In seven of the nine years, respondents 18–45 years old were more likely to approve of euthanasia than were respondents 46–65 years old. Respondents age 66+, however, did not differ from those age 46–65 in

Table 6.2. Probit Coefficients for Regression of LETDIE on Independent Variables, by Year

Variable	*1977*	*1978*	*1982*	*1983*	*1985*	*1986*	*1988*	*1989*	*1990*
YOUNGAGE	0	+	+	+	+	+	+	+	0
OLDAGE	0	0	0	0	0	0	0	0	0
GRAD	+	0	0	0	0	0	0	0	0
BACH	0	0	0	0	0	0	0	0	0
ASSOC	0	0	0	0	0	0	0	0	+
HISCHOOL	0	0	0	0	+	0	0	+	0
LOINC	0	0	0	0	0	0	0	0	0
HIINC	0	0	0	0	0	0	–	0	0
MARRIED	0	–	0	–	0	0	0	–	0
WIDOWED	0	0	0	0	0	0	0	0	0
DIVORCED	0	0	0	0	0	0	0	0	0
SEPARATED	0	0	0	0	0	0	0	0	0
LOPRES	0	0	–	0	0	–	0	0	0
HIPRES	0	0	0	0	0	0	0	0	0
BLACK	–	–	–	–	–	–	–	–	0
NOEAST	0	+	+	0	+	+	0	0	0
MIDWEST	0	+	0	+	0	+	0	0	+
WEST	+	+	+	+	0	+	0	0	+
PROT	–	–	–	–	–	0	–	–	–
CATH	–	–	–	–	–	–	0	–	–
JEW	0	0	0	0	0	0	0	0	0
MALE	+	0	0	+	+	+	0	+	0

Notes: Plus denotes a positive coefficient that is statistically significant at or below .10; minus denotes a negative coefficient that is statistically significant at or below .10; zero denotes a coefficient that is not statistically significant at or below .10. Significance was determined with a two-tailed test.

The number of respondents in the regression equations was 1218 for 1977, 1238 for 1978, 1179 for 1982, 1278 for 1983, 1240 for 1985, 1175 for 1986, 760 for 1988, 762 for 1989, and 713 for 1990.

any year. *F*-tests (not shown) comparing YOUNGAGE and OLDAGE, moreover, were significant at or below .10 in eight of the nine years. The *F*-test was even significant for the 1977 coefficients, neither of which differed from the reference group. (For YOUNGAGE, the 1977 coefficient was positive even though it did not differ significantly from the reference.) In terms of age, then, the public appears to be divided between persons 18–45 and persons 46+.

In addition to race and age, three other variables in the regression analysis need to be considered—region, religion, and sex—because table 6.2 provides a basis for arguing that each is responsible for persistent social divisions regarding euthanasia. The argument, however, is not sound for reasons that differ for each variable. With regard to region, when *F*-tests (not shown) comparing NOEAST and MIDWEST, NOEAST and WEST, and MIDWEST and WEST were examined, a clear geographic pattern failed to emerge. With regard to religion, the table suggests that Protestants and Catholics are similar to one another, that respondents who are Jewish and respondents who identify with no religion are similar, and that the former two groups thus differ from the latter two. If this were the case, however, *F*-tests should be generally significant for the differences between PROT and JEW and for the differences between CATH and JEW, but most of the comparisons (not shown) did not produce coefficients with a probability of .10 or less. Even if they had, a grouping that combined persons who are Jewish and persons who prefer no religion would have little practical importance because of its small size.[20] Finally, with regard to sex, the coefficients for MALE are significant only in a bare majority of the nine years, but more should be required to conclude that the variable durably partitioned the public with regard to euthanasia.

Age and race, then, are the only demographic attributes that reliably divided Americans on the issue of whether to legalize medically assisted death. An examination of trends in attitudes toward the issue must therefore distinguish Blacks from Whites and must also consider age differences. It is to this task that I now turn.

Table 6.3 presents the distribution of attitudes toward euthanasia at three time points for all adults and for three age groups, and at two time points for Whites and Blacks. To show change over a substantial period, the table reproduces the results of a 1947 Gallup Poll that asked the same question on euthanasia as the General Social Survey.[21] (Because respondents who held no opinion were included in the report of the Gallup Poll, table 6.3 includes them for the General Social Survey; the Gallup report also dictated the age categories used by the table for the Survey.) Data from the General Social Survey were employed for two time points: 1977 and 1990–1991.[22] The Surveys for 1990 and 1991 were combined

Table 6.3. Distribution of Attitudes (%) toward Euthanasia in 1947, 1977, and 1990–1991, by Race and Age: United States

	1947[a]	*1977*	*1990–1991*
All adults			
Approve	37	60	70
Disapprove	54	36	26
No opinion	9	4	5
Whites			
Approve	[b]	63	72
Disapprove		33	23
No opinion		4	4
Blacks			
Approve	[b]	37	52
Disapprove		57	41
No opinion		6	7
21–29 years old			
Approve	46	70	75
Disapprove	47	26	21
No opinion	7	4	5
30–49 years old			
Approve	36	59	74
Disapprove	54	38	22
No opinion	10	3	4
50+ years old			
Approve	33	54	62
Disapprove	58	40	32
No opinion	9	6	6

Note: Percentages may not add to 100% because of rounding.
[a] *Source:* 1 G. GALLUP, THE GALLUP POLL: PUBLIC OPINION 1935–1971 656 (1972).
[b] Data not available by race for 1947.

because the question on euthanasia was asked of only two-thirds of the samples in these years; an aggregation of the two years reduced sampling variability by increasing the number of respondents used to calculate the proportions.

Table 6.3 reveals a clear trend of rising approval and declining disapproval over time. The trend appears in each of the two racial groups and in each of the three age groups. Moreover, a majority in all of the groups endorsed euthanasia in 1990–1991. Blacks, the least willing to accept the practice, experienced a 15 percentage point gain in favorable views between 1977 and 1990–1991. The principal psychological factor in the marked change among Blacks may be that there has been a decrease in the proportion of Blacks who believe that Whites as a group want to harm them;[23] to the extent Blacks have opposed euthanasia out of a fear of genocide, a basis for their opposition seems to have eroded.

Table 6.3 thus suggests that American adults, both in general and in important subgroups, now support the legalization of physician-assisted death at the request of terminally ill, mentally competent persons and that this support has been increasing. But the change in social values requires further scrutiny, because it involves a population whose membership has altered over time. Every year, the adult population acquires new members as the cohort of persons born eighteen years earlier reaches adulthood, and it loses existing members as individuals die. Membership change in a population can modify aggregate attitudes if the persons who are added to the population and/or the persons who leave it possess different attitudes than the persons who remain members throughout the period under consideration. Shifts in the attitudes of the public, in short, do not necessarily occur only because individuals abandon old views and adopt new ones.

We therefore confront an important question: the extent to which the transformation of values in a society is attributable to population turnover (also termed population replacement) and the extent to which the transformation is attributable to change in the values of continuing members. The question is important for at least two reasons. First, the speed with which a society experiences evolution in its values—and hence in its law—probably depends in large measure on the magnitude of the contribution of each source; population turnover is a potentially slower force in evolution than shifts in the views of those individuals who are members of society throughout the time period under study. Second, each of the two sources of value change may be moving society in a different direction, and the evolution that takes place in the values of the public as a whole may thus mask conflicting trends. Such conflict, if substantial, may reflect deep social divisions and inhibit, or even prevent, the emergence of new legal doctrine.

Given the potential implications of the two sources of change in social values, I will estimate the contribution of each source to the shift in views on euthanasia that took place between 1977 and 1991. The estimates, which appear in table 6.4, were developed by applying a procedure proposed by Firebaugh[24] to the data from the General Social Survey. The table lists the adjoining years in which the General Social Survey included the question on euthanasia and shows the shift from one survey to the next for which individual change and population turnover were each responsible. The latter figures, it should be kept in mind, indicate the number of percentage points by which the specified source raised or lowered approval of euthanasia. Positive numbers signify that the source increased the prevalence of attitudes favorable to euthanasia between the two years designated; negative numbers signify that the source decreased the incidence of favorable attitudes.

In order to provide an overview of the data, table 6.4 reports two summary measures for the changes that occurred between adjacent surveys—the sum and the coefficient of variation—and these measures will be the focus of the discussion here. The sum indicates both the direction in which attitudes moved from 1977 to 1991 and the magnitude of the movement. The coefficient of variation, which is the ratio of the standard deviation to the mean, measures the relative amount of variation associated with survey-to-survey changes.[25] The sum will be employed to identify how each source affected attitudes and by how much, while the coefficient of variation will be employed to determine the volatility of each source.

For all adults the sums reveal that individual change and population turnover each acted to increase attitudes favorable to euthanasia between 1977 and 1991, that their combined impact was substantial (6.4 + 5.3 = 11.7 percentage points), and that individual change contributed slightly more to the aggregate shift than population replacement (6.4 versus 5.3 percentage points). However, when the coefficients of variation are examined, we see that individual change was comparatively unstable in its effect, with a coefficient three times larger than that for population turnover. Approval of euthanasia, then, was made more frequent during 1977–1991 by both sources, but population replacement provided a more consistent gain and may therefore prove to be more important for gains in the years ahead.

Turning to race, we find that, among Whites as well as Blacks, both sources worked to increase acceptance of euthanasia. Somewhat different patterns characterized the two racial groups, however. As the sums show, Whites and Blacks did not differ appreciably in the degree to which population turnover contributed to the 1977–1991 attitude shift, but individual change had a modestly larger impact on the attitudes of Blacks than on the attitudes of Whites. Individual change relative to population turnover, moreover, was moderately more important among Blacks than among Whites. Table 6.4 accordingly provides insight into why, as noted in table 6.3, favorable views toward euthanasia increased to a greater degree among Blacks than among Whites between the late 1970s and early 1990s: Blacks experienced more individual change. However, the coefficients of variation are conspicuously large for Blacks. The instability of attitude movement across time is particularly notable in the

Table 6.4. Individual Change and Population Turnover as Factors in Shifts in Attitudes Toward Euthanasia in the United States: 1977–1991

	Individual change	*Population turnover*		*Individual change*	*Population turnover*
All adults			18–45 Years Old		
1977–1978	−.033	.010	1977–1978	−.020	.014
1978–1982	.023	.018	1978–1982	.017	.032
1982–1983	.015	.004	1982–1983	−.014	.002
1983–1985	−.002	−.001	1983–1985	.027	.011
1985–1986	.021	.007	1985–1986	−.004	.006
1986–1988	−.001	.010	1986–1988	−.002	.010
1988–1989	−.011	.004	1988–1989	−.009	.010
1989–1990	.037	.000	1989–1990	.020	−.005
1990–1991	.015	.001	1990–1991	.037	−.007
Sum	.064	.053	Sum	.052	.073
Coefficient of variation	3.0	1.0	Coefficient of variation	3.5	1.4
Whites			46 Years Old and Over		
1977–1978	−.043	.008	1977–1978	−.046	−.008
1978–1982	.026	.016	1978–1982	.017	.023
1982–1983	.017	.008	1982–1983	.046	.003
1983–1985	−.011	.000	1983–1985	−.043	−.002
1985–1986	.024	.007	1985–1986	.053	−.003
1986–1988	.009	.004	1986–1988	.003	.001
1988–1989	−.018	.010	1988–1989	−.016	.003
1989–1990	.030	.001	1989–1990	.055	.013
1990–1991	.029	.002	1990–1991	−.012	.005
Sum	.063	.056	Sum	.057	.035
Coefficient of variation	3.6	0.8	Coefficient of variation	6.2	2.4
Blacks					
1977–1978	.051	.014			
1978–1982	.001	.021			
1982–1983	.005	−.019			
1983–1985	.007	.009			
1985–1986	.040	.020			
1986–1988	−.046	.015			
1988–1989	−.008	−.007			
1989–1990	.104	.026			
1990–1991	−.075	−.029			
Sum	.079	.050			
Coefficient of variation	6.0	3.5			

case of individual change, suggesting that the shift in the views of Blacks during the decade and a half being studied may not be as enduring as the shift in the views of Whites.

We come finally to age differences in the action of the two sources. The age categories employed in table 6.4 are based on the regression results reported in table 6.2, which indicated that adults 18–45 years old differed from their elders and that adults 46+ years old should be treated as a single group. Using those categories, perhaps the most important finding from the sums is that population turnover increased favorable attitudes twice as much in the younger category as in the older category. Population turnover, furthermore, had a larger impact on younger persons than did individual change.

Since they will be the most directly involved, older persons and the views they hold may attract particular attention in the political debate that can be expected on the legalization of euthanasia. While older persons do not endorse euthanasia as often as younger persons, table 6.3 reveals that three out of five adults 50+ years of age approved of euthanasia in 1990–1991 and that approval in this age group had become more common since 1977. What does table 6.4 suggest about the attitudes of older persons in the years ahead? In the age category 18–45, the succession of cohorts during 1977–1991 raised acceptance of euthanasia by 7.3 percentage points. Not only was the rise substantial; the coefficient of variation discloses that population replacement operated in a relatively steady fashion. With the passage of time, the cohorts in this age range will populate the older group. Aging, that is, will gradually move the members of the younger group into the older category, where attitudes have been less favorable, and as the aging process occurs, the level of approval will rise among persons 46+ years old, ceteris paribus. Population succession was not the principal source of attitude change in the older group between 1977 and 1991, but it is likely to contribute appreciably to attitude change in the future.[26]

To conclude the discussion of population turnover and individual change, I would like to return to table 6.3. The top panel of the table shows that seven out of ten adults believed in 1990–1991 that euthanasia should be legally available. While that level would appear on the surface to be sufficient for the legalization of euthanasia by statute and/or court decision, little is known about the threshold required for a shift in legal doctrine. Indeed, there may not be a single threshold; the level of approval needed for a transformation of legal doctrine may depend on the nature of the issue involved. Since the threshold for euthanasia in the public as a whole may be higher than the level of approval prevailing at the start of the 1990s, two facets of table 6.4 should be underscored, for they suggest that endorsement of euthanasia will become more frequent in the future. First, as already noted, the age category 46+ will gradually acquire new members from the age category 18–45 while losing present members through mortality. As the less-favorable attitudes of the older group are replaced by the more-favorable attitudes of the younger group, approval of euthanasia will rise generally in the adult population if no counteracting factors are at work. Second, the category of persons 18–45 years old will itself probably become even more favorable toward euthanasia than it was in the early 1990s. As table 6.4 shows, population turnover in this age category boosted the incidence of favorable attitudes to a substantial extent and in a relatively consistent manner. Since there is no a priori reason to think the pattern will differ in the years to come, the cohorts reaching adulthood during the decade or two ahead can be expected to endorse euthanasia more often than persons age 18–45 in 1990–1991. To the extent this occurs, support for the legalization of euthanasia will become more prevalent in the public as a whole.

THE IMPACT OF STATUTES BANNING EUTHANASIA

The impact on social behavior of statutes and court decisions is an integral concern of the thesis I have advanced, and I will therefore consider the effect of legislation that imposes criminal penalties on individuals who intentionally assist others to commit suicide. If the legislation had little or no effect on the incidence of assisted suicide, the legalization of euthanasia is unlikely to have a material influence on the number of medically aided deaths. The failure of statutes to produce appreciable change would of course be consistent with the proposition that society develops regulatory law for social issues primarily to recognize existing practices and promote internal cohesion.

The analysis undertaken here focuses on a statute adopted by the state of Pennsylvania. The statute—which became law in June 1973—provides that "[a] person who intentionally aids or solicits another to commit suicide is guilty of a felony of the second degree if his conduct causes such suicide or an attempted suicide, and otherwise of a misdemeanor of the second degree."[27] The legislation is particularly appropriate for study because data are available for Pennsylvania on the number of suicides and on several factors found by previous research to influence suicide rates. The data, moreover, cover a reasonably long period before as well as after the statute appeared. If the ban on assisted suicide altered conduct substantially, it should have been followed by a decline or deceleration in suicide frequency.

The data I use are confined to suicides committed by persons (of all races) who were 65 years of age or older.[28] Given their relatively high incidence of fatal disease, persons of this age can be expected to supply the vast majority of euthanasia cases if and when the legal system approves medical intervention to cause death. Men and women were not distinguished in my analysis, however, even though the course of suicide rates over time has differed for each gender.[29] Sex-specific suicide rates could not be calculated for individual states because, while gender-by-age breakdowns are available for the number of suicides in each state, they are not available (during the period relevant here) for the population of states. The number of suicides by older men and by older women thus could not be weighted by the corresponding number of men and women residing in Pennsylvania.

Weighted least-squares logit models were estimated to ascertain the impact of the Pennsylvania statute banning assisted suicide. The dependent variable was the annual number of suicides committed in Pennsylvania from 1963 through 1978 by persons at least 65 years old (adjusted for the number of Pennsylvania residents in the same age range).[30] While data more recent than 1978 were available, models with just the control variables that included 1979 suffered from decidedly poorer goodness of fit than models ending in 1978.[31] The 1980s were also omitted, because knowledge about and data on variables that should be controlled is noticeably incomplete for suicide among the elderly, with the result that the ability of the analysis to generate definitive conclusions was severely constrained. Given this constraint, it appeared unlikely that terminating the time series in 1978 would further harm the analysis. The results of the logit models are thus only suggestive, but since they are based on five calendar years after the statute became law, they cover a period sufficient in length to reveal a major effect on behavior.

Control variables were per capita personal income in the state (for all age groups), the ratio of the number of persons younger than 18 to the number of persons age 65 and older in the state, and the number of divorces and annulments obtained by persons at least 65 years old in the state.[32] Existing research suggests that suicide rates are influenced by each of these variables.[33] However, prior to measuring the impact of the statute, regression models with the three control variables were estimated to determine whether the relationship between them and the dependent variable was linear or nonlinear, involved interactions, and/or contained time lags. (Nonlinear relationships were assessed with the square of each variable; interaction terms were created by the product of the component variables.) The adjusted R^2 and the square root of the mean square error indicated that nonlinear relationships and interaction terms were not present but that time lags were. The existence of such lags is not unexpected in light of previous research.[34] The lags that improved model fit were two years for per capita income, one year for the ratio of the number of persons younger than 18 to the number of persons age 65 and older, and two years for the number of divorces/annulments among persons 65 and older. All three lagged variables had positive regression coefficients; their probabilities under the null hypothesis were .003, .005, and .063, respectively. The adjusted R^2 of the model with these three variables was .637; the square root of the mean square error was .046.

The impact of the Pennsylvania statute was ascertained with regression equations that included the three lagged control variables and a dummy variable representing one year. Dummy variables for every year other than the reference could not be used in a single equation (as in chapter 5) because each year in the time series appeared in only one observation and standard errors could not be calculated. Separate equations were estimated, therefore, with each equation containing a dummy variable representing a different year. The odds ratios for the dummies in these equations, their *t* values, and their probabilities under the null hypothesis are shown below. In reviewing them, two points should be kept in mind. First, each ratio has as its reference all other years in the 1963–1978 period; a ratio thus indicates for the year specified the odds of suicide among the elderly relative to the time series as a whole and not relative just to the year before. Second, since the statute was in force as of June 1973, an effect on suicide was initially possible in 1973.

Year	*Odds ratio*	*t*	*Probability*
1963	dropped due to collinearity		
1964	dropped due to collinearity		
1965	0.993	0.119	.908
1966	1.005	0.098	.924
1967	0.959	0.695	.505
1968	1.056	1.066	.314
1969	0.961	0.772	.460
1970	1.090	1.495	.169
1971	0.932	1.279	.233
1972	1.077	1.529	.161
1973	0.988	0.228	.824
1974	0.962	0.650	.532
1975	0.937	1.221	.253
1976	0.972	0.524	.613
1977	1.104	2.328	.045
1978	0.955	0.690	.508

Because the odds ratios for the dummies are derived from separate equations, they cannot be compared to determine if one differs from another. Such comparisons are unnecessary, however, given that the ratios (with one exception) are not statistically significant. That is, the suicide rate in Pennsylvania was unaffected by any year other than one, and that year (1977) was associated with a heightened rate. The incidence of suicide among the elderly was thus apparently unaltered by enactment of the Pennsylvania statute banning assisted suicide, and legislation permitting euthanasia will probably not have a major effect either.

CONCLUSION

In the present chapter, I have reviewed the available evidence on the societal context of euthanasia and have shown that the evidence strongly indicates law will formally accept the practice of medically assisted death at some point in the foreseeable future. Social needs and values are even now exerting pressure to change legal doctrine on euthanasia,[35] and that pressure is likely to intensify as time passes. Unfortunately, our understanding of the behavior of law is not presently adequate to allow us to predict with a high degree of accuracy when the change will occur in a particular jurisdiction and whether it will emerge through legislation or court decision. These and other matters are simply beyond our ability to anticipate at the moment. In time, however, a theory that generates a wide array of correct predictions will be feasible, and to promote its development, the next chapter considers issues that I believe will need to be addressed in future work on the role of law in society.

NOTES

1. *Doctor Tells of First Death Using His Suicide Device*, New York Times, June 6, 1990, at A1.

2. At the present time, approximately half of all jurisdictions in the United States explicitly forbid active euthanasia, and none have formally legalized the practice. Rosenblum & Forsythe, *The Right to Assisted Suicide: Protection of Autonomy or an Open Door to Social Killing?*, 6 Issues in Law & Medicine 3, 11–12 (1990).

3. Newhouse, *Medical Care Costs: How Much Welfare Loss?*, 6 J. Econ. Persp. 3, 4 (1992).

4. A 1989 Oregon statute requires state government to rank health services according to their "comparative benefits" and provides that, when public funds are inadequate to cover all of the services needed by low-income persons eligible for publicly financed medical care, the ranking be used to eliminate services, "starting with the least important [service] and progressing toward the most important." 1989 Oregon Laws ch. 836.

A substantial segment of the American public even now seems willing to endorse some rationing of health care. A national survey, apparently conducted in 1990, asked interviewees to agree or disagree with the following statement: "Where health care is provided at public expense, only treatments or operations with a certain chance of being successful should be allowed." The proportions agreeing and disagreeing were 40 and 54%, respectively; only 6% had no opinion. Northwestern National Life Insurance Co., Americans Speak Out on Health Care Rationing 22 (1990) (available from the Group Marketing Communications Division, Northwestern National Life Insurance Co., 20 Washington Avenue South, Minneapolis, MN 55401).

5. 1 THE GLOBAL 2000 REPORT TO THE PRESIDENT: ENTERING THE TWENTY-FIRST CENTURY (report prepared by the Council on Environmental Quality and the Dep't of State) (1980).

Population expansion and environmental degradation will constrain affluence both by creating imbalances between the supply of and demand for resources (e.g., energy) and by requiring a reduction in economic productivity in order to counter damage to ecosystems such as the atmosphere (e.g., climatic alterations caused by fossil fuel combustion). See, for example, Guruswamy, *Global Warming: Integrating United States and International Law*, 32 ARIZONA L. REV. 221 (1990).

6. Riley & Lubitz, *Longitudinal Patterns of Medicare Use by Cause of Death*, 11 HEALTH CARE FINANCING REV. 1 (1989).

7. Bureau of the Census, U.S. Dep't of Commerce, *Projections of the Population of the United States, by Age, Sex, and Race: 1988 to 2080*, CURRENT POPULATION REP. Series P-25, No. 1018, at 8–9 (1989).

8. T. MARSHALL, PUBLIC OPINION AND THE SUPREME COURT (1989); Wright, Erikson, & McIver, *Public Opinion and Policy Liberalism in the American States*, 31 AM. J. POL. SCI. 980 (1987).

9. Ostheimer, *The Polls: Changing Attitudes Toward Euthanasia*, 44 PUB. OPINION Q. 123 (1980).

10. Unfortunately, the *prevalence* of views regarding euthanasia can be determined from the General Social Survey but not the *intensity* with which the views are held. Intensity, however, is almost certainly an important variable affecting the likelihood that social values will be translated into law.

11. Johnson, Fitch, Alston, & McIntosh, *Acceptance of Conditional Suicide and Euthanasia among Adult Americans*, 10 SUICIDE & LIFE-THREATENING BEHAVIOR 157, 160 (1980).

12. Finlay, *Right to Life vs. The Right to Die: Some Correlates of Euthanasia Attitudes*, 69 SOC. & SOCIAL RES. 548 (1985); Ostheimer & Moore, *"The Correlates of Attitudes Toward Euthanasia" Revisited*, 28 SOCIAL BIOLOGY 145 (1981); Singh, *Correlates of Attitudes Toward Euthanasia*, 26 SOCIAL BIOLOGY 247 (1979).

13. J. ALDRICH & F. NELSON, LINEAR PROBABILITY, LOGIT, AND PROBIT MODELS (1984) (Sage University Paper Series: Quantitative Applications in the Social Sciences).

14. Ward, *Age and Acceptance of Euthanasia*, 25 J. GERONTOLOGY 421 (1980). The study reported no difference in findings when it utilized responses to the single question on euthanasia that is being considered in this chapter. When examining

the question by itself, however, the study evidently dichotomized respondents. *Id.* at 423. Path analysis may be applied to a dichotomous dependent variable, but the data for that variable should be in a nonlinear form. *See* Winship & Mare, *Structural Equations and Path Analysis for Discrete Data*, 54 AM. J. SOC. 54 (1983). Such a form seems not to have been used in the study by Ward.

15. Since responses to the question on euthanasia may be influenced by the presence or absence of a "don't know" alternative, a probit specification is preferable to a logit specification. L. SAYRS, POOLED TIME SERIES ANALYSIS 58–59 (1989) (Sage University Paper Series: Quantitative Applications in the Social Sciences).

Probit equations were estimated without a weight for the number of adults in the household of each interviewee. The General Social Survey gives every household in the United States the same probability of being included in the sample and every eligible individual within a selected household the same probability of being chosen for an interview. C. Stephenson, Weighting the General Social Surveys for Bias Related to Household Size (GSS Technical Report No. 3, February 1978). However, an individual residing in a large household that is selected for the sample has a lower probability of being chosen for an interview than an individual in a small household. A weight for the number of adults in the household can in principle compensate for the unequal probabilities, but weighted estimates of population parameters are in general less efficient than unweighted estimates.

16. Data on attitudes toward euthanasia were available for 1991, but the year was omitted because the Survey changed its scale for one of the independent variables in the regression analysis, viz., occupational prestige.

17. American Board of Family Practice. Perspectives on Middle Age: The Vintage Years (1990) (telephone survey with a 48% response rate conducted in 1989 with a national sample of 1200 adults selected by a modified probability sampling procedure).

18. Prestige was measured for all respondents who had worked a minimum of one year even though they were not currently employed or were no longer employed. The analysis thus included persons who were out of a job and persons who had retired.

19. *Cf.* Faia, *Selection by Certification: A Neglected Variable in Stratification Research*, 86 AM. J. SOC. 1093 (1981); Goodman, *The Economic Returns of Education: An Assessment of Alternative Models*, 60 SOCIAL SCI. Q. 269 (1979).

20. The distribution of religious preference in the General Social Survey indicates that the grouping would encompass only 8% of American adults in the years being studied.

21. The Gallup Poll did not employ probability sampling until 1950. 1 G. GALLUP, THE GALLUP POLL: PUBLIC OPINION 1935–1971 vi–viii (1972). In 1950, the Poll utilized the question on euthanasia, but the report of its findings combines responses to this and a second question on the subject. 2 G. GALLUP, THE GALLUP POLL: PUBLIC OPINION 1935–1971 887–88 (1972). Fortunately, some data from the 1950 survey are available for the euthanasia question being considered in the present chapter. Ostheimer, *supra* note 9, at 126. While these data are

restricted to the proportions favoring euthanasia (i.e., no information is provided on respondents opposing the practice and respondents without an opinion), a remarkable similarity exists in the distribution of responses to the 1947 and 1950 polls. *Id.* Since only three years elapsed between the two polls, it is likely that the similarity is the result of little attitudinal change over the interval and that the 1947 poll depicts the attitudes of Americans toward euthanasia with reasonable accuracy.

22. The proportions appearing in table 6.3 are not weighted by the number of adults in the household. See *supra* note 15. However, weighted proportions differed from the unweighted proportions shown in the table by no more than 2 percentage points.

23. In 1984 and 1988, the Gallup Poll asked the following question: "On the whole, do you think most white people want to see blacks get a better break, or do they want to keep blacks down, or don't you think they care either way?" The view that most Whites desired "to keep blacks down" was endorsed by 41% of Blacks in 1984 but by only 24% of Blacks in 1988. G. GALLUP, THE GALLUP POLL: PUBLIC OPINION 1989 234–35 (1990).

24. G. Firebaugh, Components of Change in Gender Role Attitudes, 1972–1988 (March 25, 1990) (unpublished paper presented at the 1990 annual meeting of the Population Ass'n of America); Firebaugh, *Where Does Social Change Come From? Estimating the Relative Contributions of Individual Change and Population Turnover*, 11 POPULATION RES. & POL'Y REV. 1 (1992). Respondents having no opinion were excluded from the analysis.

I would like to thank William Gould at the Computing Resource Center for writing the program for Stata that I used to generate the estimates.

25. The coefficient of variation is often expressed as a percentage, but table 6.4 specifies just the ratio of the standard deviation to the mean. The ratio can be converted to a percentage by multiplying it by 100.

26. Research has found that aging does not generally alter views on social issues. Danigelis & Cutler, *Cohort Trends in Attitudes About Law and Order: Who's Leading the Conservative Wave?*, 55 PUB. OPINION Q. 24 (1991); Danigelis & Cutler, *An Inter-Cohort Comparison of Changes in Racial Attitudes*, 13 RES. ON AGING 383 (1991). As a result, the aging that will accompany population succession should not affect trends in public opinion concerning euthanasia.

27. 18 PA. CONS. STAT. ANN. § 2505(b) (Purdon 1983). During the 1970s, two other states adopted statutes directly bearing on euthanasia, viz., New Jersey and Texas. N.J. STAT. ANN. § 2C:11–6 (West 1982); TEX. PENAL CODE ANN. § 22.08 (Vernon 1989). The two states are not considered here because of a lack of data on all of the factors that served as control variables in the regression analysis presented *infra*.

28. Suicide frequencies were obtained from *Vital Statistics of the United States*.

29. Steffensmeier, *Suicide and the Contemporary Woman: Are Male and Female Suicide Rates Converging?*, 10 SEX ROLES 613 (1984); Stafford & Weisheit, *Changing Age Patterns of U.S. Male and Female Suicide Rates, 1934–1983*, 18 SUICIDE & LIFE-THREATENING BEHAVIOR 149 (1988).

30. Population estimates were obtained from *Current Population Reports* Series P-25.

31. Ideally, both the year that starts and the year that closes a time series should have a theoretical justification. Isaac & Griffin, *Ahistoricism in Time-Series Analyses of Historical Process: Critique, Redirection, and Illustrations from U.S. Labor History*, 54 AM. SOC. REV. 873 (1989). In the present analysis, the beginning of the time series was unavoidably arbitrary (see *infra* note 32), and maximizing model fit therefore seemed preferable to seeking an end point based on theory.

32. Income data were drawn from *State Personal Income, 1929–81: Revised Estimates*, 62 SURV. CURRENT BUS. 48 (Aug. 1982) and from *State Personal Income, 1969–86: Revised Estimates*, 67 SURV. CURRENT BUS. 43 (Aug. 1987).

Data on marital dissolutions were taken from annual issues of *Vital Statistics of the United States*. Data for persons age 65 and older commence in 1963; the latter year thus became the starting date for the time series.

33. Ahlburg, *Socioeconomic Ramifications of Changing Cohort Size: An Analysis of U.S. Postwar Suicide Rates by Age and Sex*, 21 DEMOGRAPHY 97 (1984); Breault, *Suicide in America: A Test of Durkheim's Theory of Religious and Family Integration, 1933–1980*, 92 AM. J. SOC. 628 (1986); Kowalski, Faupel, & Starr, *Urbanism and Suicide: A Study of American Counties*, 66 SOCIAL FORCES 85 (1987); Wasserman, *A Longitudinal Analysis of the Linkage Between Suicide, Unemployment, and Marital Dissolution*, 46 J. MARR. & FAM. 853 (1984).

Research has identified additional factors that affect the suicide rate, but the research has aggregated all age groups or has studied age groups other than the elderly. These factors were omitted from my analysis either because they seemed irrelevant to suicide among the elderly (as in the case of unemployment) and/or because state-level data on them were lacking.

34. SUBCOMM. ON ECONOMIC GOALS & INTERGOVERNMENTAL POLICY, JOINT ECONOMIC COMM., 98TH CONG., 2D SESS., ESTIMATING THE EFFECTS OF ECONOMIC CHANGE ON NATIONAL HEALTH AND SOCIAL WELL-BEING 67 (Joint Comm. Print 98–198, 1984) (prepared by M. Brenner).

35. In November 1991, voters in the state of Washington rejected an initiative to legalize assisted suicide. S. Initiative 119, 52nd Leg., 1991 Reg. Sess., Wash. The margin by which the initiative was defeated, however, was not large: 54% of the voters opposed the proposal but 46% favored it. *Voters Turn Down Legal Euthanasia*, NEW YORK TIMES, Nov. 7, 1991, at B16. Politically, the outcome can be attributed to an expensive media campaign that was mounted against the initiative during the last few weeks before the election. *Opponents of Euthanasia Measure Gain Ground in Washington State*, NEW YORK TIMES, Nov. 4, 1991, at A16.

A measure that would have made active euthanasia lawful in California was defeated by the same margin (54 to 46%) in the November 1992 election. *California Voters Reject 9 of 13 Ballot Measures*, SAN FRANCISCO CHRONICLE, Nov. 5, 1992, at A15.

CHAPTER

7

Issues for Research and Theory

It has been my objective in this book to decipher the role of legal doctrine in American society, and to this end I have brought together what I believe to be the best quantitative research and statistical data available on the issue. The evidence is sufficient, I think, to warrant at least a few conclusions with reasonable assurance of their accuracy, and I hope those I have reached will advance our understanding of legal thought as a societal phenomenon. I realize, however, that a number of my arguments are likely to encounter resistance because they challenge assumptions that are deeply entrenched in academic and political circles. This is especially the case with the contention that law—or, more exactly, regulation—does not appreciably influence social processes and correct social problems; the contention is counter to a belief that has characterized Americans for at least a quarter-century and will probably be regarded with considerable skepticism.[1] Doubt should not be surprising, though, because established beliefs of any sort are never displaced easily. Therefore, I can only hope that legal scholars and social scientists will recognize the thesis I have outlined is supported by a substantial body of credible evidence; that they will find the thesis sufficiently promising to investigate it further; and that they will gradually accept the thesis as additional corroborating evidence appears.

By now, the reader will recognize that, as I stated in the first chapter, the book presents no more than a rudimentary theoretical framework and that a tightly knit theory of wide scope regarding the societal functions of legal thought is still to be constructed. Such a theory seems to have been attempted just once in recent years,[2] and it has been severely criticized on both theoretical and empirical grounds.[3] Given the serious social problems confronting the United States, it is regrettable a theory cannot be developed today. However, we simply do not know enough to write a macrosociological theory of law—at least one that will generate a large number of empirically supportable hypotheses—and we will not have the necessary knowledge until considerably more research has been conducted on a broad range of topics. Admittedly, I may be overly cautious in believing that attempts at theory construction are premature. But if those attempts are made and are unsuccessful, social scientists and legal scholars may be discouraged from undertaking work that would produce meaningful, albeit undramatic, progress toward a theory. Excessively ambitious efforts to build theory may therefore involve significant costs.

Our goal, nonetheless, is and should continue to be a theory of the societal role of jurisprudence—a theory that explains and predicts the many varieties of legal thought, the many situations in which such thought is found, and the many changes such thought experiences. The preceding chapters thus represent just an early step in a long journey, and if we are to be successful in that journey, a series of issues must be studied and resolved. Since the substance of my thesis has now been fully presented, it is appropriate to devote some attention to the most salient of these issues. I will deal first with issues suggested by social science research and then turn to issues identifiable on theoretical grounds.

THEORETICAL ISSUES THAT ARISE FROM EXISTING RESEARCH

Perhaps the most general of the issues arising from research involves the difference between patterns and processes that are *social* in character and those that are *economic*. The distinction between social and economic phenomena is important because my thesis is concerned only with the former. Social patterns and processes are the arrangements and forms of human interaction in a group that has a relatively impermeable boundary. Such a group—i.e., a society—contains established, complementary modes for interchanges between people that maintain group equilibrium. Configurations of human relationships are thus inherent in a society, and this book focuses on them and on the behavior of the individual that implicates them.

The social sphere, however, is conceptually distinct from the economic arena—from the medium of exchange and the possessions and skills (i.e., the wealth) for which the medium is used. While social problems are largely unresponsive to regulation by the legal system, the medium of exchange and arrangements for increasing wealth apparently can be controlled by law in some circumstances. For instance, the federal government is able to determine the cost of borrowing money and thus influence the incidence of unemployment;[4] states can affect the productivity of publicly owned resources such as fisheries by determining the manner in which those resources are utilized.[5] Research with longitudinal data extending over a substantial time period has not consistently found other economic matters to be responsive to legal intervention,[6] and further study will be required to identify the types of economic events on which law has an impact.[7] Nonetheless, those events seem to be more amenable than social events to legal controls.

Given the importance of the distinction between social and economic phenomena, the boundary of each must be clearly located, a task that is particularly important for societal problems that include both. Such problems are not infrequent, and for purposes of illustration, I mention three of them. The first is the problem of poverty and government policies to alleviate it: "Welfare" programs, as they are popularly known, provide financial assistance to poor persons—an economic process—but over time they have not had a consistent effect on the incidence of poverty[8]—a phenomenon that seems to result largely from a social process.[9] The second illustration concerns the problem of housing and policies adopted by the federal government to promote home ownership. Whether or not housing is owned by its occupants is in part an economic matter because of the financial costs of ownership; the prevalence of home ownership has therefore been affected by the federal government through tax policy. However, ownership is also tied to factors such as marital status, number of children, and place of residence (farm versus nonfarm)[10]—factors that are social in nature and that are resistant to modification by law. The third illustration arises from the need of the federal government for revenue and the annual tax levied by Congress on individual income. The revenue that is raised involves not only the receipt of money by government but also the reporting of taxable income by individuals. However, the amount of revenue obtained by government—an economic process—implicates different considerations than the voluntary reporting of taxable income—a social process. By manipulating the subjects taxed and the rates charged, Congress can determine the amount of revenue that the federal government receives, but the extent to which persons are willing to divulge the existence of taxable income that has not been reported by others to the Internal Revenue Service is affected by social structure and values rather than by law and its enforcement.[11] Thus, the proportion of persons who understate the amount of money they owe in taxes is large and rising, a situation that probably stems from increasing societal complexity and diversity. In 1982, more than one out of seven returns submitted to the Internal Revenue Service failed to report income in amounts exceeding $500.[12]

Law, then, appears capable of influencing the course of at least some economic phenomena even though its impact on social conditions is small in magnitude and/or brief in duration. But law may be useful for more than just economic patterns and processes, and the areas in which law is beneficial must be identified. There is evidence, for example, that the legal system can produce desired results when it mandates the installation or application of existing technology: Improvements that the law has required in the structural safety of automobiles seem to have reduced fatalities from motor vehicle accidents,[13] and alterations that the law insisted be made in the chemical composition of gasoline and in the design of automobile engines have evidently curbed air pollution.[14] At the same time, however, law can have detrimental effects on technology, since some types of regulation deter technological development.[15] Probably because the growth of knowledge is a social process, technological innovation may be damaged by legal controls. In the area of technology, therefore, law can produce mixed results.

Technology is not, of course, the only area in which intervention by the legal system can produce unanticipated and/or negative side effects. Social affairs also experience such effects from legal doctrine. For example, the U.S. Supreme Court decision in 1954 that the Constitution is violated by racially segregated public schools apparently caused a measurable, though brief, reduction in fertility in the South;[16] in addition, as noted in chapter 2, judicially instigated efforts to eliminate that segregation led a substantial number of white students to withdraw from public schools. Unfortunately, research rarely considers whether law directed to social matters produces unexpected and/or unwelcome side effects; the concern is almost always with the question of whether law has achieved its *desired* ends. We thus do not know when and how often side effects occur. Yet such information is critical to a theory of law; indeed, a theory will not be useful unless it allows us to understand and anticipate these effects.

Theory, however, must deal not only with the presence of results that are unexpected and/or unwanted; it must explain as well the absence of effects that are desired. Theory must therefore account for the failure of the many attempts that have been made in recent decades to use law to remedy social ills. That failure, I believe, is attributable to societal characteristics. To illustrate, when reviewing employer decisions to determine if there has been a violation of a statute banning sex or race discrimination, courts accord greater latitude to decisions that involve white-collar positions than to decisions that involve blue-collar positions.[17] The less-searching judicial scrutiny of decisions regarding white-collar jobs probably exists because the greater self-direction and intellectual flexibility associated with these jobs[18] makes candidates for them more difficult to evaluate. The ineffectiveness of legislation that prohibits discrimination in employment can therefore be explained partially by the character of white-collar occupations in the American economic system and the large and growing number of such occupations in that system.[19]

We come now to a closely related matter: At the same time we deal with the inability of regulation to alter social patterns, we must also account for the fact that our social system has relied heavily on this type of law and that the reliance continues even though the intended purposes of the law are not being achieved. Is the persistent use of a form of law that does not accomplish its express objective simply the product of human inertia? I think not. While inertia cannot be excluded as a factor, a more fundamental reason is probably that regulatory law serves some societal need. But what need does such law meet and how does it do so? The answer, I suspect, is that regulation promotes societal cohesiveness in part by providing a symbol that increases identification with the social system. Law makes people feel the system cares about their problems and endorses their values. Even though regulatory law is generally ineffective for modifying the social behavior to which it is directed, it is a symbol that increases commitment to society. Its role in this regard probably grows in importance as a population becomes more heterogeneous culturally, specialized occupationally, and dispersed geographically.

The nature (and extent) of the impact of law is unquestionably one of the central issues raised by this book, and as the preceding discussion indicates, the issue has a number of facets. I would like to mention two more of these facets here. First, the ineffectiveness of regulatory measures for social processes should not lead us to assume that all approaches adopted by the legal system are ineffective for these processes. In particular, there seems to be a marked influence on some social patterns when law provides individuals with the means to attain culturally prized goals. Theory must identify these means and the types of social processes on which they have an impact. Present research suggests that the means include government-supplied financial assistance that allows retirement, access to health care, and home ownership.[20] Also effective are legally mandated television and radio commercials describing the deleterious health consequences of smoking; by disseminating information that permits individuals to maintain good health, an important social value in the United States, the commercials reduce tobacco consumption.[21]

A second aspect of the impact of law should also be noted: Regulation, while normally unable to influence broad social patterns, can *occasionally* do so. The propositions I have advanced are generalizations, and in certain circumstances, government regulation may substantially alter social behavior. Statutes allowing the dissolution of a marriage without evidence of fault, for example, may have appreciably increased the divorce rate in a small number of states even though they had little or no influence in most jurisdictions.[22] Because deviant cases will allow us to refine generalizations, the conditions under which law has a marked effect on social issues must be identified. I suspect that one factor relevant to those conditions is social change: As change persists and/or as its rate escalates, law can increasingly act as a barrier to fulfilling social needs, and the revision of legal doctrine can permit these needs to be met. In all probability, however, social change that persists does not continue to augment the ability of law to shape events; as a society changes, individuals seem likely to learn how to evade legal requirements that frustrate achievement of their goals. In such situations, the relationship between social change and the impact of law would be nonlinear and would take the form of an inverted U. Alternatively, the relationship could involve a threshold: Change may have to reach a certain level before law can affect social processes. Unfortunately, the exact nature of the relationship is presently uncertain, but a theory of law, to be useful, must specify it.

We turn finally to a pair of related issues suggested by existing research. The first involves lags between the point in time when a belief is accepted by most members of the public and the point in time when legal doctrine emerges that is consistent with the belief; the second involves legal doctrine that develops before the public generally endorses it. The two issues have a common thread: Each focuses on the question of how social values mold law. With regard to time lags, substantial delays seem to be common. For example, by 1954 an overwhelming majority of Americans accepted the principle that women and men with equivalent jobs should receive equal compensation,[23] but federal legislation mandating such equality was not enacted until 1963.[24] The length of time required for legal doctrine to reflect popular opinion probably differs across subjects, and theory must provide the reasons that lags vary. Two likely reasons are the intensity with which the majority is committed to a belief and the degree to which the subject of a belief implicates strongly held societal values: lag length probably becomes shorter as a belief intensifies and as the subject of the belief rises on the scale of social values.

More intriguing, however, is the second issue—legal doctrines that are adopted even though they are not supported by a majority of the public. An illustration of such a situation is abortion.[25] What accounts for the appearance of law that does not have the approval of most members of society? I suspect that part of the answer is to be found in the ideologies of important societal components: Those ideologies may remain constant in the face of shifting social needs, and when social values and social needs do not coincide, social needs probably take precedence in determining the content of law. If so, an effective theory of the societal functions of legal doctrine will necessarily identify the impact on social values of the ideologies of central social institutions (e.g., the family and religion) and the circumstances in which social needs become inconsistent with social values and produce legal doctrine.

A PRIORI THEORETICAL ISSUES

We turn now to issues that I believe will be important to a theory of legal thought even though current social science research does not clearly suggest them. Strictly on logical grounds, it would seem that the issues must be addressed before a useful theory can be developed.

I begin with the conceptual distinction between societal *conditions* and societal *needs*. The former are phenomena that reduce the efficiency and effectiveness of a society; the latter are requirements of a social system that must be satisfied if the system is to maintain itself. The distinction is important because law reflects societal needs directly and societal conditions only indirectly. More specifically, legal doctrine stems from societal conditions that have created societal needs. However, the metamorphosis of a societal condition into a societal need is not automatic: A societal condition (e.g., gender discrimination in employment) may be present, but a social system may not have a need to solve it. To complicate matters, not all aspects of a societal condition may be translated into a need. For example, there may not be a societal need to rectify the economic consequences of gender discrimination in employment because the social system provides alternative forms of compensation to the disadvantaged sex, but there may be a need to reduce the alienation accompanying the discrimination.

In general terms, how can we describe when a societal condition generates a societal need? The answer would seem to have two parts: A need arises at the point where a condition impairs the equilibrium of the social system; and such impairment occurs when a condition reaches a certain threshold of prevalence and/or intensity and exists in a particular type of social-economic setting. However, societal conditions are not all of the same type, and theory must identify the different thresholds and settings required to produce societal needs and, in turn, legal doctrine.[26] Theory must also specify the impact of social values on the process. Thus, a societal need for greater predictability in human interactions develops and leads to legal doctrine requiring psychotherapists to warn of likely violence by their patients when violence frequency, social-economic milieu, and social values combine in some as yet unknown manner. Theory must describe the role of each and the way(s) in which they interact to produce law.

The development of legal doctrine is complicated further by the fact that law is not the sole form of ideology on which a social system relies in attempting to satisfy its needs. Other types of doctrine exist as well; among them are religious beliefs—which continue to be widespread in the United States[27]—and beliefs about the basis and justice of socioeconomic stratification. This raises another issue with which theory will be required to deal: A theory of the social functions of law must specify the circumstances in which legal doctrine responds to societal needs as well as the circumstances in which other types of doctrine do so. A theory of legal thought cannot, in short, be confined to legal thought.

What is such a theory likely to show? Given the present state of research, I can only speculate, and my speculation will undoubtedly omit more relevant factors than it includes. Nonetheless, I suspect that legal doctrine is utilized more readily, and other forms of ideology less readily, in a society that is culturally diverse than in a society that is culturally homogeneous. Moreover, there is likely to be more frequent reliance on legal thought, and less frequent reliance on other sources of ideology, as the rate of social change rises. Cultural diversity and/or rapid change would seem to strain social cohesiveness and reduce the predictability of behavior throughout a society. In this situation, legal doctrine would become more important because law is the only societal institution with formal responsibility for the needs of the entire social system. If only as a symbol, law serves as a centripetal force in a society.

This brings us to a related matter. I have thus far discussed legal doctrine as if it had a single source. That, of course, is not the case. Legal thought is found in constitutional provisions, statutes, regulations, and court decisions; courts, moreover, not only interpret the other sources but also fashion the common law. Since one source of law rather than another may act to meet a social need and/or since one source may be forced to displace another, it will be important for theory to treat each source of law separately and specify which responds when a particular type of social need is present. For instance, theory must permit us to understand when a legal doctrine that serves a social need will be manifested in legislation rather than in common law; in the invalidation of a statute on constitutional grounds rather than in rescission of the statute by the legislature; and in the interpretation of a statute by a court rather than in a regulation adopted under the statute by an administrative agency. The use of one source rather than another is not simply chance, and theory must identify the types of societal needs for which each is utilized.

The matter is complicated still further by the organization of our governmental system. Both state and federal governments have, and utilize, each source of law, but it is not certain that a given source (e.g., legislation) possesses exactly the same social functions at each level. The societal role of legal doctrine is not necessarily identical for the two governmental structures,[28] and a source of law may thus operate somewhat differently at the state and federal levels. Among the states, moreover, a source may vary in the functions it performs. States differ in a host of ways, and it is unclear whether, let alone how, these differences influence the social purposes of legal doctrine.

Let me turn now to another theoretical issue on which future work should focus: the role of socioeconomic stratification in the development of legal doctrine. Stratification is evidently a central feature of all social systems, and the manner in which it is linked to law remains the subject of speculation and debate among legal scholars and social scientists. Quantitative research is therefore desirable on the question of whether stratification is merely a mechanism that responds to other factors and triggers law or whether it operates as an independent cause of legal doctrine. My belief is that stratification in the United States operates primarily as a trigger: The segments of the stratification network most directly implicated by a societal need generate the legal doctrine that is required to express the need. However, in some circumstances, segments of the stratification structure may cause the legal system to misfire and produce unneeded doctrine. Since that law can be expected to undergo modification, these circumstances must be identified. In this regard, cross-national research may find that different systems of stratification affect the frequency with which unneeded law is produced in a society.

I thus arrive at the final issue that I believe theory must confront. The societal functions of law require investigation in a range of nation-states in order to determine whether they are altered by different demographic, economic, social, and technological settings. To illustrate, coercive governmental policies to decrease family size may be effective in China,[29] but they are unlikely to work in the United States.[30] To take another example, the frequency of abortion increased in The Netherlands from the mid-1970s until the early 1980s, when the statutory grounds for pregnancy termination were liberalized, and then declined.[31] In Romania, the imposition in 1966 of restrictions on access to abortion dramatically altered abortion numbers and fertility rates, depressing the former and raising the latter.[32] Legislation on abortion thus seemed to reflect established social patterns in The Netherlands but not in Romania, an inconsistency that is probably attributable to the difference in social organization accompanying the greater urbanization and more-developed technological state of the former.[33] However, even in Romania, the impact of legal doctrine may have been substantial only in the short run, for the period during which the restrictive abortion policy in that country had a material effect on childbearing appears to have been relatively brief.[34]

CONCLUSION

In ending, I would like to underscore three points. First, this book has been concerned with just one aspect of the legal system—viz., its doctrines and their role in society. Legal doctrines, however, are a salient feature of social life and are unquestionably essential to a society. The social functions of law therefore merit investigation in their own right. Regrettably, popular assumptions of doubtful accuracy currently exist about these functions, and the assumptions seem to be a substitute for an empirically grounded theory.

Second, while a theory is needed, the theory we formulate must be *useful*—i.e., it must accurately predict observations yet to be made and not merely provide interesting, intuitively appealing explanations of what has been observed already. Since a plausible explanation can always be devised for an observation, the key attribute of an effective theory is the ability to predict with a minimum of error. For the social functions of legal doctrine, unfortunately, such a theory is not on the horizon and cannot be constructed until major problems are resolved.

Third, because it is not a possibility in the foreseeable future, there may be a temptation to conclude that a useful theory of the societal role of law is at best unlikely and at worst unachievable. The conclusion is neither warranted nor wise. The data sets and statistical techniques possessed by the social sciences have improved significantly in recent years, and they will continue to do so. The belief that a macrosociological theory of law is not probable or not possible overlooks the potential for future advances in these disciplines, and I am confident that in time they will provide sufficient information to write the theory. Accordingly, much will be gained and nothing will be lost in having as our objective a theory of the societal functions of legal thought—as long as we proceed toward the objective gradually and avoid rash speculation. Our reach, as someone once said, should exceed our grasp. It is advice that is sound, at least if we proceed carefully and take only well-considered steps.

NOTES

1. Perhaps it is appropriate here to mention that my thesis should not be interpreted to discourage or disparage careers in government-funded social services. Persons delivering such services—whether through social work, law,

medicine, or a related profession—may not significantly reduce the prevalence of the problems to which they are devoting their lives, but they can assist individuals who are experiencing serious difficulties. That assistance is justifiable in its own right.

2. Simon & Lynch, *The Sociology of Law: Where We Have Been and Where We Might Be Going*, 23 LAW & SOC'Y REV. 825, 841 (1989). That attempt, according to Simon and Lynch, was D. BLACK, THE BEHAVIOR OF LAW (1976).

3. Braithwaite & Biles, *Empirical Verification and Black's The Behavior of Law*, 45 AM. SOC. REV. 334 (1980); Doyle & Luckenbill, *Mobilizing Law in Response to Collective Problems: A Test of Black's Theory of Law*, 25 LAW & SOC'Y REV. 103 (1991); Gottfredson & Hindelang, *A Study of The Behavior of Law*, 44 AM. SOC. REV. 3 (1979); Gottfredson & Hindelang, *Theory and Research in the Sociology of Law*, 44 AM. SOC. REV. 27 (1979); Greenberg, *Donald Black's Sociology of Law: A Critique*, 17 LAW & SOC'Y REV. 337 (1983); Lessan & Sheley, *Does Law Behave? A Macrolevel Test of Black's Propositions on Change in Law*, 70 SOCIAL FORCES 655 (1992); Mooney, *The Behavior of Law in a Private Legal System*, 64 SOCIAL FORCES 733 (1986); Myers, *Predicting the Behavior of Law: A Test of Two Models*, 14 LAW & SOC'Y REV. 835 (1980).

One attempt to test the theory produced results that were described by the investigator as "somewhat inconclusive." Staples, *Law and Social Control in Juvenile Justice Dispositions*, 24 J. RES. CRIME & DELINQ. 7, 17 (1987). One study has generally corroborated the theory. Hembroff, *The Seriousness of Acts and Social Contexts: A Test of Black's Theory of the Behavior of Law*, 93 AM. J. SOC. 322 (1987).

4. Chappell & Keech, *The Unemployment Rate Consequences of Partisan Monetary Policies*, 55 SO. ECON. J. 107 (1988).

5. Agnello & Donnelley, *Regulation and the Structure of Property Rights: The Case of the U.S. Oyster Industry*, *in* 6 RESEARCH IN LAW AND ECONOMICS 267 (R. Zerbe ed., 1984).

6. *Compare* Ippolito, *A Study of the Regulatory Effect of the Employee Retirement Income Security Act*, 31 J. LAW & ECON. 85 (1988) *with* Caldeira, *Changing the Common Law: Effects of the Decline of Charitable Immunity*, 16 LAW & SOC'Y REV. 669 (1981–82).

7. Law will not always have beneficial effects on economic phenomena. For example, it appears that employment is reduced and unemployment is increased by government policies mandating severance pay for employees. E. Lazear, Job Security Provisions and Employment (1989).

8. Sanders, *Public Transfers: Safety Net or Inducement into Poverty?*, 68 SOCIAL FORCES 813 (1990).

9. Moffitt, *Incentive Effects of the U.S. Welfare System: A Review*, 30 J. ECON. LITERATURE 1 (1992). *See* Fomby & Hayes, *An Intervention Analysis of the War on Poverty: Poverty's Persistence and Political-Business Cycle Implications*, 43 J. ECONOMETRICS 197 (1990).

10. Chevan, *The Growth of Home Ownership: 1940–1980*, 26 DEMOGRAPHY 249 (1989).

11. K. KINSEY & K. SMITH, INCOME TAX CHEATING: OPPORTUNITIES, PREFERENCES AND SANCTIONS (American Bar Foundation Working Paper No. 8718,

1986); Yankelovich, Skelly & White, Inc., Taxpayer Attitudes Study: Final Report (Dec. 1984) (available from the Compliance Measurement Group, Assistant Commissioner for Planning, Finance, and Research, Internal Revenue Service, Washington, D.C.).

12. American Bar Ass'n Comm'n on Taxpayer Compliance, *Report and Recommendations on Taxpayer Compliance*, 41 TAX LAWYER 329, 335, 343 (1988).

13. *Compare* Crandall & Graham, *Automobile Safety Regulation and Offsetting Behavior: Some New Empirical Estimates*, 74 AM. ECON. REV. 328 (May 1984) *with* Graham & Garber, *Evaluating the Effects of Automobile Safety Regulation*, 3 J. POL'Y ANALYSIS & MGMT. 206 (1984).

During the time that automobiles with legally prescribed safety features were becoming more prevalent, Congress enacted legislation requiring states to establish a maximum speed for motor vehicles of 55 miles per hour in order to receive financial assistance from the federal government for the construction of roads, streets, and highways. Pub. L. 93–239, 87 Stat. 1046 (1974); Pub. L. 93–643, 88 Stat. 2286 (1975). However, while the legislation may have curtailed to some extent the speed at which automobiles and trucks traveled, it had no effect on deaths from motor vehicle operation. Once the increasing safety of automobiles is taken into account, there is no evidence that the 55 mile per hour speed limit reduced traffic fatalities among automobile occupants or pedestrians. Crandall & Graham, *supra* at 329. One study concluded that the 55 mile per hour maximum avoided a large number of fatalities. Forester, McNown & Singell, *A Cost-Benefit Analysis of the 55 MPH Speed Limit*, 50 SO. ECON. J. 631 (1984). Unfortunately, the study failed to control in its statistical analysis for the greater safety of automobiles on the road; the decline in fatalities that was attributed by the study to the 55 mile per hour speed limit evidently resulted from improvements in vehicle safety mandated by law.

14. Box & Tiao, *Intervention Analysis with Applications to Economic and Environmental Problems*, 70 J. AM. STATISTICAL ASS'N 70 (1975).

15. Grabowski, Vernon & Thomas, *Estimating the Effects of Regulation on Innovation: An International Comparative Analysis of the Pharmaceutical Industry*, 21 J. LAW & ECON. 133 (1978).

16. Rindfuss, Reed, & St. John, *A Fertility Reaction to a Historical Event: Southern White Birthrates and the 1954 Desegregation Ruling*, 201 SCI. 178 (July 14, 1978); Rindfuss, Salemi, Reed, & St. John, *Intervention Analysis: The Supreme Court and Hogan*, 21 DEMOGRAPHY 679 (1984).

17. B. SCHLEI & P. GROSSMAN, EMPLOYMENT DISCRIMINATION LAW 199 (2d ed. 1983); D. CATHCART & R. ASHE, FIVE-YEAR CUMULATIVE SUPPLEMENT TO SCHLEI & GROSSMAN'S EMPLOYMENT DISCRIMINATION LAW 57–58 (1989).

18. Kohn, Naoi, Schoenbach, Schooler, & Slomczynski, *Position in the Class Structure and Psychological Functioning in the United States, Japan, and Poland*, 95 AM. J. SOC. 964 (1990).

19. Singelmann & Tienda, *The Process of Occupational Change in a Service Society: The Case of the United States, 1960–80*, *in* NEW APPROACHES TO ECONOMIC LIFE 48 (B. Roberts, R. Finnegan, & D. Gallie eds., 1985).

20. Chevan, *supra* note 10, and the references in note 39 in chapter 2.

21. Schneider, Klein, & Murphy, *Governmental Regulation of Cigarette Health Information*, 24 J. LAW & ECON. 575 (1981). A federal statute that prohibited cigarette advertising on television and radio, on the other hand, may have caused an increase in tobacco consumption. *Id.*

22. Marvell, *Divorce Rates and the Fault Requirement*, 23 LAW & SOC'Y REV. 543 (1989).

23. G. GALLUP, 2 THE GALLUP POLL: PUBLIC OPINION 1935–1971 1240 (1972).

24. Equal Pay Act of 1963, Pub. L. 88–38, 77 Stat. 56 (codified at 29 U.S.C. §206(d) (1982)).

25. Marshall, *The Supreme Court as an Opinion Leader*, 15 AM. POLITICS Q. 147, 164 (1987).

26. In doing so, theory will be forced to recognize the large-scale forces that alter society and transform law. As I argued in chapter 2, two forces that seem to be important to numerous areas of legal thought are the volume of knowledge that a society utilizes and the level of population density that a society possesses. But whatever the relevant forces, they must be specified because they are essential to explaining and predicting broad movements in law—movements that seem to have been studied thus far through verbal descriptions of historically interesting episodes but that should be subjected to rigorous quantitative analyses, e.g., analyses of pooled time-series data on different countries.

27. Hadden, *Toward Desacralizing Secularization Theory*, 65 SOCIAL FORCES 587, 599–603 (1987).

28. For a study suggesting the differences are important, see McCubbins & Schwartz, *Congress, the Courts, and Public Policy: Consequences of the One Man, One Vote Rule*, 32 AM. J. POL. SCI. 388 (1988).

29. A. Coale & R. Freedman, Fertility Change in the People's Republic of China and Selected Other East Asian Populations: Similarities and Differences (paper presented at the 1989 meeting of the International Union for the Scientific Study of Population).

30. Some years ago I authored a book arguing that law could appreciably reduce fertility and alleviate population pressures in the United States. L. BARNETT, POPULATION POLICY AND THE U.S. CONSTITUTION (1982). Given the evidence that has been reviewed in the preceding chapters on the inability of law to change social patterns, I now realize I was wrong to believe that the legal system could contribute significantly to solving what is clearly a serious problem, i.e., domestic overpopulation. In my defense, however, I should point out that the book was completed in the first half of 1981 and that the present work rests on research the vast majority of which was published subsequently.

31. The new statute was enacted in 1981 but not enforced until late 1984. It replaced a measure adopted in 1886 and amended in 1911. Rademakers, *Induced Abortion in The Netherlands, in* INTERNATIONAL HANDBOOK ON ABORTION 333 (P. Sachdev ed., 1988).

The number of abortions per 1000 women 15–44 years of age is estimated by one source to have been 5.5 in 1977, 6.7 in 1980, 6.5 in 1981, 6.3 in 1982, 5.9 in 1983, and 5.6 in 1984. *Id.* at 342. Estimates of the number of abortions performed on residents of The Netherlands are between 15,000 and 15,500 for 1975; 19,700 and 21,300 for 1980; 19,500 and 21,100 for 1981; 18,700 for 1984; and 18,250 for 1986. Letters from Frans L. Leeuw to Larry D. Barnett (May 8, 1988 and June 1, 1988). I am indebted to Dr. Leeuw, director of the Department of Policy Evaluation Research at The Netherlands Court of Audit, for providing the materials on which this discussion is based.

32. Teitelbaum, *Fertility Effects of the Abolition of Legal Abortion in Romania*, 27 POPULATION STUD. 405 (1972); David & Wright, *Abortion Legislation: The Romanian Experience*, 2 STUD. FAM. PLAN. 205 (1971). *See generally* Mehlan, *German Democratic Republic, in* INTERNATIONAL HANDBOOK ON ABORTION, *supra* note 31, at 170, 177.

33. Both the proportion of the population residing in urban areas and the consumption of energy per capita—a common measure of technological level—are substantially greater in The Netherlands than in Romania. UNITED NATIONS, STATISTICAL YEARBOOK: 1975 381 (27th ed. 1976); UNITED NATIONS, DEMOGRAPHIC YEARBOOK: 1980 169 (32nd ed. 1982).

We may also find that the antecedents and consequences of legal doctrine differ between law that *restricts* behavior, law that *permits* behavior, and law that *encourages* behavior. The first and second approaches are illustrated by the changes noted in abortion law in Romania and The Netherlands, respectively; the third approach is illustrated by the provision of public funds in the United States to cover the cost of childbirth services but not to cover the cost of abortion. Harris v. McRae, 448 U.S. 297 (1980). The antecedents and consequences of legal doctrine may, of course, vary between the three approaches depending on the subject of the behavior and the attributes of society.

34. J. Nydon, Public Policy and Private Fertility Behavior: The Case of Pronatalist Policy in Socialist Romania 94–97 (1984) (unpublished Ph.D. dissertation, University of Massachusetts). The effect of the restrictive abortion law in Romania is difficult to assess because the law was accompanied by other pronatalist policies. For example, in the same year that access to abortion was curtailed (1966), a program of monthly child allowances was implemented to promote fertility. *Id.* at 195–208. Nonetheless, the number of births in Romania per 1000 population was virtually the same in 1975—less than a decade after restrictions on abortion were imposed—as in 1960—when abortion was readily available. *Id.* at 95, 96. By 1983, moreover, the number had returned to the low it had attained in 1965. *Id.* at 95; UNITED NATIONS, 1986 DEMOGRAPHIC YEARBOOK 536–37 (38th ed. 1988).

Index